MAFIA WARS

D1328654

TIM SHAWCROSS
AND
MARTIN YOUNG

MAFIA WARS

*The Confessions of
Tommaso Buscetta*

FONTANA/Collins

First published in Great Britain
by William Collins Sons & Co. Ltd 1987
under the title *Men of Honour*
First issued in Fontana Paperbacks 1988

Copyright © Tim Shawcross and Martin Young 1987

Printed and bound in Great Britain by
William Collins Sons & Co. Ltd, Glasgow

It cannot be called prowess to kill fellow citizens, to betray friends, to be treacherous, pitiless, irreligious. These ways can win a prince power but not glory. One can draw attention to the prowess of Agathocles in confronting and surviving danger, and his courageous spirit in enduring and overcoming adversity, and it appears that he should not be judged inferior to any eminent commander; nonetheless, his brutal cruelty and inhumanity, his countless crimes, forbid his being honoured among eminent men.

MACHIAVELLI, *The Prince*

Contents

Illustrations

Preface

Tommaso Buscetta is the highest ranking member of the Sicilian Mafia ever to have betrayed *omertà* – the Sicilian Mafia's deadly code of silence. His first statements were made to Italy's leading Investigating Magistrate, Giovanni Falcone in Rome. There, under a constant armed guard, he talked continuously from 16 July to 12 September 1984. Buscetta opened up the secret world of the Sicilian Mafia as never before. His revelations covered 400 pages, and precipitated the most intensive assault on the international power of the Mafia that has ever been undertaken.

This book is the story of what he said and why he said it: his life, his confessions and the secret debriefings conducted in a heavily protected safe house to agents of the United States Drug Enforcement Administration in 1985 and 1986.

It is also the story of the men who have dedicated their lives to the fight against the Mafia in both Italy and the United States. In Italy, policemen, magistrates, judges and politicians have been ruthlessly gunned down while investigating the Sicilian Mafia. In America, undercover agents in the Police, FBI, DEA and US customs have also risked their lives to penetrate the secret world of the 'Honoured Society'. Without their assistance, patience and cooperation this book could not have been written.

Although the Mafia in both Italy and America has existed for well over half a century, it is only within the last five years that prosecutors on both sides of the Atlantic have made the unprecedented breakthrough which has resulted in the investigation and prosecution of the most powerful Mafia bosses in Sicily and America. In New York, the entire leadership of the American Mafia, the Commission, has been investigated, tried and sentenced; and the world's largest Mafia-controlled heroin network, the Pizza Connection, dealing in $1.65 billion worth of heroin, has been destroyed. In Italy, the billion-dollar heroin trade between Europe and the United States, controlled by the Sicilian Mafia, aided and abetted by some of the most powerful and respectable Italian financiers and politicians, has at last begun to weaken.

This unprecedented assault was accomplished by a new spirit of cooperation and friendship between the law enforcement communities of Italy and the United States, a relationship which has worked both at the highest levels of government in Washington and Rome, and in the day-to-day dealings between investigators in New York and Palermo. DEA, US customs, and FBI agents make frequent transatlantic trips to confer with their counterparts in Italy. Italian policemen, agents and magistrates reciprocate, the only difference being that when an American agent visits Sicily, he has to be guarded by an armed escort twenty-four hours a day.

In the lonely and deadly fight against the Mafia, the Italians and Americans have been helped by one man to achieve their greatest success ever. Tommaso Buscetta's knowledge spans the secret world of the Mafia from the Second World War to the present day. His experiences cover the operations of the Mafia from the low-level actions of a street soldier to the high-level machinations of the Mafia's secret government, the Commission. As a man who personally knew legendary gangsters like Joe Bonanno and Lucky Luciano, the architects of organized crime in the United States, Tommaso Buscetta is proving to be the most valuable witness since Jo Valachi, whose sensational revelations in the United States in 1962 first confirmed the existence of the American Mafia from the inside.

Buscetta has exposed the control of the heroin trade by the Sicilians, their connections with the American Mafia families and the intrigue and murder of the Mafia wars of the 1980s: a bitter power struggle for supreme political and financial control of the Sicilian Mafia and the supervision of the heroin trade. Tommaso Buscetta has revealed the mechanics of the Cosa Nostra from the rites of initiation and the structure of the families, to the organization of the heroin trade on three continents. He has described the buying of morphine base from the Middle East, the secret refining laboratories in Sicily, and the laundering of billions of dollars through the financial markets of the world. He has named the chief executioners and the men who controlled them.

Buscetta's statements are supported and corroborated by testimony and interviews from a variety of sources, some of whom have to remain confidential, including former members and associates of the Sicilian and American Mafia. Research and investigations were carried out in Italy, America, Canada, Brazil and Switzerland.

Among those who can be publicly acknowledged, the authors would like to particularly thank: Michael Fahy, Special Agent, US customs; Charles Rose, Assistant US Attorney, Eastern District of New York, Reena Raggi, Assistant US Attorney, Eastern District of New York; Rudolph Giuliani, US Attorney, Southern District of New York; Richard Martin, Arron Marcue, John Savarese and Louis Freeh, Assistant US Attorneys, Southern District of New York; Dennison Young, Southern District; Tony Petrucci, Mario Alessa, John Huber and Kevin Gallagher, DEA New York; Con Docherty, Frank Panessa and Tom Tripodi, DEA, Washington; Frank Storey, FBI, Organized Crime Section, Washington; Jack French, FBI Research Section, Washington; Tom Sheer, FBI, Assistant Special Agent in Charge, New York; James Kossler, Jo Valiquette and Dan Russo, FBI, New York; Joe Coffey, New York State Organized Crime Task Force, Fred Rayano, Chief Investigator, OCTF, and Ronald Goldstock, Director, OCTF. In Miami, Mike Minto.

In Italy, Investigating Magistrates Giovanni Falcone, Paolo Borsallino; from Criminalpol, Giovanni de Gennaro, Antonio de Luca and many others from the Italian police force and *carabinieri* who must remain anonymous.

For extensive research in Brazil, the authors are indebted to the tremendous contribution made by Richard House. In America and Canada, vital contributions to investigations into the life of Tommaso Buscetta, the Pizza Connection and the American Mafia were made by Marnie Inskip. In Washington, the Scott Malone Organized Crime Research Library provided invaluable assistance and reference. In Switzerland, Klaus Vieli offered insight into the Swiss banking system and the mechanics of money laundering. In Italy, Cecilia Todeschini offered expert advice and painstaking research.

At BBC Television, many thanks to Peter Ibbotson for backing an original *Panorama* programme on the Mafia; to George Carey, Executive Producer, Documentary Features; and to Christopher Olgiati.

Carol Del Signore contributed an extraordinary amount of faultless translations and vast amounts of meticulously collated information.

At Collins, thanks for the hard work of Roger Schlesinger, Dan Franklin and Ariane Goodman in guiding the manuscript into print, and thanks also to Jim Reynolds, our agent, who brought the project to fruition.

1

The 'Godfather of Two Worlds'

He was a good family man, devoted to his children. He had been married twice before, but now all his love and loyalty was reserved for his beautiful third wife, Christina. They lived together with their children in an ordinary American house in New Jersey.

In the past his life had been hectic and even dangerous. Now, as a man of leisure, he was beginning to enjoy himself for once. He passed his time listening to classical music, reading and painting. He was rediscovering the fun of playing with his children. He was learning to enjoy cooking again. When friends came to visit he would often cook fresh pasta dishes. After all, he was the one who had run a chain of pizza houses in New York. He, Christina and their friends would sit around the kitchen table, over the remains of an elegant Italian meal, and reminisce about 'the good old days' in Italy. It was the kind of scene you might witness in countless Italian–American households throughout the United States.

Except for the fact that, during that summer of 1985, every Mafia gunman in Italy and America wanted to murder him.

For he was Tommaso Buscetta, the 'Godfather of Two Worlds', the most important *mafioso* ever to break the code of silence they call '*omertà*'. His testimony to the police in Italy and America would lead to the arrest of hundreds of Mafia gangsters in both countries. He had to be killed before he could give that testimony.

So, that summer, he was more closely guarded than the President of the United States himself. Armed bodyguards watched over him and his family twenty-four hours a day. The men responsible for keeping him alive were specially selected agents from the United States Drug Enforcement Administration (DEA), a federal agency with national and international powers to investigate the trade in narcotics. Buscetta was kept in a safe house whose location is still a closely guarded secret. The armed agents were backed up by alarm sensors around the perimeter of the property. When attorneys and agents were taken to interview him even they were not allowed to know the exact location of the house. They would be taken to an unidentified collection point and then driven to the house in a van with blacked-out windows so that the route would remain a secret.

The elaborate procedure was as much for their own protection as for Buscetta's. The Sicilian and American Mafia had demonstrated only too well in the past that their assassins could penetrate the tightest of security cordons in order to reach their target. They were quite capable of kidnapping and torturing anyone they thought could reveal his whereabouts.

One of Buscetta's most frequent guests was Charles Rose, an assistant US attorney from the Eastern District of New York. Rose had helped to bring him from Italy to the United States, and was responsible too for arranging his protection. Both Buscetta and his wife hold Rose in esteem and affection, and though he is careful to keep a professional distance between himself and the Mafia boss, he would not be human if he had not succumbed to the Sicilian's worldly charm.

Becoming friendly with one of the most powerful and most feared Mafia bosses in post-war Sicily is an unsettling experience. As Rose explains, both he and his colleague, Dick Martin, a fellow attorney from the Southern District of New York, are 'probably still vulnerable because nobody's going to believe we don't know where he is . . . If somebody believed that they could find Tommaso Buscetta through myself and Dick Martin, they would have to kill us, because we don't know. They could do what they want to us. We don't know – and that's a security precaution.'

For months the DEA and FBI had been debriefing Buscetta.

He was proving to be of incalculable value. A highly intelligent and highly motivated man, his soft-spoken charm concealed a seriousness and dedication which impressed almost all his visitors. Many of those who talked to him spoke of an authority which became apparent as you got to know him – qualities which for years had commanded the respect of his peers.

The traditional qualities of the Sicilian 'Man of Honour', which had once been so effectively deployed on behalf of the 'Honoured Society' he had served, were now being used with equally devastating effect for a radically different purpose. Buscetta had sworn to himself and to the world that the sole object of the rest of his life would be 'to destroy the Mafia'.

One of the most important tests of his resolve would be his testimony at the federal court in the Southern District of Manhattan, New York, in autumn 1985. Dick Martin and his fellow attorneys from the Southern District office would finally know if their exhaustive questioning and 'prepping' was going to pay off. The stakes could not have been much higher. Buscetta's testimony could help to convict the gangsters who ran the largest narcotics conspiracy ever investigated in the United States. In the case dubbed 'the Pizza Connection', twenty-two conspirators were charged with trafficking in $1.65 billion-worth of high-quality heroin which had been refined in the Mafia's laboratories in Sicily and smuggled into the eastern seaboard of the United States. The defendants included some of the most dangerous *mafiosi* to have seen the inside of a courtroom.

Bringing Buscetta to the witness-stand was a major security operation. A special application to have an armed bodyguard in court was granted, and a few days before he appeared the courthouse was surrounded by armed guards carrying sub-machine-guns and wearing flak jackets. When the trial began, metal detectors and extra US marshals were drafted in to increase security inside and outside the courthouse and to protect the prosecuting attorneys. So good was the security that Buscetta became almost invisible. On the day of the trial no one saw him arrive and no one saw him leave. Which was precisely what everyone wished – except those who wanted to kill him.

As he was being brought to the federal court on that clear, mild autumn day, surrounded by the bodyguards who lived, ate and slept with him, another Sicilian was also being escorted to the courthouse. His recent environment had been less congenial: he was being held in the Metropolitan Correctional Center in Manhattan and the guards were there not to save his life but to prevent his escape. In his sixties, of medium height, he walked in a dignified and upright fashion, as if casting disdain on the unfortunate circumstances in which he found himself. Smartly dressed in a charcoal-grey suit, white shirt and tie, he looked fit and well. He came from a tradition in which appearances were of the utmost importance. He was a man used to commanding respect and obedience. His looks were typically Sicilian. Jet-black eyebrows above a patrician nose gave his face a Roman quality. His eyes were dark. In court he sat erect, looking ahead with an unwavering stare. This proud Sicilian, apparently untouched by a cosmopolitan life of international travel, had been one of the world's most wanted men.

His name was Gaetano Badalamenti. He was the former head of the Sicilian Mafia, the so-called '*capo di tutti capi*' – 'boss of all bosses'. Buscetta had been one of his closest associates. They had also been friends and confidants. Although Buscetta was six years younger, they had grown up together in Palermo, and their paths had frequently crossed in Italy and other parts of the world. They enjoyed each other's company in both business and pleasure. They had shared moments of great success and great tragedy. They had formed a strong, silent bond of friendship of a kind which is peculiar to Sicily and quite distinct from the nature of friendship elsewhere.

Inside the federal courthouse in Foley Square, in the formal atmosphere of Courtroom 506, Judge Pierre Leval presided over the preliminary trial proceedings with seemingly inexhaustible reserves of good humour and patience. He made his opening remarks to the jury, warning them not to judge the guilt or innocence of the defendants until they had heard all the evidence. He warned them about forming personal likes or dislikes for any of the lawyers, whether prosecuting or defending, which might influence their final verdict. And he repeated several times that the verdict they reached at the end of the trial must be calculated 'beyond reasonable doubt'.

Just before 11.30 a.m. on 29 October 1985, Judge Leval uttered the three words the packed courtroom had been waiting to hear:

'Call the first witness.'

Dick Martin, who was leading the government's prosecuting team, stood up.

'The government calls Tommaso Buscetta.'

There was an expectant pause. Those in the public seats craned forward. The US marshals became more alert, watchful for any threat, even a suicide attempt. Reporters from the three US television networks and journalists from all over the world prepared themselves for a great story. No one was sure whether they should start writing or just watch.

At last, preceded by his bodyguard, Buscetta entered through a door at the back of the court. Many of his fellow Sicilians on trial, the men he was about to accuse, leaned forward in their seats. Some of them knew him well, others were curious to see what he looked like. They saw a man of medium height, broadly built without being fat, walk slowly and carefully with the demeanour of a university professor about to deliver a lecture to his students. There was nothing in his appearance to indicate that he was a *mafioso* about to betray an organization which demands greater loyalty than any country would ever expect of the most fanatical patriot. The concentration on Buscetta in the courtroom was so intense that it was almost tangible. Some of the twenty-two defendants managed to summon up expressions which gave new significance to the phrase 'if looks could kill'. Irrespective of his words, it was this man's very presence that mattered. Here, on the side of the government, was the highest-ranking Sicilian 'godfather' ever to have betrayed the Mafia.

After Buscetta had entered the witness-box, Dick Martin asked the first question.

'Why did you decide to cooperate with the United States authorities?'

It was an important question because the standard tactic of defence lawyers when faced with government witnesses is to discredit their motives by exposing the self-serving deals which all too often had been agreed. With a female translator beside him, Buscetta replied softly in Italian, 'Because the time had come to do so.'

With those words, the jury began to listen to his testimony.

The government prosecutors alleged that a conspiracy to import, distribute and sell massive quantities of heroin had been controlled by the American Mafia in collaboration with their Sicilian cousins. The case would give a detailed insight into the machinations of the Mafia in Sicily, America, Brazil and Switzerland.

According to the numerous defence lawyers, the accused men were honest, hard-working Italian immigrants whose sole misfortune was to be Sicilian. Many of them had built up successful businesses such as pizza parlours and demolition companies. Michael Kennedy, a distinguished and well-respected lawyer who had numbered among his clients Timothy Leary, the high priest of LSD and prophet of psychedelia, told the jury that the man he represented, Gaetano Badalamenti, was 'a proud, dignified, simple yet remarkable man. A Sicilian by blood, a Sicilian by birthright.' Like many other respectable Sicilians of his generation, Kennedy continued, his client had loyally served the Allies in 1943 by fighting the fascists. After the war his client had become a farmer, a businessman and a member of 'an Honourable Society'. His only crime, Kennedy declared, lowering his voice to an attentive jury, was that he would have nothing to do with trafficking in narcotics. His principled stand led to his persecution by the Society which forced him to flee his native country. Unfortunately, this 'honourable man' was expelled by this same Society not because he trafficked in drugs but precisely because he refused to have anything to do with such a disgraceful enterprise.

The DEA, the United States customs, the FBI, the Italian police and the US government's prosecuting attorneys all told a very different version of the story. According to their evidence,

Badalamenti was one of the world's leading heroin traffickers. They had been on his trail for more than ten years. Now their task was made much simpler by the evidence of his erstwhile friend and associate.

Badalamenti and Buscetta, friends for nearly twenty-five years, were brought together here in circumstances that a few years earlier neither could have imagined – as accused and accuser. Although they sat only a few feet apart from each other, Buscetta in the witness-box and Badalamenti sitting calmly, straight-backed and expressionless at the front of the court, they were separated by a distance that was immeasurable. Buscetta had entered a different universe. The journey that had led him to the witness-box, and to the betrayal of his friend and the world that they had shared, encompassed more money and murder than most people could even conceive of. And when he took the enormous decision to break *omertà* he set in train a unique and historic sequence of events.

In Palermo, investigating magistrate Giovanni Falcone had listened to Buscetta and discovered the truth about the Mafia wars of the past thirty years. He initiated the biggest assault on the power of the Mafia that Sicily had seen since the days of Mussolini.

In the United States, US attorney Rudolph (Rudy) Giuliani and his deputy Louis Freeh, an ex-FBI agent, had already embarked on their own crusade against organized crime, in which Buscetta was an extra, crucial weapon. It is no exaggeration to say that Falcone and Giuliani are 'at war' with the Mafia, nor to say that so far they are winning. The resources involved are staggering, but then so are the rewards for victory. The confessions of the 'Godfather of Two Worlds' have so far involved the police forces of Italy, America, Switzerland, Brazil, Spain and Turkey.

In America alone, hundreds of agents from the FBI, the DEA, the US customs and the New York City Police Department have been working for years to uncover the biggest heroin racket the world has ever seen. New laws have been passed on two continents, and extradition treaties have brought Mafia crimi-

nals back to justice, among them Badalamenti from Spain and
Buscetta from Brazil.

In Italy, the *carabinieri* scour the caves of Sicily and the slums
of Palermo uncovering heroin laboratories and Mafia hideouts
in the volcanic hills. They are a paramilitary force, armed
with automatic weapons, swooping on the Mafia in helicopters,
dropping troops and tracker dogs onto the hillsides, patrolling
the streets in armoured cars. The fight against the 'Honoured
Society' is a guerilla war.

In New York, the houses and offices of Mafia bosses have
been strung with wiretaps. Every time a '*capo*' moves, a surveillance team moves with him. At John F. Kennedy airport the
FBI hand over to the US customs special agents. They see their
charge safely on the plane. He flies to Italy. The Italian customs
and the Italian police are waiting. His every moment is chronicled
and fed into the mainframe computers of the FBI in Washington
and the *carabinieri* headquarters in Rome and Palermo.

Tommaso Buscetta is not solely responsible for this outburst
of activity. But he has been the major factor in sustaining it for
the last two years by betraying the organization he once revered.

2

'I Want to Destroy the Mafia'

A good citizen ought to forget his own private
wrongs when the interests of the common good are
concerned.

MACHIAVELLI, *The Prince*

The story of how Buscetta and Badalamenti came to Courtroom
506 in Foley Square is long and dramatic.

In April 1984 Buscetta was in prison in Brazil and Badalamenti
was locked up in Madrid. The authorities in Italy and the USA
were keen to extradite them, and after considerable negotiation
it was agreed that Buscetta would be brought to Italy and
Badalamenti to the USA.

In November 1984 Louis Caprino, an Italian–American FBI
agent who specialized in undercover work, flew out to Madrid.
His mission was to escort Badalamenti back to the United States
to face trial with other defendants in the Pizza Connection case.
He had orders to sound out the Mafia boss – there was always
a chance that he might talk, and if he followed Buscetta's
example it would cause a sensation. The authorities knew that
Badalamenti had been at war with the Corleonesi faction of the
Sicilian Mafia, that there was a contract out on his life and that
he had lost many of his close relatives in the Mafia wars. If
convicted, he faced prison for the rest of his life. It was reason
enough to talk. The FBI man was empowered to offer a generous
deal if it looked as if the Sicilian were interested.

To those who met him at this time, Badalamenti appeared to
be still in control of his destiny. He was polite and respectful to

his captors and in turn commanded their respect. He was described as 'the kind of person, who, when you look at him, you know is in charge of something'.

In an attempt to gain Badalamenti's friendship, Caprino told him that there was no need for handcuffs. He knew he was an honourable man and would not make a run for it. Such consideration would be appreciated by someone well versed in the code of the 'Cosa Nostra', where 'respect' and 'appearance' are all-important. The agent accompanied Badalamenti on the long flight back to the United States in the military aircraft which the US government had provided. He worked on the Sicilian slowly and patiently. To ask Badalamenti baldly if he would betray the 'Honoured Society' would be completely the wrong approach; the question would have to be raised with the utmost tact. As Caprino continued to talk, Badalamenti seemed responsive and well disposed towards him. Finally he broached the subject. He started to talk about the investigation in America. He revealed that they had a lot of tapes in which Badalamenti was heard, that his voice had been identified, that they had bank records linking him to the conspiracy. When the case came to trial, he implied, the Sicilian would not stand a very good chance of acquittal. He hinted that Badalamenti faced the prospect of dying in jail unless he did something to help himself. Then he said, 'How about it, we want to do the right thing here?'

'Well, what is it you want from me?' replied Badalamenti.

'Well, you know, about the case . . .'

'Well, what is it you think I did?' asked the Sicilian.

'Hey, we know you're in the heroin business and we'd like to know the lines.'

As Caprino looked at Badalamenti, he saw him undergo a total change in appearance and attitude. His eyes darkened as he said, 'You can call me anything you want, call me a murderer, call me a robber, call me a thief. But never, ever, call me a heroin dealer.'

The agent, highly experienced in the codes of the 'Honoured Society', was stunned: 'I was a believer, then, just by his instant reaction. Is it good theatre? Is the guy just that good that he can react that strongly to something?' Badalamenti was either a brilliant actor, or believed so devoutly in the 'code of honour' that he could never have admitted to himself or anyone else the true nature of his business. That was something which would be left to the decision of a court of law. There the conduct of the 'Men of Honour' would be put to the test.

Just three months before that plane journey, on 21 July 1984, Tommaso Buscetta was in Italy, in a bunker in Rebibia prison in Rome. He had been successfully extradited from Brazil and was now closeted with his confessor, the Italian magistrate Giovanni Falcone. Much of what he told Falcone in Rome was new, but he also provided substantial corroboration of their most recent investigations. His evidence added up to the most crucial breakthrough ever achieved by the Italian authorities in their fight against the Mafia, and it shattered the secret world of the Sicilian Mafia.

In exposing the influence of the 'Third Level' – the politicians and financiers who were linked to the Mafia – Buscetta would help the Sicilian magistrates move in and arrest some of its most distinguished members. His statements sent shock waves through political circles as well as among the 'Honoured Society' whose members he was now driven to destroy.

As a man whose children and relatives had been brutally killed in the Mafia wars, his motives looked suspiciously like revenge on his former enemies. Those enemies were the Greco–Corleonesi faction which had fought for control of the Mafia in the early 1980s – and won. Falcone and his fellow magistrates were careful not to lose sight of the fact that Buscetta was one of the leading members of the 'losing' faction, and that his testimony inevitably concentrated on revelations about the 'winning' faction. Buscetta was quick to deny that he was motivated by revenge, yet given his character and background, and the personal trauma caused by the murder of his sons, it is difficult to believe that revenge did not play a major part in his decision to give evidence. But whatever his motives, the risks involved in doing so were high. As the Mafia's rites of initiation had made only too clear, by talking to the authorities he was committing an act of treachery punishable by death.

As a way of life and as a system of values, the Mafia 'code of honour' bears some similarities to a religious code. And just as religious practices sometimes become estranged from their original ideals, so too did the Mafia ethic decay beyond recognition. When Buscetta was flown from America to Sicily to testify in the Palermo 'maxi-trial' on 4 April 1986, he said he had decided to talk because the society had betrayed its original ideals. He told the court, 'I remain a member of the Cosa Nostra in the same spirit as when I joined. But from the 1970s onwards, the ideals of the Cosa Nostra changed and there have been acts of violence which do not correspond to the original ideals.'

The significance of his conversion was not lost on his former friends. Shortly after his extradition from Brazil to Italy, he was given permission to visit his old friend and fellow prisoner Salvatore Contorno, an intensely loyal 'soldier' who had narrowly escaped death during the Mafia wars. Like Buscetta, many of his relatives had been murdered by the Corleonesi. When he saw Buscetta inside his prison cell he was overwhelmed. He knelt down and kissed his hand. Buscetta put a hand on his shoulder and said, 'It's all right, Totuccio, you can talk.'

From that moment Contorno became another vital witness who turned his back on the Mafia's code of silence. His confession confirmed much of the evidence given by Buscetta and provided crucial testimony against the Pizza Connection.

Buscetta's decision to cooperate with the Italian authorities coincided with a new spirit of collaboration between the Italian and United States authorities. In March 1986 Michele Sindona, the Sicilian banker, died inside a maximum security prison in Italy after drinking a cup of coffee laced with cyanide. The manner of his arrest in the United States, following the collapse of the Franklin National Bank, had helped to foster the new relationship. Under the existing legislation he could not be extradited from the USA. He was desperately wanted by the Italians and his case provided the impetus to change the law. In 1982 the two governments signed an agreement on extradition and a Treaty for Mutual Assistance on Criminal Matters. In essence it enabled the two countries to exchange witnesses for interrogation, and provided a framework for their law enforcement agencies to work together much more effectively. Sindona was one of the first prisoners to be extradited from the United States to Italy to face a series of charges for his Mafia connections and financial frauds. The following year an Italian–American Working Group on Drug Trafficking was set up. The agreements made it easier to attack the Mafia on both sides of the Atlantic, and greatly improved the cooperation between the US attorneys and their counterparts in Italy, the investigating magistrates. Charles Rose readily admits that Buscetta is of greater value to Italy, but goes on to say, 'He wants to destroy the Mafia in Sicily . . . Well, if you kill it in Sicily, sooner or later the tentacles are going to start squirming here in the United States. So we don't care where you kill the Sicilian Mafia as long as it affects here – and it does. That's why we're so cooperative with the Italians: we give them our evidence, we share it with them.'

The case against the Pizza Connection was built on the foundations of that cooperation. Italian police officers and magistrates came over to America to review the evidence and help interpret some of the wiretaps (many of the suspects spoke in the Sicilian dialect), and US attorneys visited Palermo, where they were under constant guard. In general it was much safer for the Italians visiting America, although on one occasion a top anti-Mafia detective from Palermo, on his arrival in New York, made a telephone call from his hotel and was astonished to find someone else on the line threatening him. His commanding officer back in Sicily was the only other person who knew of his trip. The incident was a disturbing reminder of how effective the intelligence-gathering capability of the Mafia could be. With his cover blown, the detective returned to Italy.

The American authorities had been interested in Buscetta for a long time. Since 1973 he had been wanted on a heroin trafficking charge in the Eastern District of New York. Ten years later, after his arrest in Brazil the Americans withdrew their extradition request in the expectation that they would be able to interrogate him fully once the Italians had finished with him. When Buscetta made his decision to cooperate their interest became much more critical. His debriefing on the heroin traffic in Sicily could be invaluable in the case they were bringing against the Pizza Connection. Under the new treaty they would have access to him. Equally significantly for Buscetta, it meant that he would have access to the United States and the possibility of a safe passage out of Italy.

Although Buscetta was determined to help the Sicilian magistrates in what he recognized as their most effective attack on the Mafia, he knew that his life would be constantly at risk in Italy. Under Italian law he would almost certainly have to spend time in prison, where he knew the Mafia could kill him with ease. Furthermore, the Italians had no equivalent to the Federal Witness Program which the Americans had developed to great effect in persuading *mafiosi* and other leading criminals to cooperate. In return for total cooperation, the programme offered protection for witnesses and their families and sometimes gave immunity from prosecution together with a new identity. The Italians themselves admitted that Buscetta was too valuable a witness – and, more importantly, too valuable an example – to be exposed to any unnecessary security risks.

In August 1984, as Buscetta was in the middle of making his lengthy statements to Giovanni Falcone in the prison outside Rome, Charles Rose, who had been in charge of the original negotiations for his extradition from Brazil, flew over to meet him. Rose was apprehensive about meeting the man about whom he had read and heard so much:

It was a dingy room that he was kept in at that time – protected, I mean total protection. When I walked in there were machine-guns all over the place, and we realized how seriously they took this, the threat to Tommaso Buscetta. The guards were hand-selected by the magistrates. They lived, slept and ate with Tommaso twenty-four hours a day, seven days a week, while he was there.

We walked into a very small room: a table, a chair and a locker – not much more. Bars on the window. And I sat there, and in walked Tommaso Buscetta. He was small; at least, he was smaller than I thought he would be. He was also extremely polite – quiet, a very mild manner. We communicated for the most part in the beginning in Spanish, because it was important ... I mean, just the initial generalities: 'Hello. How are you? Nice to see you. I've been chasing you for years – nice to catch you.'

Then with the help of an Italian interpreter we got into the nitty-gritty, and that's when the first thing came out of his mouth: 'I want to destroy the Mafia.'

The two men discussed the Federal Witness Program in the United States and the way it operated. Rose told Buscetta that he could not make any promises. He pointed out that, apart from the outstanding indictment for heroin trafficking in the Eastern District, Buscetta was also wanted by the Southern District, under US attorney Rudy Giuliani, as a potential witness in the Pizza Connection case. Rose realized that there might be a clash of interests and that he would have to talk with Giuliani's people back in New York. He also appreciated that individual rivalries must not be allowed to jeopardize the successful 'turning' of this witness. As they talked, Rose began to experience Buscetta's peculiar charm:

After a while, with his magnetism, I guess I realized that this was not just an ordinary street-mob guy ... Maybe he wasn't the dope dealer that I had heard about, but he was the quintessential *mafioso*. He epitomized what he explained the Mafia code to be ...

I said, 'Do you have any questions?'

He said, 'I want nothing for myself, I don't want a lesser sentence and I'll take whatever sentence you give me, I'll plead to whatever it is you want me to plead to: I do not want people to think I am cooperating because I am getting a benefit out of this, that I'm selling out, that I'm getting a reduced sentence, that you're giving me any benefit whatsoever. I do not want that. The only thing I want is the only thing that I have left.'

It is the only thing that means anything to him any longer – his family.

Buscetta went on to confide in Rose:

'This is not revenge for my family's death. Revenge for my family's death would have been to go and kill their sons: it's not even close. I don't want revenge: I want to destroy the Mafia, I want to reveal it for what it is, what it has become . . . a criminal organization with no other purpose.'

Charles Rose is a young and determined prosecuting attorney who has seen his fair share of informers and villains. He has specialized in terrorist cases, particularly those involving the New York Puerto Rican 'liberation' movement, the FALN. He has faced a series of death threats. Six feet tall and powerfully built, he is neither easily intimidated nor easily fooled. In the time that he was with Buscetta he was impressed: 'I'd never met an informant who never wanted anything for himself before, and that was the first thing that surprised me – that he was so adamant about it. I was a believer in ten minutes.'

Before this meeting, Rose had spent several hours with Buscetta's Brazilian wife, Christina. It was time well spent. She felt she could trust him and told her husband that they would be safe with him. It was the best recommendation he could have had.

When he returned to America, he had a series of meetings with Rudy Giuliani in the Southern District and with the DEA in Washington. A deal was struck. He was accompanied back to Italy by Dick Martin from Giuliani's office, the young government attorney in charge of the prosecution of the Pizza Connection case. They gave Buscetta the good news that he could be brought over to the United States, and the bad news that he would have to plead guilty to old charges outstanding against him in the Eastern District. They pointed out that if the Italians requested it, he would have to return to testify in Italy. Buscetta agreed – it was what he wanted. As it turned out, he later negotiated an even better deal.

In great secrecy, arrangements were made to fly him and his family to the United States. The American embassy in Rome made arrangements through their military attaché for a US Air Force C–130 to be made available. It was just before Christmas 1984.

Security precautions demanded that the landing-site in America be kept secret right up to the very last moment. Not even Rose knew where it would be. On the night of Buscetta's arrival, Rose arranged to have dinner with Dick Martin, a lawyer who would represent Buscetta, a court reporter and a judge. The plan was to arraign Buscetta in a makeshift court as soon as he touched down on American soil. After dinner they were 'caravanned' to the landing-site in a fast armed convoy. They arrived at the Marine air terminal at New York's La Guardia airport and about fifteen miles from the centre of Manhattan. The area was surrounded by armed DEA agents, Port Authority officials and police. Word had somehow leaked out in Italy that the C–130 had taken off with its important passenger and several news reporters were scouting around possible sites for his landing, including La Guardia. It was a potentially worrying gap in security. In fact the C–130 landed at a separate military installation and Buscetta was then transferred to a smaller and more comfortable DEA plane and flown to La Guardia. As he got out of the plane he was surrounded by US marshals, DEA agents, New York police and a host of other unfamiliar faces. After an uncomfortable twelve-hour flight, it was a bewildering experience, and Buscetta was more than relieved when he finally recognized two familiar faces – Charles Rose and Dick Martin. They waved to him and greeted him with the words, 'Welcome to America.'

'Thank you,' replied Buscetta simply. Then, exhausted, he was arraigned by the judge in a temporary court where everyone appeared to be half-asleep. When that was finished, he looked over at Rose and Martin and said in mock seriousness, 'I thought you were trying to kill me! I haven't eaten in twelve hours, I haven't slept and now look at this!'

'Tommaso, I just wanted to see how tough you really were!' quipped Rose as the most valuable witness he had ever had was led away.

Thirteen years after having fled from New York following his arrest for illegal entry, Buscetta had returned – but as a very different sort of immigrant. The Americans put their prize into an army barracks in New Jersey. Although he was well protected, the surroundings and the security quickly became claustrophobic. Even the agents debriefing him began to get 'psyched' by the grey-painted walls, the tiny room and the strict routines. If Buscetta wanted to go outside into the exercise yard, forty counter-snipers would be deployed in firing positions. The government attorneys realized they could not prepare him for testimony in such a forbidding environment. After high-level negotiations with the Department of Justice, Buscetta was moved to a safe house. It meant that his family could visit him in nearly normal conditions. As he had told Rose, that was the most important thing in his life. For the first time in over a year he could feel that he was with people he could trust. He was as safe as he could ever hope to be. Under the protective custody of the DEA, he could finally enjoy being with Christina and their children without having the constant worry of whether they would live to see another day.

In return, the Americans and the Italians received vital evidence about the history of the Mafia, the international heroin trade, a breakdown of the Mafia families in Sicily and their relationships with the American Mafia. In the international fight against organized crime, Buscetta would help to undermine the morale of a vicious enemy and destroy the myth that the Mafia conspiracy of silence could never be penetrated. As the US Attorney-General at the time, William French-Smith, put it, 'Buscetta has destroyed the myth of invincibility. For years traditional organized crime had been able to maintain discipline in its ranks and to attract and keep associates because of the idea that the top leadership was beyond the law. They are no longer untouchable.'

One of the 'untouchables' whom the authorities had hoped might follow in Buscetta's footsteps was Badalamenti, who, as the former head of the Sicilian Commission and head of the Cinisi family, would have had a great deal to contribute. Buscetta had last seen him in Brazil, and the hope was that if Buscetta spoke to him now he might persuade him to cooperate with the authorities. If Badalamenti agreed, it would be an unprecedented coup. Although a telephone call was arranged, Badalamenti refused even to talk to Buscetta. Whatever else he had done, the proud Sicilian would remain loyal to the 'Men of Honour'.

'General Mafia'

*May my flesh burn like this holy picture if I am
unfaithful to this oath.*

Mafia initiation rite

The factors that conspired to turn Buscetta into so egregious a
traitor are rooted in the post-war history of the Mafia. During
the Second World War the Americans enlisted the support of
the Mafia in the planning and execution of the invasion of Sicily.
This combination of American opportunism and altruism was
to result in a dreadful irony. It led to the regeneration of the
Sicilian Mafia and ultimately to the foundation of the most
elaborate narcotics distribution system the world has ever seen,
from the Mafia's first involvement in drugs to the French Connection drug ring and finally to the Pizza Connection. Each of these
conspiracies damaged no nation more than America.

It was the Mafia's increasing involvement in the drug trade
that caused Buscetta's conflict between his image of himself as
a 'Man of Honour' and his natural evil. For Buscetta that conflict
began with his initiation into the brotherhood:

> The neophyte is brought to a secluded spot, which could
> even be someone's home, in the presence of three or
> more Men of Honour of the family. Then the oldest of
> those present informs him that the purpose of '*questa
> cosa*' – this thing – is to protect the weak and to eliminate
> the oppressors. Then a finger is pricked on one of the
> hands of the person being sworn in and the blood is
> made to fall on a sacred image. Then the image is placed

in his hand and is burned. At this time the neophyte must endure the fire, passing the sacred image quickly from one hand to the other until it goes out, and he swears to remain faithful to the principles of the Cosa Nostra, stating solemnly, 'May my flesh burn like this holy picture if I am unfaithful to this oath'.

This in broad outline was the method of swearing in used when I became a member of the Cosa Nostra. After the swearing-in, and only then, the Man of Honour is introduced to the head of the family, whose post he did not know about beforehand, knowing even less of the existence of the Cosa Nostra *per se*.

Despite the religious overtones of the initiation ceremony and the pledge to uphold honour and truth, the rites of the Mafia today are nothing more than a cruel parody of allegiance and honour. In Italy a young man is to be killed. Before his execution his right arm is cut off to fulfil a vendetta. In America a *mafioso* is shot in the back, then in the face, and then bundled into an oil-drum full of wet cement. He is dumped off Long Island.

A member of the New York Organized Crime Task Force reports the confession of a Mafia killer:

> He gave us the whole litany . . . he described how they cut bodies up. He went to the extent of saying that they killed two guys and they cut their testicles off and he sat there like we would talk about having a cup of coffee. He said, 'Yes, we cut his testicles off.' And he said, 'You could see the guy's balls roll across the floor like little white onions.'

Such atrocities are highlighted here as an indication of what is to follow. Throughout Buscetta's confessions there are little homilies about 'honour', about the 'ethics' of the Mafia, about the finer points of the brotherhood, and in the face of all this rhetoric it is important to remember the murders and the cruelty. According to Buscetta, even 'abominable crimes' are subject to strict rules among 'honourable' men:

Let me be clear: it has not been grasped yet that, apart from the responsibility of the actual perpetrators of the individual criminal acts, there is the definite responsibility of the heads of the families in whose territory these events take place and, going even higher, the responsibility of the Commission that has consented to, or perhaps even decreed, the commission of such abominable crimes.

Buscetta continues his confession:

No one will ever find any written codes of Mafia ethics but the rules that I have been familiar with since I became a Man of Honour are rigid and firm and universally accepted. Likewise, no one will ever find lists of members of Cosa Nostra, nor certificates of any type, nor receipts for the payment of dues.

Nevertheless, the tie that binds Men of Honour is even more solid and impenetrable than if it were written down in some document. In my view, one of the principal mistakes made in the struggle against the Mafia has been precisely to ignore this truth which is something which all Men of Honour are familiar with.

Giovanni Falcone and Rudy Giuliani have not made that mistake. The Italian and American investigators know only too well that the Mafia is in the end a secret organization which by definition is very difficult to penetrate. Hence the importance of Buscetta.

Buscetta joined the Mafia at a critical point in its regeneration after the Second World War. He was born on 13 July 1928 into the large family of Benedetto and Felicia Buscetta. He was one of five boys and five girls. He left school when he was fourteen, after he had completed his secondary education. In the years immediately after the war, the Buscetta family's glass business began to prosper. Many of the city's windows had been damaged or destroyed during the war, so glass was in great demand.

Tommaso had considerable natural charm and therefore no problem in finding girlfriends. He also had a steady job, unlike most of his friends. By the time he was sixteen, in 1944, he fell in love with Melchiorra Cavallaro, a girl three years older than himself. The relationship soon became a passionate affair and Melchiorra became pregnant. Tommaso 'did the honourable thing' and married her in the spring of 1946. Although still a teenager, he was now a husband and a prospective father, and he was beginning to feel stifled, particularly by what he perceived to be the claustrophobic atmosphere of the family glassworks. Four weeks after his wedding he had a row with his family and left Palermo for Turin to work for the Albert & Macario glass factory. He was absent from Palermo for eight months, returning in time for the birth of his daughter, Felicia, on 7 December 1946.

His rebellion against his parents was typical of his headstrong, independent nature. Although only eighteen, he had maturity and strength of character, qualities that would attract another family business in Palermo – the Mafia.

The Mafia had had a good war. The Americans, in inviting their collaboration in the invasion of Sicily, had helped rebuild the power of the organization Mussolini had done so much to diminish. Mussolini's success against them stemmed largely from his willingness to string people up from lamp-posts without the tedious necessity of a trial. The suspension of civil liberties had given many *mafiosi* the aura of freedom fighters opposed to fascism – as indeed many of them were. *Mafiosi* like 'Lucky' Luciano undoubtedly did help the American invasion, although Badalamenti's war record has been seriously discredited by the American authorities.

Luciano's reward was the commuting of his prison sentence in America and deportation to Italy in February 1946. He received a regal send-off from his American friends and was given a hero's welcome by his Italian comrades.

In the final years of the war Luciano gave assistance to officers of US naval intelligence. At the time, he was serving a thirty-year jail sentence for possession of drugs and running several brothels, so it was hardly surprising that he agreed to help the Americans. The longshoremen were already in Luciano's pocket as their jobs were Mafia-controlled. Luciano enlisted their support through intermediaries to prevent fascist saboteurs planting bombs in the New York docks. The sabotage was duly stopped. Luciano also passed the word to his friends in Sicily that they should do all they could to help the invading American forces. The Mafia naturally complied – liberation from Mussolini was at hand.

Morally dubious though it was, the alliance of the US government and the Mafia was an effective strategy.

On 20 July 1943 three American tanks broke through the Italian lines and reached the village of Villalba in western Sicily. One of the tanks was flying a yellow flag embroidered with the black letter 'L'. It stood for Luciano. Similar flags were seen all over the island. The officer inside the tank, who spoke fluent Sicilian, had come to present his credentials to Don Calogero Vizzini, the head of the Sicilian Mafia. An elderly, overweight man in shirt sleeves and braces shuffled towards the tank. As he approached he waved a yellow handkerchief with an identical black letter 'L' in the middle. Now the Americans knew they were meeting the right man, Don Calò, Luciano's counterpart in Sicily.

Don Calò climbed into the tank and was driven away. The Allies quickly dubbed him 'General Mafia'. He led the advance from the turret of his American tank, releasing hundreds of *mafiosi* from Mussolini's jails as he went.

When the Allies reached the mainland they were joined by another Mafia representative, Vito Genovese. He became the founder of one of the most powerful crime families based in New York which to this day bears his name. He helped the Americans as an interpreter and guide. He also managed to monopolize the black market in food, petrol, cigarettes and alcohol – most of it stolen from the Americans.

Genovese had escaped to Italy from America in 1937 to avoid indictment on a murder charge. In Rome he became a close friend of Mussolini. It was a classic Mafia friendship: he gave donations to the Fascist Party and generous doses of cocaine to Mussolini's son. He was awarded the title of *Commendatore*, one of Italy's highest honours. One of the 'honourable' duties he performed for Mussolini was to arrange the murder of an anti-fascist newspaper editor in New York. The contract was executed in January 1943 by Carmine Galante who became the underboss of the Bonanno family in New York.

When Genovese realized that Mussolini's days were numbered, he simply switched allegiance to the Allied Military Government (AMGOT). He proved an invaluable fixer, sharing the money he made on the black market with some senior American officers who deposited the proceeds in Swiss bank accounts.

Barely a year after the invasion the Americans found a new role for their Mafia friends. They were quick to see the potential of the Mafia in their new war – against communism. On 21 November 1944 Alfred T. Nester, the US consul in Palermo, sent a letter marked 'top secret' to the US secretary of state, Cordell Hull:

> I have the honor to report that on November 18, 1944, General Guiseppe Castellana [*sic*] together with Maffia [*sic*] leaders including Calogero Vizzini, conferred with Virgilio Nasi, head of the well-known Nasi family in Trapani, and asked him to take over the leadership of a Maffia-backed movement for Sicilian autonomy.

The letter was followed six days later by another top-secret dispatch to Washington. It referred to a 'meeting of Maffia leaders with General Guiseppe Castellano and formation of group favouring autonomy'. Nester then quoted from an intelligence report compiled in Sicily by the OSS (Office of Strategic Services), the forerunner of the CIA:

> After a series of secret meetings with exponents of the Maffia in Palermo for three days, General Guiseppe Castellano, commanding the Aosta division in Sicily, has struck a tentative agreement on selection and support of a candidate for High Commissioner to replace incumbent

Salvatore Aldisio of the Democratic Christian Party ...
the candidate is a dark horse, a famous Sicilian, Virgilio
Nasi, 'boss' of Trapani Province, who was approached
by General Castellana [sic] after broaching his plan to
high Maffia leaders during the week.

Recognizing what they regarded as disturbing trends towards
communism in northern Italy, what they called 'the wind from
the north', the Americans were taking an interest in a bizarre
scheme to turn Sicily into an American state or a British colony.
The island was attractive to both nations because of its strategic
position in the middle of the Mediterranean and its tradition
of independence from mainland Italy. Both factors had been
important in Churchill's decision to persuade Roosevelt that
the invasion of Italy should be started from Sicily. As British
intelligence had reported, 'Sicilians consider themselves as distinct from continental Italians ... a good many Sicilians have
been in the US and have picked up some English. They are highly
individual and vengeful.'

Today the idea of a Sicilian separatist movement seems far-
fetched, but at the time it was taken seriously. Although the
movement petered out, the Mafia remained a powerful force for
the suppression of communism in Sicily.

Tommaso Buscetta first came to the attention of the Mafia at
the age of fifteen when he killed some German soldiers. The
heads of the Mafia families needed new talent and it was a good
time for prospective candidates to prove that they had the right
qualities. Some of the tough street kids from the Palermo slums
would loiter by the squares in the town centre waiting to catch
the eye of a local 'Man of Honour' so that they could run an
errand. They might be asked to deliver a message or they might
be called on to carry out a murder; if they proved competent
and loyal, they stood a chance of being enrolled as soldiers in
one of the families. Gaetano Filippone, head of the Porta Nuova
family, one of the most prestigious Mafia families in Palermo,
had already received recommendations about Buscetta, the
young lad who had killed the enemy.

In the 'Honoured Society' the murders meant that he had 'come of age'. He was sworn in to the Porta Nuova family through the ritual he describes, and became a fully-fledged member of the Mafia. But he did not stay in Sicily for long. After two more years in the family business he began to get restless again. His frustration surfaced in a curious way. Towards the end of 1948 he began to work as a trade-union activist, encouraging his fellow workers in the Palermo glass factories to organize themselves against the management. It was hardly logical behaviour for the son of a family business, and unthinkable for a 'made' member of the Mafia. His family was not amused, so he decided to leave Sicily.

With his wife and daughter and his son Benedetto, who had been born in September 1948, Buscetta travelled by ship to Argentina, settling in a suburb of Buenos Aires called Temperley. There he set up his own glass factory. Melchiorra found it difficult to adjust to life in Argentina and, after the birth in August 1950 of their third child, Antonio, the family decided to move to São Paulo in Brazil. Buscetta opened another glass factory called Conca d'Oro which seems to have prospered, but Melchiorra was still unhappy. She did not like São Paulo either, and she urged Buscetta to return to Palermo. When his brother, Vincenzo, came to visit them in Brazil, he also exhorted Buscetta to return. Reluctantly, he gave in.

In 1951 they went back to Sicily. It had been the first of many voyages to South America.

The island they returned to had changed radically in the three years they had been absent, and the Mafia had expanded dramatically. 'La Piovra' – 'the Octopus' – was more pervasive than ever before. The expansion of their power was attracting a new type of mafioso, young, ambitious and scornful of the old ways – men like Luciano Liggio, a ruthless killer from the Corleone family. Liggio's ambition and outlook were radically different from the rural traditions of Don Calò.

Buscetta's criminal career coincided with the activities of the new Mafia, but in his confession he claims his 'spiritual' allegiance lay with the traditional 'Men of Honour'. He speaks movingly of Gaetano Filippone, his family head who exemplified the tradition. He also singles out Dr Maggiore, the owner of a clinic for mental patients, and Giuseppe Trapani, the licensed distributor in Sicily of Messina beer and town councillor in Palermo. One of the two was the deputy head and the other the '*consigliere*' (literally 'counsellor', usually the third highest-ranking member of a Mafia family):

> They were both very dignified people, gentlemanly and inherently good. These two were just the sort of people I was modelling myself on, as well as Gaetano Filippone. He never made much money – even when he was seventy he still used to travel by public transport. I very quickly realized though that the Costa Nostra was not really inspired by principles of honesty and moral rectitude as I had once believed, but that it was in fact a conspiracy whose sole end was to protect the members from being caught in their criminal work. This went so far that violence was becoming almost a daily occurrence among us.

By the time the Buscettas returned to Sicily the immensely overweight and ageing Don Calò had become a respectable public figure as the mayor of Villalba. The Americans continued to be his benefactors. In return he dealt with the threat of communism, and he dealt with it uncompromisingly. Certainly, he said, the new trade unionists could have headquarters in Villalba. Certainly the communists could set up their centre as well. There was only one condition – one of Don Calò's men must be in charge. It was an offer that they had the nerve to refuse. So Don Calò, as a true Sicilian, bided his time. When the communists asked the mayor's permission to hold an open-air meeting in the town square, Don Calò consented. When the communists assembled, Don Calò's men greeted them with a hail of machine-gun fire.

It may not have been subtle but it worked.

A new source of revenue for the post-war Mafia was property speculation. The post-war building boom provided a bonanza for crooked politicians and *mafiosi* alike. In effect this meant buying land at agricultural prices in the knowledge that it was due to be given planning permission. Close contacts within the 'Third Level' were vital. The politicians designated the areas for development, and local builders, who were Mafia front men, bought the land and took the contracts.

The Mafia's other main source of income after the war was tobacco smuggling. The Italian government had a monopoly over the sale and distribution of tobacco. Everyone wanted imported American cigarettes. So the Mafia either bought or, more simply, stole American cigarettes outside Italy, smuggled them into the country and sold them at an enormous profit. In order to expand this trade the Mafia formed an alliance with some powerful Neapolitan gangsters – men like Michele Zaza, a leader of the Camorra, the Naples version of the Mafia. Naples was important as an alternative port of entry to Palermo. It was also the new home of Lucky Luciano, the architect of organized crime in America, and the instigator of the Sicilian Mafia's wholesale involvement in the narcotics trade. Much of Luciano's post-war career is still unknown. His importance to the Sicilian Mafia was only recently revealed by Tommaso Buscetta. He had met Luciano in Palermo shortly after his return from South America in 1951. Buscetta was greatly impressed by his fellow Sicilian. The two men formed a firm friendship and the young *mafioso* was particularly keen to hear about Luciano's experiences in the United States. Luciano explained to Buscetta the details of the New York Commission of the Mafia. It was a ruling council which had the power to adjudicate disputes between families and to order Mafia executions. As long ago as 1937, Luciano had organized the twenty-four Mafia families into a national Commission based in New York. The founder members included Luciano himself, Giuseppe 'Joe Bananas' Bonanno, Vito Genovese and Albert Anastasia. Now he was returning to Palermo as the 'war hero' who had helped the Americans to liberate Sicily.

The Commission was so successful that it was not until 26

February 1985 that the US authorities were finally able to bring an indictment against the heads of the five New York families who supervised the operations of the American Mafia. The Sicilian Mafia had no such Commission and, to make matters worse, they had a reputation for long and vicious vendettas. Luciano confided in Buscetta that it was essential that the Sicilian Mafia should get themselves organized along similar lines. The more Buscetta thought about it, the more it made sense.

Another important voice endorsed this advice. In 1957, on a visit to Sicily, the American boss Joe Bonanno put his considerable weight behind the idea of a Sicilian Commission. It seems to have been a favourite structure, mostly because it made killing people a more orderly and controlled affair.

Joe Bonanno landed at Rome's Fiumicino airport in the late summer of 1957. As one of the bosses of the five New York families, he was received like a visiting statesman. Bernardo Mattarella, the Italian Minister for Foreign Trade, was among the welcoming party. Mattarella was one of the ruling Christian Democrat politicians. He had grown up with Bonanno in Castellamare in Sicily.

On the evening of 12 October 1957, at a private room in the Spano restaurant in Palermo, Bonanno was fêted as the guest of honour. His host was his old friend Lucky Luciano. Luciano introduced an up-and-coming young man to Bonanno – Tommaso Buscetta, already a success in the Porta Nuova family, particularly for his skill at smuggling. Among the other guests were Carmine Galante, Bonanno's *consigliere*; Angelo and Salvatore la Barbera, friends of Buscetta who were making fortunes in real estate; Salvatore 'Ciaschiteddu' Greco, a family boss; and Gaetano Badalamenti, a morose dark-haired young man who would succeed in the Cinisi family.

During dinner Bonanno took Buscetta and Greco aside. 'It would be to everyone's advantage if you had a Commission, like the one we have in America,' he said. 'Since we started in 1937, the Commission has approved all the hits against Men of Honour, and the system has worked very well.'

Buscetta was now convinced that it was a good idea and,

more importantly, that it would also serve to enhance his reputation and prestige.

Bonanno also attended a major Mafia summit meeting while in Sicily that year. It took place in the Hotel des Palmes in the centre of Palermo on 14 October. The other guests at the summit included Bonanno's 'underboss', John Bonventre; Carmine Galante, a tough gangster called 'Lillo' – 'Little Cigar' – who supervised a major heroin network for the Mafia; Cesare Manzella, the head of the Cinisi family before it was taken over by Badalamenti; Calcedonia di Pisa, a brash gangster who headed the Noce family and was one of the early heroin traffickers; and Genco Russo, the heir to Don Calò. Buscetta and Luciano Liggio were almost certainly also there. Liggio, like Buscetta, was earning a considerable reputation for himself; he was the youngest *mafioso* to run one of the feudal estates, and he was already an expert killer by the age of twenty.

Although the Hotel des Palmes summit was clearly a gathering of the *illuminati* of organized crime, the details of it are still shrouded in mystery. It is now believed that one of the main topics on the agenda was the organization of the heroin trade on an international basis. According to the FBI, it was this meeting which established the Bonanno family in the heroin trade, an involvement which continued all the way through to the Pizza Connection.

Another part of the agenda concerned the next summit meeting of the American Mafia, to be held in Appalachin in New York State. However, before 'the board' could reconvene there was another killing. Albert Anastasia, the original boss of 'Murder Incorporated', ran his operation with a combination of maximum terror and minimum intelligence. This reign of terror came to an end on 25 October 1957. He was gunned down sitting in a barber's chair at the Park Sheraton Hotel in Manhattan.

The subsequent Appalachin summit proved to be a disaster. The police raided it and arrested a number of top *mafiosi*. More importantly, the Mafia and its national leadership was now exposed for the first time.

Vito Genovese had been responsible for organizing the summit, and back in Italy Luciano made as much capital as he could out of the disaster. He was glad to have escaped, not least because there was substantial opposition by some of the Mafia leaders to the prospect of wholesale involvement in the narcotics business. Luciano was now presented with the opportunity to dominate the trade himself.

During his time in Italy, Luciano had been establishing a complicated network for the supply and distribution of heroin. Morphine base, the first stage in refining the gum drawn from the opium poppies, would be brought in from the Middle East, usually from Beirut, refined into heroin in European laboratories mainly situated in Marseilles and Sicily, and then transported to America.

The success of the trade can be gauged by the fact that not once was Luciano's network interrupted by the authorities, and by the sheer growth of the number of addicts in the United States during his heyday: from an estimated 20,000 at the end of the war to 60,000 by 1952, and by 1965, three years after his death, the number had tripled to 150,000. Although the increase was not totally attributable to Luciano, he undoubtedly helped.

Luciano's initial source of supply was one of Italy's most respectable pharmaceutical firms – Schiaparelli. At that time, controls over the manufacture of pharmaceutical supplies of heroin were very lax. Luciano simply bribed some of the company's executives and secured more than 700 kilos over a four-year-period. American investigators from the Federal Bureau of Narcotics eventually uncovered the conspiracy and pressured the Italian government to tighten up their pharmaceutical regulations. Luciano had no difficulty in finding alternative sources of supply. He turned to the world's biggest supplier of morphine base, Sami-El Khoury, a Lebanese with highly placed political connections in Beirut. There, with the active assistance of Lebanese customs, the Narcotics Police Division of Beirut and the director of Beirut airport, raw opium in large quantities was smuggled in from Turkey and exported to Sicily and Marseilles.

The methods of shipment and the geographical networks that

were used then are remarkably similar to those used by the Mafia today. Then, as now, small fishing boats would set off from Palermo harbour or a remote spot on the Sicilian coastline, rendezvous with a Middle Eastern freighter in international waters, pick up the consignment and smuggle it back ashore. Once it was landed, the morphine base was taken to a laboratory for refining into heroin. One of Luciano's main laboratories was a confectionery factory in Palermo which had opened in 1949. It functioned smoothly until 11 April 1954 when a daily newspaper in Rome published an article and a photograph of the factory under the headline 'TEXTILES AND SWEETS ON THE DRUG ROUTE'. The factory was closed that evening, and the chemists smuggled out of the country.

From Sicily, the refined heroin entered the United States through a variety of routes. Luciano, using associates in Milan, Hamburg, Paris and Marseilles, would ship it in cargoes of fruit, vegetables or olive oil, or have it taken in by couriers, usually Italian immigrants who frequently had no idea what they were carrying. From Europe, the heroin was shipped either directly or via Canada or Cuba, both ideal transit points for heroin destined for the North American market.

But Luciano was beginning to experience 'business problems'. The main difficulty was the refining process. Although it is relatively easy to convert raw opium into morphine base, the chemical process of turning morphine base into heroin is considerably more complex. The technical name for heroin is diacetylmorphine: the morphine is acetylated by reacting it with acetic anhydride or acetyl chloride. The morphine base has to be heated to a precise temperature with acetic anhydride, then filtered through alcohol, charcoal and acetone. The final stage is the drying and crushing, using hydrochloric acid to make the hydrochloric salt of heroin. This makes it soluble in water – an important property as heroin cannot be used for injection until its salt has formed. A bad chemist with poor equipment could turn out heroin of such poor quality that there would be difficulty in selling it, and if he was a real amateur, then getting the temperature wrong by just a few degrees during the heating stage would result in a lethal explosion. Good chemists were at a premium. Although the Sicilians were skilled smugglers, for the most part they lacked the necessary expertise to run sophisticated refining laboratories. For those skills they had to turn to the chemists of the French Connection based in Marseilles. Like Palermo, Marseilles is a dockyard city dominated by a secret criminal organization: the Union Corse. Many of its members had also been fierce opponents of the German occupation.

One of the most famous of the Resistance fighters was Antoine Guerini. He had worked as an agent for both British and American intelligence. He worked as the contact man for British agents parachuted into occupied France and his organization helped to smuggle the arms dropped by British aircraft to the Resistance.

At the end of the war, the fragile alliance that had existed within the Resistance between the socialist and communist factions disintegrated. At the same time, the communists were attracting growing support throughout France, particularly in Marseilles. Their success was accompanied by a series of street battles and civil unrest. In 1947, American intelligence analysts in Washington, already faced with the communist threat in Italy, also feared an imminent communist coup in France. The CIA poured money and agents into Marseilles. It was there, they decided, that the battle for France would be won.

A CIA psychological warfare team was set up to liaise directly with Antoine Guerini, who was able to provide considerable resources of manpower – although the skill of his men tended to the physical rather than psychological. The eventual victors were the socialists backed by the CIA and the Union Corse. With control of the port and an abundant supply of strong arm men, Guerini and his associates took over the heroin trade. They dominated the French Connection throughout the fifties and sixties, carefully ensuring that none was peddled inside the country for fear of upsetting powerful political friends. Using the best chemists and laboratories to produce heroin of the highest purity, they became central to the world-wide market.

Luciano was quick to appreciate the advantages of the French Connection, and when his supplies from Schiaparelli were closed down the Corsicans filled the gap.

Tom Tripodi, now one of the DEA's most experienced operators, who worked in France during the height of the French Connection, has few illusions about its origins:

> Prior to World War Two, the laboratories were in Sicily. The war displaced all the laboratories there, then they were established in the Nice/Marseilles area. This was a fortuitous thing politically because the American State Department and the intelligence services were very active in Marseilles and Nice in combating the very strong pro-communist labour movements at the dock. The support that we achieved from the French people was amongst the Corsicans, who were traditionally active in the underground during World War Two. They formed the backbone – the *Barbouzes*.
>
> The laboratories were set up there and some people would argue that our own financial peripheral support cultivated that. Whether it's true or not, we'll never know or even care. But the Italians always controlled the morphine base flowing from the poppy fields into Marseilles. They always controlled the heroin coming from those laboratories into the States.
>
> During the period of the French Connection, in the late sixties and early seventies, it's no coincidence that we arrested over forty former French intelligence officers.

Heroin has always been an international trade, connecting the poppy fields of the Third World with the backstreets of the affluent world by a route stretching through France, Turkey, the Lebanon and Italy. *Mafiosi* like Luciano helped to set up those connections, to establish the world market.

The old Mafia, epitomized by Don Calò, was eclipsed by Luciano, who in turn laid his evil blessing on Buscetta. Although Buscetta found himself torn between the obvious profits of the drug trade and the sense of honour he had inherited from the old guard, he was nevertheless to become one of the principal beneficiaries of Luciano's legacy.

4

The First Mafia Wars

Success in war is obtained by anticipating the plans
of the enemy, and by diverting their attention from
our own designs.

FRANCESCO GUICCIARDINI, *Ricordi*

Shortly after their grand dinner at the Spano restaurant in
Palermo, Tommaso Buscetta and Salvatore 'Ciaschiteddu' Greco
conspired to set up a Commission system in Sicily. Buscetta was
still only twenty-nine, with the nominal rank of 'soldier', so his
involvement with its foundation was a considerable honour. The
fact that the Commission proved to be a success endowed him
with an unofficial power and prestige, and though he did not
actually sit on the Commission, his status within the 'Honoured
Society' was now assured. The fact that he was instrumental in
setting it up enabled him to influence many of their decisions.
He has explained to agents who have been debriefing him in
New York that his instructions and advice to Commission
members were often accepted.

Instead of a single commission as in America, Greco and
Buscetta set up a series of provincial commissions with represen-
tatives who were soldiers rather than bosses. The Palermo Com-
mission became the supreme ruling council. In his confession
Buscetta reveals the complexity of the structure of the Sicilian
Mafia:

> The word 'Mafia' is a literary creation, whereas the
> *mafiosi* are simply known as Men of Honour; each one
> of them is part of a village – the *mafioso* organization

taking its name from the area itself. Within the family there are: the *capo* [boss], chosen by the Men of Honour; he in turn names a *sottocappo* [underboss], one or more *consiglieri* [counsellors]; if, however, the family is very large, even the counsellors are elected, but no more than three; and the *capidecina* [heads of ten]. The boss of the family is called the representative of the family.

Above the families and serving the purpose of coordinating the different groups is a collegial structure known as the Commission, made up of members each one of whom represents three families that are geographically close together. This member is one of the bosses of the three families, named by the bosses of those families. The members of the Commission, in my day, held office for three years, but I don't know if these rules still apply. At the present time, the profound degeneration of the main leaders of the Mafia has resulted in the fact that these rules are respected only formally, because in reality the Commission is the instrument through which the individual or individuals who dominate impose their will. Overall, this organization is called Cosa Nostra, as in the United States.

It was a state within a state, comparable to a central government body with regional affiliates. The centre of power was Palermo, to which the provincial commissions would defer. For a time the system worked effectively, but not well enough to prevent a series of rivalries from erupting into a bloody civil war between the Mafia families of Palermo in the early 1960s.

It was no coincidence that the war followed shortly after the death of Lucky Luciano on the evening of 22 January 1962 at Naples airport. Luciano was waiting to meet a Hollywood film producer, Marvin Golsch, who was planning to make a film about him. His American Mafia friends were not wild about his questionable life being immortalized on film, and had warned him that if he went ahead with it there would be dire consequences. Dire indeed – he died after drinking a cup of coffee, raising the possibility that he had been poisoned. (Drinking poisoned coffee is known in the Mafia as 'taking a bitter coffee'.) Agents of the narcotics bureau of Interpol were also waiting for him at the airport. Although the official cause of death was given as heart failure, there were rumours that he had been silenced because of the film project and as an insurance policy against any revelations he might have made if he had been arrested.

In Sicily, Mafia wars come and go in cycles, like a volcano which is constantly smouldering and occasionally erupting. In fact there is a war going on virtually all the time – it is the intensity with which it manifests itself that varies. This perpetual conflict is due to the Sicilian tradition of vendetta: death and dishonour have to be avenged. The ritual may take a long time. The Sicilian will savour his enemy's false sense of security, then kill him when he least expects it. According to a well-known Sicilian proverb, 'Revenge is a dish best eaten cold.'

The reason for the war in the early 1960s was, as ever, money, and in particular drug money. There was a power struggle to control the enormous profits from the drug trade and from building speculation. It led to increasing conflict between the old and the new Mafia, the traditional and the modern. The former tended to be established members of the community, who came from a rural background. The latter emerged from the slums of Palermo, and their power depended on streetwise cunning and a total disregard for human life. These modern *mafiosi* took their cue from the Chicago school of American crime, characterized by sharp suits, sub-machine-guns and wallets full of dollars. They had seen too many Cagney movies. The traditional 'Men of Honour' on the other hand favoured a low-key approach, dressing in the shabby clothes of the Sicilian peasant and responding to an almost tribal code of conduct. They used the traditional methods of persuasion accompanied by veiled threats before resorting to physical violence.

Luciano Liggio, a fast-rising and almost unbelievably blood-thirsty *mafioso*, epitomized the new Mafia. Just as Lucky Luciano paved the way for the Mafia's wholesale move into the narcotics trade, so did Luciano Liggio pave the way for a new spiral of violence. His rapid rise to power was consolidated by a series of vicious murders which he personally supervised, many of them aimed at the destruction of the trade-union movement in Corleone. The boss of his own family in Corleone was Dr Michele Navarra, a highly respected member of society. He exemplified the traditional 'Man of Honour'. As well as being inspector of health for the area, he was President of the Cultivators' Association of Corleone and chairman of the local branch of the Christian Democratic Party. In addition he was a genuine doctor who, on one infamous occasion, administered a fatal injection to a twelve-year-old shepherd boy who had seen Liggio murder a trade-union activist.

Corleone is a small but sprawling village which lies beneath the main mountain road from Palermo where it appears to have settled by accident. It is surrounded by some of the most spectacular countryside on the island. The town square is watched over by an imposing statue of St Francis whose hands are raised to the sky in a gesture of hope or, more likely, desperation. Old men with flat caps gather round the benches outside the small strip of land which passes for the municipal park, and talk endlessly with scarce movement of their lips. They gesticulate wildly with their hands, displaying an energy that belies their years. There is one bar which has been named The Godfather, and a stallholder sells a variety of goods including plastic guns to the few children who venture onto the streets. Torn, faded posters denouncing the violence of the Mafia hang on the village walls. Corleone means 'Lionheart', but for the most part it has the desolate air of a ghost town – shuttered blinds, deserted alleys, crumbling buildings. Elderly widows in black dresses scurry down narrow streets like frightened spiders. The only other signs of life are the endless rows of washing strung from one narrow balcony to another.

Corleone was the fictional name of the Mafia family in Mario Puzo's novel *The Godfather*. It was well chosen. Between 1953 and 1958 there were 153 murders in the town, a statistical tribute to the rising terror of Luciano Liggio.

Liggio came from a very different background from Dr

Navarra. He was almost illiterate, having never gone to school, though later in life he did make an attempt to educate himself, extracting lessons from a schoolteacher – at gunpoint.

He began his career as a rural bandit, protecting the feudal estates of the aristocracy, and ended up presiding over a multi-million-dollar empire, which he still controls from behind the bars of Ucciardone prison in Palermo. Characteristic of the new breed of *mafioso* was an impatient ambition which would not be held in check by traditional deference to their elders. Liggio was intent on diversifying as fast as possible into new and more lucrative rackets: transport, cattle smuggling, slot machines, kidnapping, construction and eventually drugs. If his boss did not approve, that was his problem. The doctor would have to be eliminated. The final confrontation came when Liggio spotted an opportunity to make a lot of money out of a project to build a dam. The conservative Dr Navarra tried to oppose it. As Navarra now stood between Liggio and the prospect of a huge fortune which could be extorted from the contractors, there was only one solution. A fifteen-man ambush was set up on a road along which Liggio knew Navarra would be driving. Liggio and his men took no chances. Navarra's body was found inside the car ripped apart by 210 bullets.

Liggio then systematically set about killing Navarra's supporters.

According to Buscetta, it was this murder which began to undermine the traditional codes of conduct observed between 'Men of Honour'. By killing his boss for personal gain, Liggio was openly flouting the conventions of the 'Honoured Society' where rank was determined by elections and the position of the *capo* was both sacred and unchallenged. In Buscetta's words:

> . . . the underlying cause of the crisis that afflicted the Mafia organization goes back to when Luciano Liggio, without the knowledge of the Commission, killed Dr Navarra, who was then the boss of the Corleone family. Liggio was called in to answer for this serious infraction by the then head of the Commission, Salvatore Greco,

known as Ciaschiteddu; Liggio explained it to the latter on the basis of personal grounds that I know nothing about, and asked Greco to believe him.

From that time on, Liggio has systematically and scientifically pursued all those who had supported the rigorous and consistent approach of Ciaschiteddu and all of them have been eliminated or, at any rate, pursued.

With no one daring to challenge him, Liggio went on to become the undisputed king of the melancholy little town of Corleone and one of the most fearsome killers that the Mafia has ever seen. In the years to come, so many succumbed to his power that his henchmen and family associates became known as 'the Corleonesi'.

While Liggio was consolidating his power, other forces were at work which would produce a different faction within the Mafia. When Lucky Luciano died the man who took over much of his narcotics trade was Cesare Manzella, a traditional Mafia *capo*, who sat on the Palermo Commission. He was the head of the family based in Cinisi, a small seaside town on the way to Punta Raisi airport. As the airport was in their territory it was an invaluable asset for the import and export of contraband, including narcotics. His deputy was Badalamenti, already a leading *mafioso*. Manzella loved children. As he sauntered down the narrow streets of Cinisi, often wearing a wide-brimmed American-style hat, he would hand out pocketfuls of sweets to passing orphans and street urchins. He devoted a proportion of his profits from the heroin trade to building an orphanage. His charity was rewarded by his election as president of the Catholic Action Group in Cinisi.

In February 1962, Manzella's family had arranged for a consignment of heroin to be delivered by their normal supplier, a notorious Corsican smuggler known as 'Goldfinger'. His men operated out of almost every port in the Mediterranean, smuggling everything from cigarettes to heroin. Normally, when delivering heroin to Sicily, Goldfinger would simply bring his yacht close in to the port of Palermo and hand over the heroin to one of the Mafia's many small fishing boats. Recently, the transfers had become so blatant that the authorities had objected. For this shipment it was decided that a little discretion would be in order. The transfer would take place on the south side of the island. The man who Manzella asked to collect the shipment was Calcedonio di Pisa. Di Pisa has been described by Norman Lewis, author of *The Honoured Society*, as 'a garish young freebooter, habitually be-gloved, shirted in a puce silk and with a coat of the palest camel hair . . . He drove a butter-coloured gadget-festooned Alfa Romeo.'

Despite his colourful appearance he was a considerable figure in the Mafia, being both a member of the Palermo Commission and head of the Noce family.

Di Pisa hired a boat from Agrigento and made the rendezvous with Goldfinger, after which he delivered the package to Manzella. The heroin was then smuggled out of Palermo to New York via a crewman on the transatlantic liner *Saturnia*. When the syndicate financing the deal received their money they discovered that they had been shortchanged. Manzella contacted his partners in New York, who told him that the package which had been delivered was underweight. Di Pisa was immediately suspected of double-crossing his partners, and was summoned to appear before the Commission. Skilfully, he managed to convince them that he was not the guilty party. But the case was bitterly contested by two members of the Commission – the la Barbera brothers. This was the start of a vicious rivalry between the la Barberas and di Pisa's supporters.

Angelo and Salvatore la Barbera had raised themselves out of the slums of Palermo via petty thievery and murder to become the heads of one of the most powerful groups of the new Mafia. They had risen to prominence on the tide of money flooding in from building rackets and drugs. They had gone into partnership with Lucky Luciano and another gangster with American connections, Rosario Mancino. With powerful friends behind them, they had fought their way to the top over a pile of corpses.

Police reports suggested that Buscetta had become one of their principal enforcers and hit men. The brothers were certainly closely allied to Buscetta's Porta Nuova family. Salvatore la Barbera was the district representative on the Commission and Buscetta, the driving force behind the Commission, had become one of its trusted associates. Already Buscetta's authority was considerable, not least because of his many powerful friends. Other *mafiosi* would think twice before showing disrespect to a man who was on intimate terms with Lucky Luciano, Salvatore Greco and the la Barberas.

Throughout his career in the Mafia, Buscetta's prestige was enhanced by the respect he commanded among the most powerful Men of Honour. His close association with the power-brokers endowed him with an almost legendary reputation, part built on myth and rumour and part owing to an innate confidence, intelligence and strength of character which enabled him to impress all those with whom he came into contact. When Buscetta applied for the return of his passport, which had been taken from him after his arrest on charges of tobacco smuggling in 1958, he was able to produce a letter from an Italian Member of Parliament to support his claim:

> To the very kind Doctor Jacovacci,
>
> I strongly ask that you approve the renewal of the passport of Tommaso Buscetta, a person whom I have great interest in. Certain of your personal attention, I thank and greet you cordially.
>
> The Honourable Barbaraccia

Buscetta's passport was returned on 23 May 1961, valid for three years.

In a profile of Buscetta prepared by the Italian parliamentary Anti-Mafia Commission, he was described as an 'individual totally devoid of scruples, a bully, haughty and vain, who brags a lot of friendships and relationships in high places'. They were not all idle boasts. In the civil war that was to develop in 1962–3, he had close connections with both sides. His relationship with the la Barberas covered the whole range of Mafia activities, from extortion, blackmail and murder through to threats and harassment aimed at building contractors and other businessmen who were foolish enough to refuse the generous offers made by the la Barberas in their redevelopment of Palermo.

Some evidence of Buscetta's early criminal career comes from the same Anti-Mafia Commission report:

> His life of crime began in the year of 1956. On the night of 28–29 March two trucks, carrying 3815 kilos of cigarettes, were confiscated at Torre Ciachia di Capai. Among those named in the incident were Gioacchino Testa, known to the Ministry of Finance police to be closely tied to Tommaso Buscetta as well as Vincenzo Mancino. On 28 March 1958, Buscetta was charged with 'criminal conspiracy to smuggle cigarettes'. He was acquitted.
>
> In another incident gleaned from wiretaps on the phone of Giuseppe Amerta, police heard that Amerta had asked the notorious smuggler Molinelli on behalf of 'the friend of Nino Camporeale', for the 'same merchandise', that is 'this beautiful piece of work'. To the police it looked as if a major heroin deal was under way. On 17 March 1958, the police discovered from another wiretap that Michel de Val, a messenger from Molinelli, had arrived in Rome bringing 'the merchandise' in a suitcase.
>
> The police raided the house of Wanda Persichini, one of Tommaso Buscetta's lovers. They could not find the suitcase but they did find a small set of scales normally used to weigh drugs. In the house they found de Val, Camporeale, Amerta and Buscetta. Although he had his passport confiscated and was 'warned' by the police headquarters in Rome, Buscetta was acquitted. There was insufficient proof.

Twenty-seven years later Buscetta admitted to Falcone that he knew de Val was the lover of Wanda Persichini but denied that there was any heroin involved. For example, he says, 'Now, about the suitcase de Val had with him, I would like to point out that he was followed by the police from the moment of his arrival at the Rome railway station until he entered Persichini's house. If he had had a suitcase with him I do not see how he could have managed to hide it, since the police broke into the apartment just about the same time as de Val.'

On 19 March 1959, Buscetta was charged with conspiracy to evade customs inspection in Taranto, Sicily. The police had confiscated a truckload of cigarettes and Buscetta was arrested.

Although Buscetta's criminal record at this stage was inconclusive, with the exception of the conviction for tobacco smuggling, the police were convinced that he was an accomplished killer and an influential power-broker within the new Mafia. Although never convicted of murder, circumstantial evidence linked him to a number of killings. One of them was on behalf of the la Barberas.

In September 1959 Giulio Pisciotta and Vincenzo Maniscalco, two small-time Palermo gangsters, decided to pay a call on a builder named Girolamo Moncada. They told him that they wanted his property as they were planning to open an electrical shop and his site was the perfect spot. Moncada, however, was a 'friend of friends'. The site was in the la Barberas' territory and his Palermo construction business was a front for their building rackets. He referred the matter to the la Barberas, who told Maniscalco and Pisciotta to lay off – they were in la Barbera territory and Moncada was not to be touched.

They ignored the warning. Maniscalco was connected to some of the older *mafiosi*, who disliked the upstart la Barberas and may even have set up this act of provocation. Maniscalco proposed that the problem be discussed at a meeting of the Palermo Commission. Before the meeting could be held, Maniscalco was attacked in the centre of Palermo, shot several times and wounded. He refused to name his attackers and was later gaoled. Three days after the shooting one of his close friends who had been preparing to avenge the attack was killed. A child who got in the way also died.

On 2 October 1960, Pisciotta, who had by now opened a shop on Moncada's site, and his bodyguard were on their way to Palermo East railway station to collect some goods in a small Fiat. As they got out of the car they found themselves face to face with the la Barberas and, according to a witness, Buscetta. At gunpoint the two men were forced into another car which left at high speed. They were never seen again. Angelo la Barbera denied any involvement and, when the case came to trial, he and Buscetta were acquitted.

Another incident illustrates both Buscetta's role as power-broker and the undercurrent of tension that was beginning to threaten the Mafia's new system of government. In the late summer of 1962, Rosario Anselmo, a soldier in the Porta Nuova family, came to Buscetta to seek his advice. Anselmo had fallen in love with the daughter of a soldier in the Noce family. The Noce family boss, Calcedonio di Pisa, opposed the marriage. Buscetta told Rosario that he and the woman should go ahead and get married, which they did. Di Pisa was angry at Buscetta's interference and proposed to the Commission that relatives in a conventional family should always be members of the same Mafia family. Now that Rosario Anselmo had married into the Noce family he should be reassigned to that family. Such was Buscetta's status that he was able to veto di Pisa's proposal, and his voice carried the day. The Commission pronounced that di Pisa's scheme would be impractical and impossible to enforce. The decision made sense, but di Pisa had lost face.

On the surface it appeared to be a minor, almost pathetic disagreement but, according to Buscetta, it was to tear the Commission, and subsequently the Sicilian Mafia, apart. Buscetta believes that the issue was seized on and exploited by a group of older Mafia bosses, led by Michele Cavataio, who were jealous of the increasing power of the younger members of the Commission, notably the la Barbera brothers. In their turn, the la Barberas were insisting that members of the Commission, delegate bosses, should be distinct from family bosses – indeed that the delegate boss should be a junior member of the family nominated by the family's boss. This move struck directly at Cavataio and his allies, who all combined roles on the Commission with their positions as family bosses.

With a curious respect for democracy, the Commission endorsed the proposal. The ruling exacerbated the tensions between the *capi*, who did not like the idea of seeing their power diminished by the junior ranks. Some of them even resigned their positions as family heads to take seats on the Commission. Cesare Manzella had already agreed to be replaced by his deputy, Gaetano Badalamenti, and Calcedonio di Pisa was also about to submit to the ruling. But he never got the opportunity to stand down. On Christmas Day 1962, he parked his car in Palermo's main square and got out. As he walked towards a tobacco kiosk, three men fell in silently behind him and shot him with a sawn-off shotgun and a revolver. When questioned by the police none of the bystanders in the square could even recall hearing any shots.

Who had killed him? Buscetta himself was suspected because of the argument over Anselmo's marriage. It could have been Michele Cavataio, attempting to shift the blame on to the la Barberas. The prime suspect, however, was Angelo la Barbera. He had never been happy with the Commission ruling that exonerated di Pisa over the shortfall from the heroin deal. It was reason enough for the 'contract'. In Buscetta's words:

> It was immediately felt that the one who had given the order for this killing was Angelo la Barbera, who among the young family bosses was the most violent and determined.
>
> It was even said that he had used Men of Honour from the Porta Nuova family to commit the murder, specifically the grandson of the family boss. The latter protested that he had absolutely nothing to do with the murder and his position was supported by his grandfather. These denials were not believed and the entire Porta Nuova family was put 'out of commission'.

Whether or not Angelo la Barbera was guilty, the Mafia now turned on the brothers. The Porta Nuova family, previously allies of the la Barberas, not least because of Buscetta's friendship with them, now found themselves in the middle of a highly charged situation, suspected as accomplices and implicated in the di Pisa hit. It is a tribute to Buscetta's diplomatic skills that he survived the ensuing struggle, although he has been accused of merely switching sides and offering his allegiance to the forces now ranged against the la Barbera organization. Although he had a powerful friend in Salvatore Greco, the head of the Commission, it is more than likely that he would still have been called on to demonstrate his loyalty by some act of violence against his former friends.

With a powerful alliance ranged against him, Angelo le Barbera fled to Milan. His brother was not so lucky. On 7 January 1963, eleven days after di Pisa's murder, he disappeared, never to be seen again. The Palermo police suspected that Salvatore 'l'Ingegnere' ('the Engineer') Greco (Ciaschiteddu's cousin) had arranged a deal whereby Buscetta betrayed his former friend, killed him and disposed of his corpse in the furnaces of his glass factory. This could have been the price Buscetta had to pay for his new alliance. The body was never discovered and Buscetta claims to know nothing about the disappearance. He points out that 'the responsibility . . . had to rest with the Commission as a whole. You have to remember that la Barbera was a member of the Commission and that no other body, without the risk of severe reprisals, could have decreed his death. Everyone knows that the entire Cosa Nostra organization mobilized against Angelo la Barbera, and this horrific crime could not have happened without the unanimous decision of the Commission.'

When the Commission turned on the la Barberas, the members of Buscetta's family, ostracized because of their close relations with the brothers, held a crisis meeting. They agreed that it was advisable to scatter to avoid a vendetta. In fact the Commission, according to Buscetta, 'generously refrained from attacking the Porta Nuova family, mistakenly considered an ally of the la Barbera people'.

There is an obvious discrepancy in Buscetta's account: if the Porta Nuova family was not allied to the la Barberas, why were they shunned by the Commission? Buscetta denies that he was one of Angelo la Barbera's lieutenants. He also denies that he arranged the disappearance of Pisciotta and his bodyguard, or of Salvatore la Barbera.

The winners of the first Mafia wars were the immensely powerful Greco family, who forged an alliance between elements of the old and the new Mafia which put unlimited firepower at their disposal and gave them great reserves of political and financial strength.

The Grecos were the most powerful Mafia family in Sicily, a position held today by relatives bearing the same name. L'Ingegnere 'The Engineer' and Ciaschiteddu ('Little Flask' or 'Little Bird', apparently because he had very narrow shoulders and broad hips) controlled the area around Ciaculli and Giardini, south of Palermo. They had entered the drugs business early, first appearing in police records in 1955. They were the main threat to the la Barberas' power. With Salvatore la Barbera dead and Angelo on the run, victory seemed certain. But Angelo la Barbera could still retaliate.

What happened next literally blew the Mafia apart. On 12 February 1963 a stolen car packed with dynamite exploded in Ciaculli. It had been parked outside the house of Salvatore l'Ingegnere Greco. He escaped unhurt.

On 1 April, in bright morning sunshine, a Fiat 600 drove slowly past a fishmonger's shop in Palermo. The windows shattered as a fusillade of bullets poured from the car. One of la Barbera's main lieutenants was killed. It was rumoured that Angelo la Barbera himself, now back in Sicily, was wounded. When the police arrived they found an arsenal of weapons in the shop.

On 26 April, Cesare Manzella was returning home when his bodyguard was surprised to see a brand-new Alfa Romeo parked inside the wrought-iron gates of the courtyard. Manzella and his driver got out of their car to take a closer look at it. When they opened the door of the car they triggered a massive bomb. All that was found of Manzella was his wide-brimmed American-style hat and a single shoe. His companion disappeared completely. The Mafia had discovered a new if somewhat noisy and expensive method of killing their enemies and disposing of their corpses at the same time.

In a tree some twenty yards away the police discovered a satchel belonging to Manzella. Its contents revealed a great deal about the inner workings and the current strategy of the Mafia. The documents showed that the Commission was extremely worried about the Italian parliamentary Anti-Mafia Commission which had just been set up, and that a meeting had been held to declare a truce between all the Mafia families. The last thing they needed now was further bad publicity which might increase the Italian Parliament's determination to crack down on them. They also resolved to strengthen their political ties and their connections with prominent people. The Commission had noted that the argument over di Pisa and the missing money from the heroin deal would put all this in jeopardy.

They were right.

It was Manzella, *capo* of the Cinisi family, who had convened the Commission that sentenced Salvatore la Barbera to death. Now Angelo had made him pay for his brother's murder. Having got his revenge Angelo did what anyone would do in such circumstances. He ran away – but he was not fast enough. At 1.20 a.m. on 24 May 1963 he emerged from his mistress's house in Milan's Viale Regina Giovanna and slid behind the wheel of his Opel. Further along the road two cars were parked with their headlights on. Before he could start his car, the doors of the two cars opened simultaneously. Two men leapt out and emptied the contents of their revolvers into the *mafioso*. Hit by six bullets, he still managed to draw his own revolver and fire back, wounding at least one of his attackers. An ambulance arrived and took him to hospital, where he gradually recovered.

The war reached its climax at the end of June 1963. On 30 June the Questura, the police headquarters in Palermo, received a telephone call alerting them to a suspicious-looking Alfa which had been left in a lane in Ciaculli, the area controlled by the Grecos just outside Palermo. A few minutes later a second telephone call was logged in which the anonymous caller said,

'Don't touch the Alfa Romeo.' The police did not need warning – only the day before an Alfa Romeo had blown up in Villabate, killing a man on his way to work and crippling another for life. The Palermo headquarters dispatched a police patrol and a squad of army engineers to investigate the car. To their relief they discovered that the device placed in the rear seat of the car was very primitive. It had a fuse which had been lit but had gone out. One of the car's rear tyres was flat, which explained why it had been abandoned. The police carefully removed the device from the back seat and opened the boot.

Then the real bomb exploded. Seven soldiers and policemen were killed. The back seat device had been a decoy.

The Alfa had been parked opposite the house of l'Ingegnere Greco. Suspicion for the attack fell on Pietro Toretta, a rising Palermo *mafioso*, and also, once again, on Buscetta. The incident became known as the Ciaculli Massacre. It shocked the Italian people and precipitated a massive crackdown on the Mafia.

It is doubtful, however, whether Buscetta had anything to do with this outrage. He claims to have fled from Italy in February 1963, going first to Mexico and then to the USA. While there he heard of the attack on Manzella and the massacre at Ciaculli:

> I believe there was another attack aimed at Ciaschiteddu. These attacks were blamed on Angelo la Barbera but it didn't quite fit because one of the attacks took place when la Barbera was in Milan and had himself been seriously wounded in an ambush.

In Buscetta's version the murder of di Pisa is also seen in an entirely different light:

> The cleverness of Cavataio and his allies consisted in killing di Pisa at the time when the Anselmo romance was current so that the blame for the murder would fall on the la Barberas. The end result, in addition to the killing of district leader Salvatore la Barbera, was the disbanding of the Porta Nuova family as a punishment and Rosario Anselmo being taken into the Noce family.

The flaw in Buscetta's account is that he makes no mention of the disagreement over the heroin deal which clearly played a major part in the first Mafia war. Nevertheless, he gives an accurate account of the consequences of the internecine conflict and the effect that it had on the Mafia:

> The exodus abroad of Salvatore 'Ciaschiteddu' Greco and of so many others and the dissolution of some of the Cosa Nostra structures was caused by the knowledge that there had been a mistake in pinning the responsibility for the killing of Calcedonia di Pisa on la Barbera – as well as other serious acts of blood. Ciaschiteddu left everything and went abroad because he felt that the Mafia was obliterating all its traditional principles right in front of his eyes and turning itself into an organization of criminals.

Buscetta's version of the first Mafia war is a story of Machiavellian intrigue and fiendish complexity. It differs from the accepted version not only in omitting the Manzella heroin deal but also in that Buscetta himself emerges as relatively innocent. He admits that l'Ingegnere Greco tried to persuade him to murder Salvatore la Barbera but says he refused, that he played no role whatsoever in the disappearance of Salvatore la Barbera or the ambush of Angelo in Milan.

When reading Buscetta's confessions one ceases to be surprised at his denial of any involvement in criminal acts. He may be betraying the Mafia, but he clearly has no intention of betraying himself. Asked by Giovanni Falcone whether he knew that di Pisa dealt in drugs, Buscetta expressed complete surprise. His emphasis too on the 'Romeo and Juliet' version of the background to the first Mafia war is equally unconvincing. Most of the participants in the war are now dead and the exact truth died with them. The most plausible explanation is that Buscetta's story of Anselmo's romance is true as far as it goes, but that he deliberately exaggerated its importance, using it as a smokescreen to disguise his own involvement in the murder. There were clearly a number of overlapping disputes which destroyed the peace the Commission had so far maintained, and left the Mafia in total disarray. Buscetta himself emerged unscathed, with an even greater aura of power and prestige.

Angelo la Barbera, having had eight bullets removed from his body, was taken from hospital to prison. A dummy, dressed in one of Cesare Manzella's finest suits and wearing the hat and shoe that were the sole remains of their owner, was buried in a sumptuous coffin. The Porta Nuova family broke up, most of its members going abroad. Ciaschitteddu Greco went to Brazil, which would become a resting place for many *mafiosi* on the run. Meanwhile police pressure in Sicily became so intense that the Mafia almost ceased to function. The Ciaculli Massacre had provoked so many arrests that there was a chronic shortage of soldiers on the streets.

In 1967 many of those who were arrested came to trial at Catanzaro in Calabria. There were 114 defendants including Angelo la Barbera, Luciano Liggio, the Grecos and Buscetta. Buscetta was tried in his absence, as he was safely out of the country. The trial was a farce. When the court reached its verdict on 22 December 1968, sixty of the defendants were acquitted, and many of those convicted were sentenced on minor charges.

One of the acquitted was Michele Cavataio who, according to Buscetta, had masterminded the overthrow of the la Barberas. Cavataio's career was also nearly over but before it ended more blood would be spilled.

One of Buscetta's closest friends in the Mafia was Stefano Bontate. A young, good-looking Sicilian, nicknamed 'the Falcon', Bontate had become the *capo* of the Santa Maria di Gesù family at the early age of twenty, an accomplishment made all the more remarkable by the fact that he was unanimously elected by the members of the family itself. According to Buscetta, Cavataio had a grudge against Bontate and his family and decided to order the murder of Bontate's deputy, Bernardo Diana. Giuseppe Sirchia was given the contract and Diana was shot down and killed.

Bontate was furious – it was a grave insult to his authority. But he waited.

In 1969 Sirchia was banished to Castelfranco Veneto in the Treviso province. When Bontate found out that he was there he began to plan his revenge. He commissioned a four-man team to drive to the area and keep Sirchia under observation so that they could work out the best method for a hit. Sirchia became suspicious when he saw some cars cruising around which he had not noticed before. Contrary to the Mafia code, he telephoned the *carabinieri*. They sent a patrol car which stopped the two suspicious-looking cars. Inside they found the four men armed with sawn-off shotguns and sub-machine-guns. Three of them were members of the Porta Nuova family, which by 1969 was back in business. Their presence was an indication of the close relationship between the Porta Nuova family and Bontate, to whom Buscetta was almost like a brother. The new head of the reconsolidated Porta Nuova family, Giuseppe 'Pippo' Calò, also maintained a close relationship with Bontate.

Some years later, when he was in prison in Palermo, Buscetta learned more details of the plot against Sirchia. His informant had been part of the team. Buscetta recalls:

> He explicitly told me that, on the orders of Pippo Calò, he went to the town of Castelfranco Veneto to identify the house of Giuseppe Sirchia, who was living there under house arrest. They cased the joint, so that an expedition could be sent later so that they could get rid of Sirchia.
>
> Sirchia, who had become Michele Cavataio's deputy, was going to be killed because he had been an accomplice in all of the crimes committed by Cavataio, in particular the murder of Bernardo Diana, who was actually killed by Sirchia's own hand.

Sirchia survived this attempt but not the next. He was killed outside the Ucciardone prison. His wife was caught in the hail of bullets and also died. The hit had been ordered by Bontate but, according to Buscetta, 'he was never happy about the way in which the murder was perpetrated, especially with regard to the murder of Sirchia's wife'.

On 10 December 1969 several policemen entered an office in the Via Lazio, a modern street in one of the redeveloped areas of northern Palermo. The office belonged to the real-estate developer and former front man for the la Barbera brothers, Girolamo Moncada, the man whom Pisciotta and Maniscalco had leant on ten years before. When the reign of the la Barberas had come to an end in 1963, Moncada's services had been taken over by the successors to their property empire. Chief among them was Cavataio, who happened to be in the office at Moncada's desk when the policemen arrived. As they entered Cavataio suddenly realized that one of the men in uniform was not a policeman at all but a rival *mafioso*. Cavataio pulled out his gun and shot him. The other 'policemen' started firing and a ferocious gun battle followed. Cavataio and three others were killed. The bogus policemen fled, taking their dying companion with them. He was flung into the boot of one of the two new Alfa Romeos which had been left outside. The killers faded into the Palermo traffic and disappeared. They left behind more than a hundred bullet holes, a 7.65 Beretta, a 7.63 Mauser, a Colt Cobra revolver, a 38A Zanotti shotgun, a 38/49 Beretta machine-gun and an MP40 machine pistol.

Cavataio had paid with his life for the subtlety of his moves against the la Barberas. As Buscetta relates in his confession:

> Not only did the hostilities lead Angelo la Barbera and his family to the abyss, destroying their power, but also the entire Mafia organization as a whole. Consequently, some groups of the dissolved Mafia families felt it necessary to punish and eliminate Michele Cavataio, who had been the cause of this cataclysm. Finally, Cavataio's punishment came in the notorious massacre of Via Lazio.

Angelo la Barbera eventually died in prison in a Mafia killing described by Gaia Servadio, who knew him well and wrote his biography:

> When in July 1975 he was moved to Perugia prison, he was interned in the prison's hospital (although it had

been officially closed for a year), had various rooms at his disposal on the third floor, windows without bars, could ring up – he talked to his mother every night – and gave banquets (sometimes even champagne was served) to the inmates, who readily recognized him as a man '*di rispettu*' – of respect. The meals came from a restaurant near by. But lately la Barbera's men, eight of his bodyguards, had been transferred to another prison and the boss was on his own. An odd arrangement. When three killers left their isolation cell with surprising ease and knocked out the prison guard who was on duty at la Barbera's building, the boss only just had time to ask, 'What's the matter, *picciotti*?' La Barbera was stabbed eight times by the three Sicilians and died immediately.

Buscetta followed the example of Ciaschiteddu Greco. He fled the country. He was just in time, as the police had issued a warrant for his arrest in connection with the disappearance of Pisciotta and his bodyguard. Although there was now a murder warrant outstanding, at this stage the only successful conviction against Buscetta was for cigarette smuggling. The man who had played both ends against the middle, the man reputed to have taken part in several murders, had escaped yet again.

5

The Quiet Sicilian

> It should be borne in mind that the Man of Honour
> never ceases to belong to the family and until such
> time as he withdraws or is removed he maintains
> his membership in the family itself and in the Mafia
> organization in general.
>
> The confession of Tommaso Buscetta

While the Mafia families in Sicily were embroiled in civil war, their American cousins were enjoying a period of peaceful criminal activity. The one exception was the Bonanno family, which was split by its own war.

When Buscetta left Palermo in February 1963, he went first to Mexico. In Mexico City he acquired a false identity and papers under the name of Manuel Lopez Cadena. He also met a man who would play an important role in his future – Giuseppe 'Pino' Catania. Catania was a fellow Sicilian who had left Sicily in the fifties for South America. The exact circumstances of their meeting are mysterious. Buscetta says that accounts of the Mafia wars had appeared in a Mexican newspaper and that Catania recognized him from one of the pictures. Catania claims that they were introduced by another Italian living in Mexico. Whatever the truth, they became close friends and within three months Catania had invited Buscetta to come and live with him and his wife. Buscetta, who by this time had been joined by his mistress Vera Girotti, accepted the offer. In the early part of 1964 they all moved to Toronto, where Buscetta worked with Catania as a 'fabric salesman' before moving to New York in late 1964. Catania stayed on in Toronto for about a year before returning to Mexico City. Buscetta maintains he did not engage in any criminal activity while in North America:

> I deny that I received any help of any sort from the American Mafia during my stay in the USA. I entered the country with Giuseppe Catania and in order to buy the bus ticket from Buffalo to New York, Catania pawned his watch, receiving the amount of five dollars for it.

His statement is scarcely credible when it is remembered that he was a major Sicilian Mafia fugitive and that on his arrival in New York he received the sponsorship of Carlo Gambino, head of the Gambino family. Furthermore, Catania's connections were a little too good for an innocent Sicilian who just happened to recognize Buscetta while browsing through a Mexican newspaper. He was, for instance, very close to Frank Cotroni, brother of Vincent Cotroni, head of the chief Mafia family in Canada. The Cotronis worked in collaboration with the Bonanno family in New York, whom they consulted on matters of importance. Their relationship was much like that of a subsidiary company in a neighbouring country which had a great deal of independence but would defer to the parent company on matters of policy. Montreal had all the necessary qualifications to become a Mafia capital: it was close to the United States, in particular New York; it had a large Italian immigrant population, although mainly Calabrian rather than Sicilian; and it was the main route for the shipment of heroin into the United States from Europe. Also, Canada's historical relationship with France had made it an attractive refuge for French and Corsican gangsters from Marseilles.

In 1947, a thick-set, olive-skinned young man, suave, good-looking and fluent in five languages, had arrived in Montreal. His passport bore a false name — in fact he was Antoine d'Agostino. Like many of his Marseilles colleagues, d'Agostino was a former Gestapo agent and black marketeer. He had owned four Paris night clubs and several brothels. The Algerian-born Corsican had also been part of Luciano's heroin network. He received the refined heroin in Montreal and supplied it to Jean 'the Silver Fox' Laget, who was the New York liaison man between the Corsicans and the Mafia. Their clients included Anthony Strollo and Jo Valachi of the Genovese family. Another Mafia associate in the ring was Eugenio Giannini, a Luciano protégé. Giannini has been credited with the now standard smuggling technique which has been dubbed 'Gino's European Tours'. It involved a steady flow of Italian–American tourists visiting Europe by luxury liner along with family and car, all expenses paid by the Mafia. In garages in Italy and France heroin would be concealed inside the cars, which would then be shipped to Montreal or Quebec and driven across the border. A lot of the heroin coming in from Quebec would go to New York and back up to Toronto through Niagara Falls, where Stefano 'the Undertaker' Magaddino and his brother owned a funeral parlour. Magaddino was a New York Mafia boss and a member of the Commission. His territory included Buffalo, upstate New York, Toronto and Hamilton. His extensive interests in Canada would later bring him into conflict with fellow New York *capo* Joe Bonanno, who was a cousin. D'Agostino helped to organize and consolidate Montreal's position in the post-war heroin traffic. The Cotroni family dealt with them for both the domestic market and for export across the border to the vastly bigger market in the United States. When d'Agostino was chased out of Canada, he fled to Mexico City, from where he found it even easier to smuggle heroin into America. In 1954, Carmine Galante, one of Bonanno's men, filled the vacuum left by d'Agostino. He took over the 'Montreal Connection' in concert with Giuseppe 'Pep' Cotroni, the younger brother of Vincent Cotroni. At the height of the operation, couriers for Cotroni and Galante were driving fifty kilos a month across the border, using specially constructed Cadillacs with hidden back-seat compartments that could only be opened when several electric gadgets were switched on at once. Cotroni's operations came to an end as the result of an undercover agent infiltrating the gang. The agent was so convincing that Cotroni even gave him helpful instructions on preparing the car: 'This is the one [screwdriver] you need for the Chevy,' he pointed out to the agent while rummaging through a bag of tools:

> You take off the arm rest and you put the load down there in the well. Then you cover it with tar paper and put the arm rest back. Never miss getting across the border at night. If a customs guy gets it into his head to look in there, all he sees is that black tar paper and he thinks he's looking down into empty space ... some of the boys that had been in this business a long time they got special traps built in their cars. Like Big John Ormento. You first turn on the heater, then the ignition and a compartment in the rear drops open under the seat.

Galante and 'Big John' Ormento, a lieutenant in the Genovese family, sold to the biggest independent retail rings in the East, Mid-West and the South. By 1956, an estimated 60 per cent of the continent's heroin was coming in through Montreal. The network ran smoothly for at least five years until finally broken by a joint operation between the US Bureau of Narcotics and the Royal Canadian Mounted Police. One of the reasons for their uninterrupted success was the political protection which the Cotronis had bought. During a Quebec Police Commission inquiry into organized crime in February 1973, the former police director of Montreal testified that Vincent Cotroni was one of a number of 'untouchables' in organized crime who could not be prosecuted. He revealed that he had been fired twice because he had refused to follow orders to lay off.

When the ring was eventually caught, several of the top Mafia controllers in Canada and America were gaoled, including Galante, Giuseppe Cotroni and Big John Ormento.

Buscetta knew Luciano, Bonanno and Galante, having met them in Palermo and taken part with them in important meetings about Mafia policy and operations. In addition he would spend a considerable amount of time in Canada, associating directly and indirectly with the Cotronis.

On his arrival in New York, like thousands of Sicilians before and after him, Buscetta worked for a short time making pizzas. One of those who helped him get on his feet was Salvatore 'Sacco' Catalano, a member of the Sicilian Mafia who was living in America at the time. Buscetta began to manage a successful pizza restaurant. According to some of those who have been debriefing him in the United States, he is an extremely good cook.

He became involved in the pizza business through another friend called Filippo Casamento, who ran the Eagle Cheese Company. A small, bespectacled, grey-haired man with the unassuming appearance of a taxi-driver, Casamento was indicted in 1985 as one of the principal heroin dealers in the Pizza Connection case, along with Salvatore 'the Baker' Catalano, a relative of Sacco Catalano and an underboss in the Bonanno family. Eagle Cheese did not just deal in mozzarella – it was one of the front companies used to arrange the exchange of grocery bags full of heroin for grocery bags containing thousands of dollars.

Buscetta worked next as a labourer on construction sites in Brooklyn and Queens. The building industry was of course deeply infiltrated by the New York Mafia families, particularly through their control of concrete supplies and of the labour unions.

In 1965 Buscetta was joined by his wife and children. Although he still loved his family, his affection for Melchiorra had long since faded in favour of Vera Girotti. Buscetta's love for women and the night-life of big cities had earned the disapproval of the Porta Nuova family, and it was typical of the warped sense of 'honour' among the Mafia that he was censured for being too blatant about his infidelities, while the same organization would think nothing of instructing him to murder people: a Man of Honour may not cheat openly on his wife and children, yet he can turn wives into widows and children into orphans with impunity.

Buscetta had met Vera in Italy. She was an attractive and intelligent blonde. They met frequently in Rome when Buscetta was visiting various hotels in the city, often in the company of other *mafiosi*. Having a mistress was something of a status symbol within the Mafia, but a certain amount of discretion was called for. Buscetta, with the strong independence and scorn for hypocrisy that would often get him into trouble, paid little attention to such conventions. At the same time he took care not to abandon his responsibilities to his family. When Melchiorra and the children arrived, he arranged a separate apartment for them so that he could live with Vera.

In 1966 he decided to move full time into the pizza business. He borrowed $5000 and bought the Pizza Den on Pitkin Avenue, which he ran for two years and then sold. With the proceeds he bought the Pizza Master's pizzeria in Jamaica, Queens, with two business partners. The partnership also bought up Pizza City on Eighth Avenue in Manhattan. They ran these restaurants until 1971.

Among his circle of friends was Peter Castellano, brother of Paul Castellano, who was a powerful Mafia lieutenant in the Gambino family. 'Big Paulie' had been helped in his rise to power by marrying the sister of his boss, Carlo Gambino. It was a shrewd marriage, as Gambino, a small, slight man with an enormous nose, wielded great influence. The Gambino family was acknowledged to be the biggest and most powerful in New York, and members of the other New York families would always defer to Gambino during Commission meetings. (He once complained that there were so many people in his family that he did not know who was in and who was not.) Gambino's brother, Paul, was also a close friend of Buscetta. The two men met in Palermo in the fifties when they were neighbours – in fact Gambino had lived on the top floor of Buscetta's house. When they arrived in New York, Melchiorra and the children were put up at the house of Rosario Gambino, Carlo's cousin. Like the Bonanno family, the Gambinos maintained strong links with many of their relatives still living in Sicily. In the mid 1970s the Sicilian branch of the Gambino family was up to its neck in heroin trafficking mainly through the clan headed by Salvatore Inzerillo and Rosario Spatola, both relatives of the Gambinos. It has been estimated that by the late seventies the Inzerillo–

Gambino–Spatola network was smuggling $600 million worth of heroin into America each year.

Although Buscetta is careful to play down his activities in New York, he was, as ever, well connected. The story from underworld informers and low-level Mafia gossip is that he was not a man to be trifled with: he may have been playing the quiet Sicilian, but he was also well informed about the Mafia, its hierarchy and operations. Peter Castellano, for example, was known by Buscetta to be an active member of the Gambino family with the rank of soldier. Similarly, Buscetta's partners in the pizza business were also soldiers, one from the Gambino family, the other from the Lucchese family.

Buscetta points out that visiting members of the Sicilian Mafia could not engage in criminal activities without first seeking and receiving the approval of the American family in whose territory they wished to operate. Given the Mafia's long history of the use of small front companies like restaurants and pizzerias as a cover for a wide range of crooked operations, and Buscetta's status and credentials, it is almost inconceivable that he was entirely innocent of involvement with them during his stay in America. Moreover, his friends in the New York Mafia belonged to the Gambino and Bonanno families, those most deeply involved in the heroin traffic between Palermo and New York. Buscetta also kept in touch with visiting members of the Sicilian Mafia, including Antonio Salamone, head of the San Giuseppe Iato family. Buscetta reveals that Salamone started a pizza business with Giuseppe Ganci, a 'soldier' in his family. Ganci later became the principal organizer of the billion-dollar Pizza Connection heroin network, reporting directly to Salvatore Catalano, the Sicilian underboss of the New York Bonanno family. Throughout his career in the Mafia, Buscetta maintained close links with Salamone, whose family played a leading role in the narcotics trade. Characteristically, Buscetta has been extremely reticent about any illicit activities that they may have been involved in together. Later Buscetta became a crucial link between the Corsicans of the French Connection, who had moved to Brazil, and the Sicilian Mafia in New York.

6

The Latin American Connection

Al reported to Washington. He said, 'Hey, the French are shipping the stuff to South America – cars up to Mexico – and then driving it across the border.' The reaction was, 'Al's been in Marseilles too long and we'd better bring him home, he's been out in the sun.' Several years later, we started getting some breaks and we found out, oh goodness, we've been knocking our brains out.

Kevin Gallagher, DEA special agent, Manhattan

When France became too hot for them, many of the leading gangsters from the Marseilles heroin trade moved to South America. By a strange coincidence Tommaso Buscetta decided to move there too. The man who began the exodus and founded the new network was Auguste Ricord, a former Nazi collaborator who fled from Marseilles after the war. Slight in stature, with a face like a weasel, Ricord reached the very top of the heroin trade.

He began his career as a pimp and petty crook during the reign of fellow Marseilles gangsters and Nazi collaborators Carbone and Spirito in the 1930s. A police report of the time condemned him as 'quite unscrupulous. Sole interests: food, girls and money. No sense of humour, decency or dignity.' What he did have was a sense of the vast amount of money to be made from heroin. On 8 December 1947, under an assumed name, he sailed from Spain aboard the *Argentina Star* for a new life of wealth and crime in Buenos Aires. Apart from a minor interruption when he was jailed for white slavery and drug trafficking, he was to preside over one of the most successful heroin trading operations the world has ever had the misfortune to experience. Basing himself in Buenos Aires and Asunción, Paraguay, Ricord and his associates organized the smuggling of an estimated 11,000 pounds of heroin into America, valued at more than $1 billion, over a ten-year period. Known variously as '*el Viejo*' – 'the Old One' – or 'Monsieur André', and enjoying political protection from one of Paraguay's corrupt generals, Ricord built up a network of pilots, couriers and strong-arm men to transport his heroin to the North American market. One of the central figures in his network was Christian David, known as 'Beau Serge', a Marseilles gangster who was wanted in France for the murder of a policeman. David had freelanced for French intelligence and for de Gaulle's secret army, the SAC. The most infamous intelligence operation that he took part in was the abduction of Mehdi Ben Barka, the Moroccan opposition leader who was kidnapped and murdered in October 1965 while on French soil.

On 2 February 1966 Beau Serge was playing cards in a bar in Marseilles with Belkachem Mechere, the deputy Prefect of the Interior Ministry Police. Such a liaison was typical of Beau Serge's semi-official status as a gangster. But outside, the new head of the Serious Crimes Squad, Inspector Maurice Galibert, was waiting. He had been tipped off that a man involved in the Ben Barka affair was in the bar. Two other policemen arrived and walked into the bar with Galibert. Beau Serge continued his game of cards. The bar was not crowded. The police carefully approached the other customers before coming to the table where David sat. When they asked his partner, Mechere, for his papers he rapidly got angry, waving his official identity card at the policeman. When they asked Beau Serge for identification, he produced his official SAC identity card. Galibert looked at it but was unimpressed:

'I must ask you to come with us to the police station,' said the inspector, 'for an identity check.'

Beau Serge got up and let one of the other policeman frisk him for a concealed weapon. He wasn't carrying one. As they were leaving, Beau Serge asked if he could go back and collect the raincoat he had left in the bar. He returned with the coat, and they walked down the street towards the waiting police car. Beau Serge continued to protest his innocence:

'It's not me. You've got the wrong man.'

Suddenly, he reached into the pocket of the raincoat and pulled out a 7.65 mm automatic. He fired point blank at Galibert and the other policemen. Galibert died on the spot. His two companions were badly wounded. The police driver returned fire but missed. Beau Serge disappeared. But his underworld contacts were not good enough to get him off a murder charge. Although there was then an international alert for him, he was able to make use of a well-organized escape run from Marseilles. After hiding at a motel called Le Kentucky, which often acted as a transit lounge for criminals, he was driven to Genoa and sailed for Latin America. Among the few possessions he carried with him was a letter of introduction to Auguste Ricord.

He scarcely needed it, for his reputation had preceded him to South America, where he was warmly welcomed by the growing band of exiled Marseilles gangsters, most of whom were wanted on murder charges back in France. David's main associates were Lucien Sarti, who had also killed a policeman, and Michel Nicoli, a debonair and conspicuously well-dressed drug peddler.

Another major figure in Ricord's network was Claude Pastou. He had started off as one of Ricord's 'mules', carrying the heroin strapped to his body across international frontiers. Using this method he could carry three or four kilos at a time, earning $1000 per kilo. For larger shipments, the group would usually fly the narcotics to Mexico. South American *contrabandista* pilots specialized in flying light aircraft laden with South American contraband to Miami. They would return with American contraband, mainly whisky and tobacco, which they could sell for huge profits in Paraguay or Argentina. Often they would fly heroin to Mexico, where it would be hidden inside a car and driven across the border into the United States. There was so much traffic that the odds were stacked in the courier's favour. The car would be met in Texas, where another courier would collect the heroin, put it into a suitcase and take a commercial flight to New York. Both methods worked successfully for at least ten years. The DEA did not catch on to the Latin American Connection until Ricord and his men had sent thousands of kilos of heroin into the United States.

It was Pino Catania, the man Buscetta had met 'by chance' in Mexico in 1963, who would introduce him to this circle. While Buscetta was living in New York, Catania was travelling to Italy, New York, Canada and Mexico – an extensive itinerary for someone who had to pawn his watch to buy a ticket for a Greyhound bus. On a visit to New York in 1965, he introduced Buscetta to Carlo Zippo, known as 'the Baron', who ran an import–export company called Brasitalia. Buscetta was working at that time in the construction industry, courtesy of the American Mafia. Leaving his friend in New York, Catania visited Frank Cotroni in Montreal.

After meeting his Canadian Mafia friends Catania flew to Mexico, where he set up a business selling shirts with the backing of a prosperous Mexican businessman called Jorge Asaf y Bala. Part of Asaf's wealth came from the textile trade, but most of it came from narcotics. Known as the 'Al Capone of Mexico', he was the country's biggest heroin trafficker. Catania borrowed $1400 from Asaf and set up a boutique called Comiseria le Duc. It was an appropriate front – in the coded language the Sicilian Mafia used to arrange heroin transactions over the telephone, one of the most frequently used code words for heroin was 'shirts'. Shortly after meeting Asaf, Catania received a telephone call from Buscetta. They arranged to meet each other in Laredo, Texas. There Buscetta explained that he needed Pino's help. He wanted to go to Mexico to have plastic surgery. He was still using a false identity in New York and was increasingly worried about being caught. There was a warrant out for his arrest in

Palermo which would, of course, have been circulated to Interpol and the FBI. Towards the end of March 1967, Catania and Buscetta left for Mexico City, where Buscetta had plastic surgery at the Santa Fe Clinic. The operation does not seem to have been a great success: when he returned to New York three months later his children did not notice any difference.

In March 1969 Asaf asked Catania whether Buscetta would take twenty-five kilos of heroin from them in New York. Catania did not want to discuss the deal on the telephone, so he took an Eastern Airlines flight the following week to New York to find out if Buscetta had any customers who might buy the shipment. According to Catania, Buscetta said that he did. He would buy the heroin from Asaf for between $10,000 and $12,000 a kilo.

Vera Girotti was in the apartment at the time although she does not seem to have taken part in the discussion. Although separated from Melchiorra, Buscetta had been unable to divorce her without declaring his true identity, so he had married Vera under his false name, Manuel Lopez Cadena. His best man was Giuseppe Tramontana, a fellow Sicilian.

Buscetta warned Catania not to talk about the heroin deal in front of his American partners in the pizza business. This may have been because he wanted to avoid cutting them in on the deal – or because he knew that the American Mafia did not like the Sicilians operating without their permission, particularly in narcotics. Some of the heads of the American families disapproved of the narcotics trade. They felt it was a degrading business and attracted too much attention from the authorities; such disapproval rarely deterred members of their families from dealing in drugs – the money was too attractive.

Catania returned to Mexico City; Buscetta arranged for Tramontana to go to Mexico to make the arrangements and to meet the courier who was to drive the heroin over the border into the United States. It was arranged that Tramontana would meet Catania in a coffee shop in Mexico City called the Duca Desti, conveniently near Catania's clothes shop. The courier was a fifty-five-year-old Mexican Arab, Felipe Deguer. Balding, bespectacled and with a limp, Deguer was a close friend of the

Mexican police chief. His job was to take the heroin across the border in his Mercedes – just the sort of car and driver guaranteed to attract least suspicion from US customs.

When Tramontana arrived in Mexico City he gave Deguer an address in Pennsylvania where he was to deliver the heroin.

The gang then waited anxiously. The merchandise was carried safely across the border, but they still had to find a customer. They were sitting on at least $250,000 worth of heroin, and there were a lot of people wanting a piece of the action. Presiding over it with his customary calm was Buscetta. Most nervous of all was Catania, who was worried that their first major shipment might be seized or that they had been double-crossed somewhere along the line. The heroin business was like that – fast profits and 'sincere' friendships soon gave way to double-dealing and betrayal.

The telephone call came four days later: 'The merchandise has arrived safely.' Catania felt better – the run had paid off. In the middle of April he went to New York to collect the money, but Buscetta told him just what he did not want to hear: there was no cash because the merchandise was no good. Catania began to get extremely jumpy. During the next two months he visited his old friend twice and was told the same thing. He began to despair of getting any money for the shipment. Frantic for the share he had to pay back to Asaf, he flew to Montreal to contact one of his Mafia associates, Guido Orsini. Orsini was an impresario in a night club called the Club Circolo, owned by the Cotroni organization. He was later implicated in an illegal-alien smuggling operation which was investigated by the Royal Canadian Mounted Police and the New York State Police. It was an operation run by the Mafia which involved bringing Sicilians illegally to Canada and then smuggling them across the border to New York. Although it has not been proved, it is highly likely that many of the immigrants acted as couriers for heroin being sent to the United States by the Sicilian Mafia. This method has been used ever since the heyday of Lucky Luciano – a pedestrian version of 'Gino's European Tours'. Among the suspected organizers were Carlo Zippo and Buscetta, and although no heroin shipments were discovered, Buscetta was one of the common denominators in the extensive investigation.

At the same time that the illegal-alien ring was operating between Canada and New York, civil war was raging within the ranks of the Bonanno family. One of the main reasons was that Salvatore 'Bill' Bonanno had been elevated in the Mafia family by his father against the wishes of a faction led by Gaspare di Gregorio. The investigators believed that many of the immigrants were being used as soldiers in the Bonanno war. Sicilian immigrants were often used by the American Mafia as hit men. They were more skilled in this than their American colleagues, some of whom no longer had the stomach for such distasteful work. And as illegal aliens, there would be no record of their presence in the United States.

Other names that turned up in the investigation were Giuseppe Tramontana and Giuseppe Romano. Romano, known as 'the American', was a Sicilian hit man.

When Catania met Guido Orsini in Canada he proposed that they try to find a source of supply of heroin or cocaine in Mexico, which they could then sell in Montreal. If Orsini came in, Catania would split the proceeds fifty-fifty. Catania explained the desperate problems he was having with Buscetta's twenty-five kilos. Orsini was sympathetic, and he consoled his friend by offering to look around for a buyer. Word must have got round: Orsini could not find anyone.

Meanwhile, in Mexico City, Asaf was also searching for buyers for the heroin that no one wanted. A Cuban called Alcibiades Garcia Vasquez seemed interested. As soon as Catania was told he telephoned Buscetta and instructed him to send somebody to the San Antonio Inn in San Antonio, Texas, to meet Vasquez.

Once again Buscetta's best man acted as his sales representative. Tramontana met the Cuban and Catania at the hotel, then returned to New York with Vasquez. The Cuban appears to have bought about a kilo because a week later Buscetta's son Antonio flew to Texas to meet Catania and hand over $14,000. Catania does not seem to have done very well out of this transaction, considering the amount of travelling he was doing between Mexico, Canada and New York. When he got back to Mexico City he handed the money over to Asaf.

Buscetta then told Catania that their friend Guido Orsini from Montreal had turned up and had bought half a kilo for $4000. The tireless Catania flew to Montreal and collected the cash from Orsini. Once again he handed it over to Asaf. He then flew to Italy and on to Munich, where he met Buscetta, who was in Europe probably in order to attend a Mafia meeting.

In the late summer of 1969 the Sicilian Mafia was beginning to recover from the trauma of the family wars. Although police action after the Ciaculli Massacre in 1963 had decimated their ranks, many families had continued to operate in their places of exile, notably the United States and South America. The Commission was back in business. It consisted of a new triumvir- ate, headed by Salvatore Riina from Corleone, with Stefano Bontate and Gaetano Badalamenti. When Bontate and Badala- menti had been arrested during the course of the big trial of 114 mafiosi at Catanzaro in 1967, Riina was replaced by Luciano Liggio.

Liggio stopped what was in effect a state of emergency and got the 'business' going again. But in reality he was building the foundation for the second Mafia wars. He started to appoint his own place men as district bosses, causing resentment and ill feeling between himself, Bontate and Badalamenti.

At the beginning of 1970 Buscetta, using yet another alias, flew again to Europe and returned to Mexico City. He told Catania that he had bought a shipment of heroin in Europe which would arrive shortly in Mexico. He wanted Catania and Asaf to handle it in Mexico City. When Catania agreed, Buscetta confided that it was going to be a big shipment – between eighty-seven and eighty-nine kilos – and it would be coming via Panama. Two weeks later it arrived. Buscetta, who was staying at the Suites Parioli Hotel in Mexico City, told Catania to drive to Calle Paris, a street near the Hotel Reforma, and leave the keys in the car. Catania took his Chevelle Malibu, and parked near the Hotel Reforma, leaving the keys under the mat as instructed by Buscetta. Thirty minutes later he returned to collect it and drove to rendezvous with Asaf. There the Mexican collected a suitcase and drove off. Catania returned to his shop. They had successfully transferred over twenty kilos of heroin in broad daylight in the middle of Mexico City. Street value: $2 million.

It was the first delivery – a third of the total shipment.

But, once again, there was a problem. Asaf could not locate his buyer. They decided to send the merchandise to New York. The unprepossessing Deguer was again recruited to take it across the border in his Mercedes. Soon afterwards the other shipments arrived. In total, eighty-nine kilos. Street value: nearly $10 million.

On 27 March 1970 Buscetta, still using his alias, flew to Texas and on to New York, leaving his heroin in Mexico City. A few days later another key member of the Buscetta network, Carlo Zippo, arrived in Mexico. He told Catania that he had come to meet the person who would be delivering the heroin to New York. Zippo was introduced to a courier who later crossed the border without a hitch. The rest of the heroin was taken up afterwards by another courier.

Who bought the heroin from the Buscetta network is unclear, but Zippo almost certainly sold it to his American contacts via Filippo Casamento, the Sicilian who had helped Buscetta get into the pizza business.

During the summer of 1970 a series of Sicilian Mafia summits were held. The main item on the agenda was the reorganization of the heroin trade. At one of these meetings, on 4 July 1970 at the Hotel Sole in Palermo, it was decided during a twelve-day discussion that South-East Asia would replace Turkey and Marseilles as the main source for opium and heroin. Mexico would be used as a 'safety valve'. Two weeks later there was another summit in Milan. Among those in attendance were Buscetta, Badalamenti, Liggio and Gerlando Alberti, a powerful figure in the Porta Nuova family and a known trafficker in tobacco and drugs. He had been a fellow defendant with Buscetta in the Catanzaro trial.

Buscetta flew from America for the summit using a Canadian passport in the name of Adalberto Barbieri. He was very nearly caught, along with Badalamenti, Alberti and Salvatore Greco, when the police stopped his Alfa Romeo on the way out of Milan for speeding. The police let them go after they gave false identities, but later ran a check on the names. Then they realized their mistake.

Exactly what Buscetta was discussing with his colleagues in Milan is not clear. When Giovanni Falcone interrogated him about the speeding offence he denied that he was involved. He suggested that someone else was impersonating him. In fact his presence in Milan was confirmed by the US Bureau of Narcotics and Dangerous Drugs (BNDD) and commented on in the Italian Parliament's Anti-Mafia Commission report in 1971:

> It is true that Buscetta was never accused of crimes regarding drug trafficking, but it is equally true that only the friendship and the mutual interest of organized crime dedicated to this activity and related crimes could have enabled Buscetta to live under false names, to leave and re-enter the country clandestinely, to bring his wife, children and lover with him to the United States and take care of them there. It remains to analyse the trip made by Buscetta to Italy in July 1970.
>
> The presence of Buscetta in Milan along with Badalamenti and Alberti must be weighed by two factors: the necessity of a direct meeting and the extreme secrecy and importance of negotiations regarding the drug traffic between Italy and America. Only by taking into account these two factors is it possible to explain why Buscetta decided to run the risk of returning to Italy, knowing that he had been hunted since 1963.

The report expresses the hope that Buscetta will eventually stand trial in Italy, and it ends on a heavily ironic note, saying that because of his role in the first Mafia wars, and his suspected involvement in the attack on Angelo la Barbera, 'the vendetta of the Mafia could also bring him down'.

One month after the Milan summit, on the morning of 25 August 1970, an intelligence unit of the New York State Police was on surveillance at 247–253, 149th Drive, Rosedale, New York. The eight-man intelligence team was under the command of state police investigator Mike Minto. It was part of the group set up at the initiative of New York Governor Nelson Rockefeller to 'target' major narcotics traffickers in New York City. They were working alongside other federal agencies and their investigation coincided with separate inquiries being made by the Organized Crime Strike Force of Brooklyn. The strike force concept successfully brought together the intelligence, personnel and organized crime investigations of different federal agencies under the overall direction of a US attorney. In particular, this investigation had gained valuable information from the Immigration and Naturalization Service (INS). As part of their investigation into the illegal-alien racket, the INS had been painstakingly monitoring the movements of several suspects who were regularly driving across the Canadian border at the Champlain crossing. One of their most interesting discoveries came when they ran a check on someone purporting to be Roberto Cavallaro who had presented a birth certificate claiming that he was born in San Francisco on 13 July 1928. Cavallaro was the maiden name of Buscetta's first wife, Melchiorra. Buscetta's date of birth was 13 July 1928.

'Cavallaro' was in a car with Giuseppe Tramontana. The INS were suspicious and when they searched 'Cavallaro' they found an Italian passport in his jacket in the name of Rinaldo Sarracino. They found several other passports all bearing the name Roberto Cavallaro. They also found a pornographic film and a Playboy Club credit slip in the name of Frank Cotroni. While they were making their examination, 'Cavallaro' managed to escape from the inspection office and sneak back across the Canadian border. When the INS later obtained pictures of Buscetta and compared them with the Cavallaro passports, they were unable to make a positive identification. But 'Cavallaro's' papers contained names that revealed an 'extensive involvement' with other narcotics traffickers and with a whole host of individuals and travel agencies which had figured in other investigations. Significantly, they included aliases that were used by Michel Nicoli and his associates in the Auguste Ricord network.

Carlo Zippo also surfaced in the investigation. Zippo was already known to the authorities as a smuggler of pornographic films and counterfeit Omega watches. As their investigation progressed they received a valuable tip-off from an informer that Zippo had moved into something much more dangerous than imitation watches: the BNDD got word that 200 kilos of heroin were going to be smuggled into New York by Zippo's company, Brasitalia Inc. The heroin would be concealed inside a 'specific item' imported by Brasitalia, probably wooden statues of the Christ of the Andes. The tip-off also revealed that 'an important LCN [la Cosa Nostra] figure was involved in this and prior transactions'.

Although the agents did not fully appreciate it, they had come across some raw intelligence linking the Buscetta network with the Ricord organization down in South America.

Carlo Zippo now appeared to be the central figure in both the illegal-alien racket and the heroin network, and Mike Minto put him under intense surveillance. The organized crime connections were beginning to look extensive: Giuseppe Tramontana was connected with various businesses run by the Bonanno family; the Cotroni family in Canada was clearly involved and was known for its heroin connections and its links with the Bonanno family; and the name Tommaso Buscetta kept coming up.

The house in Rosedale which the agents were watching was used by Zippo and some of his associates. The surveillance team saw two men come out of the house and get into a 1969 Ford Thunderbird which was registered in Zippo's name. A young member of the team looked closely at the men, thinking that he recognized one of them. He exclaimed, 'Jesus, this looks promising.'

The Thunderbird drove off and was discreetly followed to the Woodstock Hotel, where Zippo was living. The two men got out, met Zippo and then went round the corner to a coffee shop on West Forty-sixth Street, the former office of Brasitalia. After a few coffees the three men went into the Brasileira boutique at 10 West Forty-sixth Street. The surveillance team radioed for back-up. They needed to cover all the exits. The State Police surrounded the area, putting men halfway along each block to tail and identify the suspects in case they did not get back in their car.

About half an hour later the men came out. Zippo returned to the Woodstock Hotel, the others towards their car. Mike Minto recalls what happened next:

> He finally walked to a parking lot where he got into the white Ford Thunderbird – and he was being driven by a young man; there was a young boy and a young girl. The boy was eight or nine and the girl in her early teens – and they went down the Westside Highway. We decided we'd let the car get out of the area. We stopped the car on the Brooklyn end of the Brooklyn bridge. The driver produced identification saying he was Benny Cavallaro – a known alias used by the Buscetta family. The older man had no identification but readily admitted who he was.

The older man was Tommaso Buscetta, the driver his son Benedetto. The young boy in the back of the car was Buscetta's youngest son, Domenico, and the girl was his daughter Felicia. The children were driven back to the house in Brooklyn where they were staying with the Gambinos. Because of their false papers, Tommaso and Benedetto were turned over to the INS. One of the most dangerous members of the Sicilian Mafia had been arrested.

It was a major break in the strike force investigation. The arrest was the result of extensive coordination between the New York State Police, the US customs, the BNDD and the INS. The main target of the operation had been Zippo and his driver Antonio Settimo, who had also been monitored crossing the Canadian border several times.

The Americans believed that they had cracked the illegal-alien network. According to Mike Minto this was how it worked:

It was like an underground railroad for illegal aliens coming into the United States . . . it was a sophisticated system where, if you were, for argument's sake, a legitimate Italian immigrant that wanted to come to the United States, you couldn't get into the United States by legitimate means. They would charge you a fee. They would bring you into the United States and give you a job in a pizza parlour . . . You were given some kind of promise that if everything worked out well you would be given 20 per cent of the business – and the guy and his wife and his kids worked there all day trying to make a go of this thing. But you were paying exorbitant rates for the oven to be installed, or whatever. If the business did take off, became a great financial success, they would just take it back off you. If it failed, so what? It was no skin off their noses – it didn't cost anything.

The day after Buscetta's arrest, the Italian authorities were notified. The BNDD then received a message from Interpol in Rome:

Please be informed that the subject is wanted on warrant of arrest 203/63 issued on 8.13.63 by the Examining Magistrate of Palermo for Conspiracy–Complicity in a double murder and being in possession of forbidden weapons. For your information in Palermo on 10.2.60 he participated in the shooting of Giulio Pisciotta and his bodyguard and in the destruction of their bodies. On 5.28.63 firearms were found in his house in Palermo.

Subject belongs to the Mafia which is a criminal association responsible for numerous cases of murder . . . please keep him under arrest in view of extradition which will be requested by Italian government.

We inform you that our authorities consider this case a very important one considering that Buscetta is a very dangerous criminal.

Wearing a striped T-shirt, long sideburns and a serious expression, Buscetta was photographed, fingerprinted and jailed in Bergen County, New Jersey. Proceedings for his extradition began.

Benedetto Buscetta was let out. He, like his father, had gone into the pizza business, but unfortunately his father also seems to have involved him in something rather more dangerous. When Buscetta had escaped from the wars and the warrant for his arrest in Palermo in 1963, he had reluctantly left his family behind, intending that they should join him as soon as they could. Benedetto remembers that his father later wrote asking him to meet an Italian–American called Joseph Rizzo who was visiting Palermo. To make the arrangements secure, his father sent him the torn half of a paper napkin of which Rizzo would have the other half. When Benny met him, Rizzo was accompanied by Pino Catania. They matched the halves of the paper napkins, and discussed plans to get the family out of Palermo. A few days later Catania picked up Benny and his younger brother Antonio and they all caught a train for Genoa. There they were met by Rizzo, who took them to a ship which was going to New York. Rizzo got them on as stowaways. In New York, Rizzo smuggled them ashore and took them to his girlfriend's house, where they had a much-needed wash and change of clothes. Then he took them to meet their father. Buscetta was overjoyed to see his boys again.

Both boys soon went to work at the Pizza Den in Pitkin Avenue, Brooklyn, and it became a family business. Their father then left for California before going on to Mexico to have the plastic surgery.

When he got back to New York he sold the Pizza Den and the boys went to work in another pizza parlour owned by Tony Settimo, Zippo's right-hand man. Benny first met Zippo through his father towards the end of 1969. They got on well and, after Buscetta's arrest, Zippo helped to look after the family. Sometimes he went with the boys when they visited Buscetta in gaol. On one occasion, when Zippo could not come, he asked Benny to pass a message to his father: he was to tell him that 'his friend who was sick would be feeling better in a few days'.

When Buscetta heard this message he told Benedetto, 'Stay close to Carlo. He will be going to a hotel in a few days' time and you must make sure that no one is following him.'

Sure enough, within a few days, Zippo asked Benny to drive him into Manhattan. He asked to be dropped at the McAlpin Hotel, saying he would catch up with Benny later at the hotel where he was staying, the Woodstock. Remembering his father's instructions, Benny waited and watched outside the McAlpin Hotel. Half an hour later he saw Zippo come out of the hotel with two suitcases and get into a yellow cab. Benny drove to the Woodstock, where he found Zippo waiting for him at the front of the hotel.

On their next visit to his father Benny overheard Zippo say, 'It's OK, Tommaso – the sick one is better. He will be all right in thirteen days.'

Benny noticed that his father became extremely angry when Zippo said this. He thought it might have been because Zippo was talking openly over the detention phone. He need not have worried: so far the authorities had no idea of his drug-smuggling activities.

Buscetta was let out just in time for Christmas 1970. His bail was set at $75,000. As soon as he was home, Zippo came over to talk to him. As he was leaving Zippo asked Benny to come with him. When Buscetta protested that Zippo did not need Benny, Zippo explained that he only wanted Benny to drive him home. He was not familiar with Brooklyn and was worried he would get lost.

Benny drove Zippo to a house belonging to a man called Emmanuel Loguidice. Zippo and Benny got out of the car and went into the house for a short time. They came out accompanied by Loguidice and his cousin. They got into the car, and Zippo turned to Benedetto for the keys as he wanted to get some things out of the boot. Inside the boot Benny saw two suitcases. Zippo took one and gave the other to Benny, who handed it to the cousin. The three men took the cases into the house, and a few minutes later Zippo came out with a different case which he put back in the boot. As Benny and Zippo were leaving, the cousin called out, 'Say hello to your father for me!'

Although he had not seen what was inside the suitcases, Benny had just assisted Zippo in one of his numerous heroin transactions. Not surprisingly, Benny soon learnt that his father was involved with Zippo in the narcotics business. On one occasion he was with them in a coffee shop on Thirteenth Avenue and Seventy-third Street in Brooklyn when he overheard his father to say to a man called 'Monoco', 'Are you interested in thirty pairs of shoes for fourteen dollars a pair?'

Benny remembers that Monoco answered 'Yes', but he did not hear the rest of the conversation. Buscetta was using the Sicilian clothing code.

Benny's suspicions were later confirmed by a friend of Zippo called Felice Bonnetti, who revealed that he was in the heroin trade and had delivered drugs to Zippo. He also said that he was a good friend of Michel Nicoli and Lucien Sarti, the French Connection exiles in South America.

Benedetto confronted his father about his involvement in drugs. Buscetta's response was to tell his son not to worry because the only time that he had been involved was when he had driven with Zippo to the Loguidice house in Brooklyn.

Although the American authorities had received the background intelligence on Buscetta's Mafia career from Interpol, the Italians seemed to have missed their chance to extradite him. Early in 1971 he was allowed to leave the USA for Mexico. Once across the border he was met by Pino Catania. They drove to Guatemala, and from there Buscetta travelled to Paraguay and on to Rio de Janeiro. Since the false identity Buscetta had been using in America had been exposed, he needed new documents and a new passport. He went to Rio to see Guglielmo Casalini, a mysterious Brazilian–Italian who provided a variety of services to Zippo's clients and the Ricord network – David Nicoli and Sarti. Casalini claimed that he was working for the Brazilian police and could fix things with them if there were any problems. He also had political connections who may have helped him to supply false documents and passports.

Although Buscetta denied any involvement with the narcotics trade of the French Connection exiles, there is little doubt that he was deeply embroiled. Not least through Casalini and Zippo, who had been buying heroin from the Frenchmen in New York commuting between North and South America to set up the deals. Buscetta claims that what he had in common with them was nothing more than the fact that they were all fugitives — hence the common link with Casalini, since they all needed to protect their identities. This 'alibi' collapses under the weight of too many indisputable facts and the mutual corroboration on a multitude of points from the statements of Catania and Nicoli. His own son saw quite enough to be convinced that his father was involved in drugs.

In the spring of 1971, shortly after Buscetta's arrival in Brazil, Nicoli was approached in Rio by Claude Pastou seeking a potential buyer for thirty kilos of heroin to be delivered in New York. Zippo was contacted and agreed to take the lot. Pastou was working for Christian David, who had organized the shipment and hired Pastou as his agent. David, as ever, was staying in the shadows. He instructed Pastou to go to the Sheraton Hotel on Fifty-seventh Street and Seventh Avenue and to stay in the lobby until his contact turned up.

David's contact was Roger Delouette, a former French Secret Service agent. Delouette, wearing a brown suit and a raincoat, entered the lobby. Pastou made contact, then they walked to the bar of the Taft Hotel. Delouette explained the method for bringing the heroin in. He had already shipped over a Volkswagen camper which he was going to take through customs. It was loaded with the heroin. They would take the merchandise out and drive it down to Mexico. He asked Pastou if he had a place in the city where they could take the drugs out of the car. Pastou told him that he did not have anywhere at the moment, but that he knew the city very well and had a buyer for the shipment. David had instructed Pastou to pay Delouette off with a commission from the money that he was going to get from Zippo, the rest of the money to be returned to David. Pastou arranged to rendezvous with Delouette the next day at 1 p.m.

and 6 p.m. at the same bar at the Taft Hotel when he had got the Volkswagen through customs. The second meeting was a fallback in case Delouette was delayed.

The next day Pastou turned up but Delouette did not appear. Pastou returned at six o'clock and hung around for another hour. There was still no sign of Delouette. Pastou was beginning to get worried – Delouette's absence made it seem increasingly likely that he had been picked up by customs or the police. He searched for the camper outside the Taft and the Sheraton Hotels then, convinced that the police might be after him, he took flight – literally, three flights – to Canada, to Germany and then to Brazil. It was a roundabout route, but if Delouette had talked, Pastou knew the authorities would be watching direct flights to South America.

Delouette's smuggling career came to an end because of the diligence of twenty-two-year-old Lyn Pelletier, one of the youngest customs inspectors in the service. On Monday 5 April 1971 she was reminded of a memo that all customs inspectors had recently received, which pointed out that vans and minibuses were increasingly being used to smuggle drugs, mainly hashish, into the United States. So she looked with more than casual interest at the brand-new Volkswagen camper which had just come off the cargo boat *Atlantic Cognac* from Le Havre. It was awaiting clearance at Port Elizabeth, New Jersey. When she glanced at its owner she saw a tall Frenchman with a round face, rather overweight, with brown hair beginning to go grey. He was dressed in a brown suit with a fashionable Mao collar. She asked him for his licence and was surprised to see that it bore the address of the French Embassy in Cuba. When asked about his licence, he replied that he was being posted to Cuba to work for a French agricultural organization. She mentioned that his van seemed to be fairly new. Trying to conceal the nervousness that he felt, Delouette replied, 'Indeed – I bought it in Paris on 1 March. It had done a thousand kilometres, accounted for by a trial run I did after a running in, before putting it on the boat on 26 March.'

As they talked, Miss Pelletier began to search the camper,

looking under the seats, over the dashboard and beneath the arm rests. It was a new vehicle, so she was puzzled to find a screw missing from one of the panels to the right of the dash. She felt behind the panel and her hand touched something. She pulled it it out and found a plastic bag full of white powder.

She summoned the help of another inspector. By the time they had finished their search, they had pulled out forty-eight bags, each containing 500 grammes of 92 per cent pure heroin. The total haul was forty-five kilos with a street value of $10 million. A French-speaking special agent from US customs read Delouette his rights and explained the seriousness of the prison sentence that he was now facing – unless he talked. Delouette did not need much persuading. He confessed that he was working as a courier for French intelligence. American agents working for BNDD could do little more than register resigned astonishment. Later investigation confirmed that Delouette was indeed connected to SDECE but their involvement in the transaction was never resolved. In Brazil, David remarked that they had nothing to do with it.

Following the seizure the French exiles were worried that the Americans might have gained valuable leads into their network and would persuade the Brazilians to round them up. Although they had connections with corrupt policemen and politicians, it could work both ways. The men protecting them could just as easily betray them. But their worries did not disrupt the dynamics of their trade for longer than necessary. David and his friends, determined to make up for the setback caused by the arrest of Delouette, resumed negotiations for further shipments of heroin. Eight weeks later they successfully organized a thirty-kilo shipment via Zippo in New York. It netted them $300,000.

As well as being a convenient base of operation, the countries of South America in general, and Brazil in particular, provided a congenial new home for the gangsters of the Union Corse and the Sicilian Mafia. São Paulo, where Buscetta would spend most of his time, was a city with a powerful Italian heritage, built on successive waves of immigrants mainly from Reggio Calabria and the south. The first major influx had come after the First

World War, when Brazil's coffee barons were accumulating vast fortunes and investing them in the first generation of industrial ventures in the city. São Paulo was then a thriving market town of 400,000 inhabitants. Italians came to work as stevedores on the docks at Santos, loading aromatic sacks of Brazilian coffee bound for Europe. As the city became more industrialized, many Italians moved into mainstream commerce. Others, lower down the social scale, went to work on the construction of the Edificio Martinelli, South America's first skyscraper.

After the Second World War, a fresh wave of Italian immigrants left Reggio Calabria for a new life in Brazil, a nation which had prospered during the war. With its large Italian population, São Paulo became a favourite place of exile for a variety of Italian fugitives. Licio Gelli, Grand Master P2 – 'Propaganda Due', the sinister sect of Italian Freemasons – has been a frequent visitor to the city, and his right-hand man, Umberto Ortolani, lives there permanently.

One of Buscetta's first ports of call after leaving New York was Asunción, the capital of Paraguay. The corruption in other South American nations pales into insignificance compared to Paraguay. It had been a transit camp for many top Nazis who escaped after the war on the 'Odessa' route from Europe to South America, among them Josef Mengele, the former SS concentration camp doctor. Asunción became a haven for a wide variety of international gangsters, thieves, murderers, smugglers and ex-Nazis. One man who managed to combine most of these occupations was Auguste Ricord, and the fact that Buscetta became so involved with his lieutenants in São Paulo and Rio de Janeiro in the early seventies suggests strongly that on leaving New York he went to Paraguay to do business with them. Buscetta is reported to have spent a long time in Asunción, apparently becoming a naturalized citizen there with documents in the name of Tomas Roberto Felice. According to him, he changed his name because Buscetta, in Portuguese, is the slang word for vagina.

His arrival in Paraguay coincided with the imprisonment of Ricord, who had been arrested on 25 March 1971. The American authorities eventually persuaded Paraguay to agree to Ricord's extradition. During a year of tough negotiation he lived a life of comparative luxury inside one of Asunción's better jails. He had sufficient freedom to continue planning his operations with Lucien Sarti and it has been suggested that Buscetta went to Paraguay to discuss moving the network to Brazil now that Paraguay was no longer safe. Other sources have claimed that Buscetta was acting as an ambassador for the Sicilian Mafia, which wanted to control the operations previously dominated by the Union Corse. This theory is partially reinforced by the fact that the French Connection was beginning to lose its dominance as the laboratories and the financing moved increasingly to Sicily. Given their history of cooperation, it is unlikely that Buscetta would have been involved in a takeover bid for the Union Corse operations in South America. He would have needed too much money and firepower to do that. The approach was much more subtle: the Mafia was already deeply involved with the Union Corse, so all they had to do was to become even more indispensable. When the remnants of the Ricord organization were eventually smashed, those who stood to gain the most would be the Sicilian Mafia. A substantial gap would appear in the market, and no one else would be better placed to exploit it.

Soon after arriving in Brazil and abandoning his two wives in New York, Buscetta had fallen in love yet again. Christina Guimarães, a beautiful and intelligent blonde Brazilian woman, came from a family which was well connected in Brazilian society – her father was a friend of the former president of Brazil – but her apparently respectable background did not prevent her from having an affair with a man whose lifestyle was notorious. Although at first her family seem to have opposed the relationship, they were soon converted by Buscetta's confident and easygoing manner. He got on particularly well with Christina's brother, Homero. They set up an insurance-broking partnership with some of Homero's friends in São Paulo. One of the other partners was a high-ranking officer in the Brazilian army.

In the years to follow Christina remained a faithful companion. She and Buscetta settled into a comfortable lifestyle that included a weekend home at the coastal resort of Ilha Bela, and a string of properties including a farm called Rancho Alegre – 'Happy Ranch'. But their happiness would always depend on the next heroin deal – and on not being caught.

7

Operation Springboard

It is necessary to destroy this band of criminals
who have perverted the principles of Cosa Nostra
and dragged them through the mud.

The confession of Tommaso Buscetta

Following the death of Lucky Luciano in 1962, the most obvious
candidates for the succession to his narcotics empire were Vito
Genovese and Luciano's close friend Meyer Lansky. However,
Genovese was serving a fifteen-year sentence in the Atlanta
Federal Penitentiary on a heroin-trafficking charge, and Meyer
Lansky, the financial genius of organized crime, was too clever
and cautious to get directly involved with narcotics; so eventually much of Luciano's business passed into the hands of Santo
Trafficante Jr, whose family power base was the city of Miami,
then, as today, one of the chief crossroads of the international
narcotics trade. Miami was particularly well situated for access
from Cuba, the Caribbean and South America. Trafficante's
father had been a close associate of both Lucky Luciano and
Meyer Lansky, so Santo Jr was a natural inheritor of Luciano's
business.

The influx of Cuban refugees into Florida after Castro's
takeover gave the Trafficante group an unlimited supply of
manpower. Cubans would be recruited as couriers in the drug
business and as hit men. Other Cuban refugees, drifting into the
slums and ghettos, became the consumers. Although the supply
of morphine base from Turkey seemed to be drying up, there
were alternative sources of supply in Mexico and South-East

Asia. Asia had become the biggest source for opium and refined heroin, and French colonial involvement in Vietnam and Cambodia introduced a plentiful flow of Corsican gangsters who, with their friends in Marseilles and Sicily, lost little time in harvesting the profits of the region. Ironically, as the Americans filled the political vacuum created by the French abandonment of South-East Asia, the heroin trade was boosted even further. CIA support for the hill tribes of Laos in counter-insurgency operations against the communist-backed Pathet Lao involved the agency's proprietary airline, Air America, in the transport of substantial shipments of raw opium. Once again, a sinister alliance emerged between the Mafia trade in heroin and the American war against communism. The heroin, refined in clandestine laboratories in Bangkok, Hong Kong, Laos and Saigon, would find a rich new market among the thousands of GIs being sent to Vietnam.

The political conditions were ripe for wholesale exploitation of the narcotics trade by the leaders of organized crime. Political corruption in Saigon eased the path for hundreds of heroin deals, many of which were financed by South Vietnamese generals. The Mafia was quick to spot their opportunity. Santo Trafficante Jr made a 'good-will' tour of South-East Asia in 1962, stopping off in Saigon, Hong Kong and Singapore, the principal refining centres for the high grade 'Number 4' heroin from the 'Golden Triangle' of Burma, Laos and Thailand.

As the flow of heroin to America increased, and as drug abuse among GIs in Vietnam reached alarming proportions, political pressure forced the Nixon administration to launch a new initiative in the war against narcotics. Nixon announced a series of measures to curb the international traffic in the summer of 1971. The government reached an agreement with Turkey to ban the opium crop, in return for which the United States would subsidize alternative crops for the Turkish farmers. (It was an initiative doomed to failure, as no substitute crop could ever hope to match the profits from the opium fields.) Agreement was also reached with the French government to coordinate their fight against the international drugs traffic. This was more promising. The French authorities, particularly in Marseilles, had previously failed to cooperate fully with the Americans who were trying to break the French Connection – political protection bought by the Union Corse had paid dividends. And in South America, the State Department put pressure on several countries including Paraguay, where their diplomatic moves resulted in the arrest of Auguste Ricord on 25 March 1971 and his eventual extradition to America in September 1972. After his arrest the network dispersed into Brazil and Argentina.

In the middle of August 1971, Tommaso Buscetta and Carlo Zippo renewed contact with their old friend Pino Catania. They telephoned him from Rio and asked him to come down and see them. Pino flew down, checked in at the Hotel Riviera, and met them in an apartment they were renting together around the corner from the Copacabana Palace Hotel. They told Catania that they were expecting a fifty-kilo shipment for delivery in Mexico and that they needed him to go to Naples to finalize the arrangements. Neither Buscetta nor Zippo would risk going to Italy for fear they would be arrested. In Naples Catania would meet someone calling himself Carlos Silveira, who was in fact Michel Nicoli. The heroin was to be supplied by French Connection contacts of Nicoli and Sarti and sent from Naples to Mexico. The plan was to ship it in a trunk by air freight disguised with material for Catania's shirt business.

In October the trunk duly arrived and was delivered to the buyer, Asaf. A few days later Zippo and Catania picked up the money from Asaf – $450,000. Nicoli then flew to Mexico City to meet them. Pino was paid off for his part in the deal and some money was put aside for Zippo and Buscetta. Nicoli says he received only $200,000, and that when he asked them where the rest was he was told that there had been a problem at the airport.

Somewhere along the line, a quarter of a million dollars had gone missing. Oddly enough, no one seems to have been over-concerned about it. Nicoli flew to Rome to hand over the cash to his suppliers, keeping $10,000 for himself and $10,000 for Sarti. When he returned to Rio and gave Sarti his share, Sarti told him that he was going to set up a 120-kilo shipment with Zippo for sale in Mexico. According to Nicoli, Buscetta once again acted as a middle-man. Again the buyer was Asaf.

Over the next two weeks Sarti received $840,000. Nicoli received between $35,000 and $40,000. How much Buscetta received is unclear, but Catania says that some of his own share was used to buy Sarti a diamond ring for $8000. If he could afford to spend that much on presents then their cut must have been considerable. In return, one of Sarti's associates bought Piaget watches for Zippo and Catania.

Sarti soon ran into a series of problems and was arrested in Bolivia as the direct result of the success of 'Operation Springboard', the US government initiative which was gaining support from the Latin American countries where the French Connection exiles were operating. Several thousand dollars,' worth of bribes to the police helped to solve his problems, and once out of prison in early 1972, he returned to Mexico City. He told Catania and Zippo that he was expecting a large shipment. He was not exaggerating. He intended to import 300 kilos, worth more than $30 million at street level.

The deal never came off.

On 17 April 1972, as Sarti and his wife were getting into his car, they found themselves surrounded by Mexican policemen. Sarti grabbed his gun and fired. The police killed him. They had been on his trail for months.

A few months later in Brazil, Nicoli found that he too was being watched. He called his home in Rio and was told by his wife that the neighbourhood was crawling with police. He took a bus to São Paulo and made for the house that Buscetta was staying in, only to find that everyone had left in a hurry the day before. He then went to a mutual friend's house where he managed to contact Benedetto Buscetta, who arranged a meeting in a supermarket in São Paulo. Benny told Nicoli that his stepmother's parents had both been arrested and that the police were now looking for his father.

Nicoli returned to the friend's apartment, where he was joined by Pastou. But Pastou arrived with a police tail. A squad burst into the apartment and arrested the Frenchmen. The remnants of the Ricord organization were virtually destroyed.

At around the same time, sixty kilos of heroin were seized in Buenos Aires, and a few days later Brazilian port officials discovered an eighty-kilo shipment. The heroin was hidden inside some religious statues and was destined for Carlo Zippo. The earlier BNDD intelligence about the Christ of the Andes figurines had been remarkably accurate. By this time the investigation had linked Zippo with Buscetta, and further evidence had been gathered when the police picked up Homero Guimarães, Buscetta's brother-in-law.

The resourceful David and the elusive Buscetta were now the only criminals still on the run. David, realizing that time was running out, had escaped to a scruffy hotel in a remote part of Brazil, Feira de Santana in the Bahia province. On his trail was a man with an equal reputation for ruthlessness and brutality – Sergio Paranhos Fleury, the head of the Brazilian police and also the suspected leader of a Brazilian anti-communist death squad. In Feira de Santana two Brazilian policemen had noticed an attractive woman whose expensive clothes and smart appearance were suspiciously out of place. They took her in for questioning. It did not take them long to discover that she was David's girlfriend. Fleury was notified and a patrol was sent to the hotel that she identified. Six armed policemen burst through the door, surprising David, who was in the middle of packing. He was grabbed before he could reach for his gun but his reactions were still fast. He leapt on his assailants and fought like a madman. 'He was a master of karate,' one of the policemen later reported. 'He threw us around like balls. If there had only been four of us, I don't see how we could have handled him.'

They needed handcuffs and footchains to restrain him. Even then he did not give up. First he tried to bribe the policemen by offering them $100,000 each plus tickets to anywhere in the world for their families. Then, on the way out of the hotel room, he managed despite the handcuffs to grab a glass and cut his wrists. He hoped to be sent to a hospital where it would be easier for him to escape. His wounds were stitched up and he was thrown into a cell.

In his attaché case they found a 9 mm Browning, a silenced Beretta, a short-barrelled Smith and Wesson, ninety cartridges of different calibres, three phials of a lethal poison and a Uruguayan diplomatic passport in a false name. The photograph was of Christian David.

Next in line was Buscetta. On 2 November 1972 he was picked up by Fleury at the beach resort of Itapema, near Camboriu in the Brazilian state of Santa Catarina. With Nicoli and David he was tortured by the Brazilian military police: Buscetta claims he was the only one who did not talk.

This is his account of his stay in Brazil and his arrest, as told to Giovanni Falcone:

> I went to Brazil because, after I had gone to Argentina, I had moved there in 1951 and set up a mirror factory called the Conco d'Oro; as a result, I had acquired Brazilian residency but had returned to Palermo soon afterwards for family reasons. Well, when, in 1971, I needed to leave the USA and didn't know where to go – having made the acquaintance of Carlo Zippo in New York, I learned from him that he was the friend of a Brazilian police officer, Guglielmo Casalini, from whom he could find out whether I still had my residency. He found out that I did, so I went back to Brazil, entering the country on a false passport because the Italian consulate in New York had refused to give me an authentic one. It turns out that Casalini, who I thought was a member of the Brazilian police force, was instead being looked for by the US authorities for drug trafficking between France and America. Casalini, possibly because he was dropped by the French, denounced them to the Brazilian police, who, after questioning him, arrested him too. When they searched his home, they found a book on the Sicilian Mafia in which I was discussed, among others, and my name had been underlined. When he was asked about the reasons for the

underlining, he told the police about his contacts with me and they arrested me.

So I was arrested – not because I was in any way involved in the drug traffic (Casalini had nothing to say against me) but because I was considered a dangerous Sicilian *mafioso*. I should explain that the investigations were conducted at that time by the military police. I was tortured for a long time in the army prison called the DOPS to get me to reveal my connections with the Sicilian Mafia. I was given electric shocks on my testicles, anus, teeth and ears, and the nails of my big toes were pulled out – I've still got the marks from this torture, because the nails grow very stunted and irregular. Also I was often left hooded and tied to a stake for hours under a scorching sun.

Buscetta, ever eager to justify himself as a Man of Honour, added:

In spite of this, I never said a word about Cosa Nostra, and I would like to emphasize this, because my present conduct in these proceedings is not the result of fear for my physical safety nor a personal matter – it comes from an awareness that it is necessary to destroy this band of criminals who have perverted the principles of the Cosa Nostra and dragged them through the mud.

During his debriefing in America, Buscetta claimed that Sarti's mistress and Casalini were persuaded by the Brazilian police to implicate him in the operations of the French Corsicans, which he maintained he had nothing to do with. But the statements of Catania and Nicoli corroborate each other on too many important issues for Buscetta's claims to carry much weight. He has dismissed Catania's statements and many others by saying that he is a victim of his own infamy, that his reputation as a drug dealer comes from exaggerated press reports and from gangsters hoping to clear themselves by naming him.

There are some within law enforcement, both in Italy and the

United States, who believe that Buscetta may be telling the truth. Others describe him as 'trash' and a 'known trafficker in heroin'. Certainly there is a noticeable lack of hard evidence for his alleged crimes, even for those for which he was convicted. Yet the same can be said of many other high-level Mafia narcotics traffickers.

Charles Rose, the prosecuting attorney from the Eastern District of New York, where the heroin case involving Catania, Nicoli and Asaf was handled, has studied all the evidence and talked to Buscetta at great length. Before they met Rose was convinced that Buscetta was the major *mafioso* and heroin trafficker described in so many police files and intelligence reports. Now he is not so sure. At one of their early meetings Buscetta told Rose that he had never touched or even seen heroin. Rose remarked cynically, 'I would be very disappointed if you had!', meaning that no top-level narcotics trafficker would ever be found anywhere near the drugs themselves. But Buscetta continued to protest his innocence. Rose summarizes Buscetta's defence:

He says 'No'. But every person around him has been indicted, convicted or suspected of heroin dealing. His explanation is: because my reputation has been as a man you can respect, if someone were to come and say, you know that Tommaso Buscetta, I am with him, then you could deal with him and there would be no questions asked. You would not try or attempt to, you know, screw him in any way during the business deal. I mean, you don't mess around with someone who's hooked up with Tommaso Buscetta. So he says, what happened in his opinion, he said people used his name.

Giuseppe Tramontana, we believe, was a courier for Tommaso Buscetta, or in any case he was very close with Tommaso Buscetta. Tramontana and Buscetta's sons were together constantly. Giuseppe Catania said that he delivered heroin for Giuseppe Tramontana. Giuseppe Catania said that heroin was delivered to, for example,

Filippo Casamento, a very close friend of Buscetta – and we seized heroin from Filippo Casamento back in 1970 – clearly in the heroin business. Tramontana said he worked for Buscetta. Buscetta said, 'Tramontana is a nothing – he was a nobody, he was not a Man of Honour, he was not a main man. I dealt with him because, you know, he knew my son, he was a friend of my son. Tramontana probably went and said, "You know how close I am with Tommaso Buscetta, you know you can trust me . . .".'

It is some kind of 'brokering' of his name – which is not unknown to have happened – that could happen in numerous instances. The problem is it's happened all over the world! He's been convicted in Italy for narcotics. 'I did not do it.' He essentially has denied criminal activity all over the world, wherever he is. When he goes back to Brazil after serving his sentence in Italy, who does he hook up with? Badalamenti, who we know to be a heroin dealer; Sansone, we know is wanted for heroin. The people he is in business with are fugitives from heroin trafficking charges in Italy. And again, he explains it, that they are fugitives: 'I am a fugitive, they are Sicilian and I am a Sicilian – there's the bond, it is very strong, but I am not in the heroin business.'

The senior policemen and lawyers who have dealt with Buscetta are divided over the question of his guilt or innocence. Research shows that Buscetta's name was indeed exploited by certain people to enhance their own reputations, and that some reports of his work as a heroin trafficker are false or exaggerated. In a secret, criminal world that is inevitable. But the evidence is overwhelming that in his dealings with Catania he was involved in heroin traffic at a very high level.

The US government certainly thought so too. The extradition document, presented in 1984, based on the Eastern District indictment of 1973, stated:

Giuseppe Catania and Michel Nicoli were two of Buscetta's most trusted associates in this conspiracy. Catania and Nicoli were Buscetta's specialists and without them his conspiracy could not have succeeded. When Catania and Nicoli were finally arrested and cooperated with the US government, they provided a specialist's view of a complex consortium which was powerful and well-financed and was able to reinvest its profits to provide a continuing supply of heroin from numerous sources. Its organizational integrity enabled it to smuggle large quantities of heroin from these sources to Mexico City and then on to the United States, with rigid controls and supervision being provided by Buscetta and Zippo through trusted lieutenants such as Catania and Nicoli, at every step of the process.

After his arrest in Brazil in November 1972, Buscetta was extradited to Italy. As he boarded the plane he turned to reporters and said, 'São Paolo is the best city in the world to live in.' It had certainly been a congenial haunt for him up to the time of his arrest. He promised them that he would come back – a promise he would keep.

In Italy he was charged with Mafia association and sentenced to three years. A year later an indictment was served in the Eastern District of New York naming him as one of the principal defendants in a grand jury case alleging conspiracy to import a total of 170 kilos of heroin. The Italian authorities received a request for his extradition, but instead of handing him over to the Americans, they used the charges as a reason for another court case in Italy in which he was sentenced to a further ten years in prison, although this was reduced to eight years on appeal. The US extradition was denied.

In December 1972 at Ucciardone prison in Palermo, a gloomy legacy of the Bourbon era, Buscetta was welcomed in a manner befitting a visiting statesman. Ucciardone, as well as being a prison, was a centre for the most powerful members of the Sicilian Mafia when they had the misfortune to reside within its ancient walls. Well guarded though it was – indeed, there was an agreement which the Mafia enforced that no prisoner should try to escape lest the regime be made more uncomfortable for their fellow inmates – it was a headquarters from which operations could be planned and discussed, old scores settled and murders arranged. And because of the diversity of its inhabitants, it was probably the best-informed centre in Italy for gossip and intelligence about the operations of organized crime throughout the world.

8

The 'Illustrious Corpses'

No one will stop this thing. The most you can ever
do is to keep it within bounds. This is a game. It's
like chess. I give a piece here and I take a piece
there, but I know it's a game I'm never going to be
able to win.

Boris Giuliano, Escuadra Mobile, Palermo

Once the Mafia had recovered from the chaos of the wars of the
1960s, the Commission came back into operation led by the
triumvirate of Salvatore Riina, representing the Corleone family,
Stefano Bontate, boss of the Santa Maria de Gesù family and a
close friend of Tommaso Buscetta, and Gaetano Badalamenti,
capo of the Cinisi family. Representatives of the different families
were given a place on the Commission under the title 'district
bosses'.

While Buscetta had been in Brazil, Liggio had murdered his
way to the top of the Sicilian Mafia, investing heavily in the
kidnapping industry and the heroin trade. A stockily built man,
with a taste for large cigars and dark glasses, his reign was
frequently interrupted by bouts of illness caused by Pott's disease
(tuberculosis of the bone). Despite this he managed to hold on
to power even when in prison. He took care to appoint district
bosses who would support him, a move which was deeply
resented by Bontate and Badalamenti.

Badalamenti was appointed head of the Commission, but, for
reasons which have never been explained, he was ousted and his
place as head of the Cinisi family was taken over by his cousin
Antonio. This *coup d'état* was almost certainly orchestrated by

Liggio and the Corleonesi. Although Buscetta has not revealed why his friend was expelled, he has this to say about the procedure:

> A Man of Honour can be expelled for reasons relating to the family he belongs to or the Mafia organization as a whole. It is considered a very grave mistake for a Man of Honour to continue to deal and even to talk to a member expelled for not being worthy.

Badalamenti's seat on the Commission was taken by Michele Greco, a close friend of Liggio and a relative of the Grecos who had been caught up in the first Mafia wars. His Ciaculli family became, along with Liggio, the dominant power in Sicily, with connections to the highest political and financial circles. His nickname was appropriately powerful – 'the Pope'.

The Commission guarded its powers of life and death jealously, and there were many rows over the way decisions were being reached on assassinations.

One of the first state officials to be murdered was the *procuratore generale* – the chief public prosecutor – of Palermo, Pietro Scaglione. Scaglione's career was riddled with allegations of corruption, and although he was investigated for links with the Mafia, the tribunal declared him innocent. He had custody of numerous dossiers relating to Mafia crimes which were mysteriously shelved or lost. One of them was a report from the *carabinieri* on the involvement of all the Mafia families in the narcotics trade. Nothing was done for four years until the *carabinieri* agitated for a Mafia trial, and the entire Mafia from Castellamare, Joe Bonanno's birthplace, was charged, including Bonanno's lieutenants Frank Garofalò and John Bonventre and his associate Frank Coppola. After a long and tedious trial, all were acquitted for lack of proof. Scaglione's position was a powerful one, from which he could threaten those he chose to protect. But when he chose no longer to serve the Mafia's interests, they decided to kill him.

On 5 May 1971 he made his daily visit to his wife's graveside in a Palermo cemetery. As he turned to leave, he and his driver were shot dead. No one saw anything, though of course plenty of people knew what had happened.

It was only when Tommaso Buscetta broke the code of silence fourteen years later that the police could confirm their suspicions. He told them that Liggio was quite ill at the time with Pott's disease, which made it difficult for him to walk but not, apparently, to kill. He had himself driven to the graveyard where Scaglione was mourning his wife, and fired from the seat of the car, killing Scaglione and his driver. According to Buscetta, Salvatore Riina was Liggio's accomplice in this double murder.

In his confession Buscetta is again concerned to uphold the propriety of Mafia decision-making:

> The murder in question took place on Via Cipressi in a section controlled by the Porta Nuova family, whose head was Pippo Calò. No murder, in particular the murder of Pietro Scaglione, chief public prosecutor, could have been committed in that area without the consent of the family boss – and this is not just for reasons of prestige, but because this sort of murder inevitably arouses strong pressure from the police authorities in the territory where the crime has taken place and that may have repercussions on the family's operations in their territory.

In this case the rule was observed and, according to Buscetta, Calò's power and status grew after the murder.

Scaglione's death came almost a year after the Milan summit of July 1970 which Liggio and Buscetta had attended. As well as discussing the drug trade, the meeting may have been held to authorize that murder. It may also have arranged for the murder of Mauro de Mauro, a journalist who worked for Palermo's crusading newspaper *L'Ora*.

The disappearance of de Mauro remains a mystery. No one doubts that he was murdered, but Buscetta claims it had nothing to do with the Mafia. The mystery is further clouded by the fact that de Mauro was mixed up with the neo-fascist movement. He had been investigating the mysterious death of Enrico Mattei, the Italian oil magnate whose plane crashed in Sicily possibly as a result of sabotage. At the time, Mattei was seen as a threat to the American oil companies and it was alleged by some that the Mafia was contracted to carry out his assassination on behalf of 'political interests'. The disappearance of de Mauro and the death of Mattei were the first of the long list of what have become known as the *cadaveri eccelenti* – the 'illustrious corpses'.

Over the next decade the Grecos and the Corleonesi eliminated anyone who seemed to threaten their interests, from the most insignificant Palermo villains to the highest officials of the state. Corpses, illustrious and not so illustrious, would become an everyday sight on the streets of Palermo.

Giuseppe Russo, a dedicated *carabinieri* colonel, was drafted in to Sicily from northern Italy in 1977 to investigate the Mafia. He had already taken part in the investigations into the murder of Pietro Scaglione and the disappearance of Mauro de Mauro. But Russo too was to die. As Buscetta has now revealed, he was shot by Pino Greco.

After Russo the murders became more frequent – frequent enough to establish a pattern. They usually took place in broad daylight in Palermo, and involved anyone who threatened the Mafia's heroin trade. Their monopoly of the business had been confirmed when they built a number of refining laboratories. Anyone who knew about these laboratories and was foolish enough to broadcast the fact was effectively signing his own death warrant. And anyone trying to investigate the millions of dollars which were being 'laundered' back and forth from Italy to America was also likely to be killed.

The powers of investigation available to the judiciary were very limited. The Mafia's political protectors had ensured that their bank accounts, like those of the law-abiding citizen, remained strictly private. The power to investigate finances would inevitably lead to discovery of the drug traffickers. It might also reveal the politicians and financiers who supported them. That, of course, was why the power was being withheld. Those who were brave enough to attempt investigation into the sources of finance and the location of the refineries realized that they were no longer dealing with a Sicilian problem. The narcotics trade was international, and the police and investigating magistrates would require major assistance from overseas in order to tackle it.

Boris Giuliano, the leading detective in Palermo's *escuadra mobile* – flying squad – was one of the first to realize that law-enforcement agencies throughout the world had to cooperate if they were going to defeat the Mafia. In particular he recognized the value of working with the Americans, and was involved in the investigation of a major heroin case with the US customs and the DEA.

On 19 June 1979 a cheap blue plastic suitcase had arrived at Palermo's Punta Raisi airport, twenty-five kilometres outside the city. The case had come via Rome from New York. When Giuliano intercepted it he found $497,000 in small-denomination bills – the currency of the narcotics trade. The money was wrapped in several pizza aprons. They were later traced to a pizzeria in New Jersey run by a Sicilian called Salvatore Sollena.

Sollena was the nephew of the recently deposed Palermo Commission boss, Badalamenti. When the DEA in New York infiltrated the operation they discovered that Sollena had not only lost the money confiscated at Punta Raisi, which was payment for drugs he had already received, but that he had recently suffered another blow when a twenty-four-kilo shipment of heroin had been seized at John F. Kennedy airport in New York. His supplier had been his uncle.

Badalamenti was not the only *mafioso* to suffer from the attentions of Boris Giuliano. In the months before his death Giuliano and his associates were getting dangerously close to the centre of another smuggling ring. It could implicate not only criminals in Sicily but respectable leaders of society in Rome and elsewhere.

From 1976 to 1980 the heroin trade between Sicily and New York was dominated by the smuggling network controlled by the Inzerillo–Gambino–Spatola ring. Between 1977 and 1979 the Italian police tracked $4 million which had been transferred from New Jersey to a bank in Palermo. They also discovered a $1 million transfer made by Frank Castronovo, owner of the Roma restaurant in New Jersey (who in 1985 would be one of the principal defendants in the Pizza Connection trial). The money was used by Salvatore Inzerillo for a property transaction, the favoured method of recycling Italian drug money – the 'narco lira'. This operation was easy because Rosario Spatola ran a construction company as a front. Among the public contracts he was awarded was the building of a local school. Inzerillo's company specialized in porcelain and lavatories.

But other connections were about to cause problems. In the seventies, Michele Sindona had been a useful man with his skill in setting up front companies, but when his Franklin National Bank crashed the reverberations ran deep into the Mafia. As the shattered pieces of his financial empire were put into receivership, traces of the recycling of heroin money from the Inzerillo–Gambino–Spatola ring were uncovered in Italy. It was 'black' money, which ran into billions of lire. Shortly after the seizure of the suitcase at Punta Raisi, Giuliano met Giorgio Ambrosoli, the government-appointed liquidator of Sindona's financial network. It is thought that Giuliano provided Ambrosoli with proof that Sindona was laundering heroin money through Swiss banks. Three days after their meeting Ambrosoli parked his car outside his Milan apartment, got out and locked it.

'Are you Giorgio Ambrosoli?' asked a voice from behind him.

He turned around and said, 'Yes.'

Three gunmen then shot him five times in the chest.

Working alongside Giuliano in Palermo was Tom Tripodi, one of the DEA's most experienced undercover agents. He worked in Palermo and managed to develop a network of Mafia informers whom he 'ran' like secret agents. Meetings would be arranged on remote hillsides where they could ensure they were not being followed. Tripodi is tall, powerfully built and unmistakably American. It is hard to believe that he could have worked successfully undercover against the Mafia, but he has. On one occasion he set up a meeting with Badalamenti himself:

I had an informant who took us to a guy he said was Tommaso di Maggio and this guy took us out to Cinisi where we went to a little bar. He introduced me to a guy named Badalamenti and we sat and we talked for a few minutes. I told him I was American and was looking for some business and he said, 'What kind of business?' I said, 'Well . . .' and he said, 'I know what kind of business.' And then he said, 'Where are you staying?' I told him I took a hotel room at the Presidente Hotel. He said, 'Well, someone will be in touch with you.'

The informant is dead and di Maggio is dead. It was dark, I couldn't even make Badalamenti out.

In fact, no one contacted him later, Badalamenti was too cautious to make a connection after only one meeting.

Working undercover in Sicily might seem a short-lived occupation. Tripodi survived and remains relaxed about his experiences:

The success of any undercover operation depends upon the informant. That means it's not a question of my going into Naples or Palermo and just hanging around bars, you know, because no one's going to trust me. Someone has to vouch for me. A person who's going to vouch for me is going to be someone who is in place. We recruit somebody who is in the target area, who has established bona fides, and he takes me in and he introduces me. So, when people deal with me, they deal with me because that individual has vouched for me – and he is going to be held accountable if I am a cop.

One case we were able to prosecute for drugs in Sicily came about because we gave them four kilos of morphine base to home-process. Hopefully they would lead us to a laboratory. They didn't at the time, but we arrested them.

Tripodi was working with Giuliano on a joint investigation codenamed 'Operation Caesar'. The priority was to locate the heroin laboratories and some of the chemists that were operating them – hence the undercover deal with the morphine base. Giuliano had grave reservations about trying to pass off the morphine base. He voiced his misgivings to Tripodi, saying that it was like planting heroin on someone and then arresting them. Nevertheless, the two men went ahead with it.

Although dealing in morphine base is comparatively rare, it is standard practice for the DEA to buy heroin, sometimes spending as much as $250,000 or more on a 'buy' that will give them a lead to the wholesalers and possibly the manufacturers. It is not a practice which is followed by the Italian police, for whom Tripodi has the highest admiration.

Giuliano was a Sicilian and knew the ways of the Mafia better than most. He once spoke about the rules of the game to Norman Lewis, author of *The Honoured Society*:

> In my trade you have to be a realist. No one will stop this thing. The most you can ever do is to keep it within bounds. This is a game. It's like chess. I give a piece here and I take a piece there, but I know it's a game I'm never going to be able to win. I have to do business with them, and they can be helpful in small ways. Among other things they hate to have small-time villains spoil the atmosphere of the place. You can leave your car unlocked in the parking space outside this hotel. Can you think of any hotel on the mainland where you could do that?

Lewis pointed out that the Mafia still killed judges and policemen. They, said Giuliano, are:

> outsiders who don't bother to learn the rules of the game. We try to explain to them, but they refuse to listen. It's a great help to have been born here.

But not, as it turned out, help enough. When Giuliano received the customary threatening calls, he was not unduly worried, as he and Tripodi had just rounded up a number of *mafiosi*. When Tripodi was due to leave Sicily, he made sure his American friend was well protected. Tripodi drove to the ferry accompanied by a helicopter and a two-car escort with police roadblocks lining the route. On the ferry itself another police patrol was waiting.

A few days after Tripodi's departure on 21 July 1979, Giuliano left his apartment for his usual early-morning *cappuccino* in the Bar Lux. It was eight o'clock on a Saturday morning and there were not many people on the street. He had received a phone call from someone he knew and arranged to go down to meet him a little earlier than usual on this particular morning. According to the only witness in the bar who came forward, this is what happened:

> I noticed a man who was trembling. He was white in the face. He must be ill, I thought. My first impulse was to offer to help. When the Commissario Giuliano went towards the door the man followed him. He drew a pistol and shot him three times in the neck. Signor Giuliano fell face downwards, and the man then shot him four more times in the back.

Giulano did not even have a chance to pull his own gun.

The killings went on. Michele Reina, the Provincial Secretary of the Christian Democratic Party, was murdered in 1979. A political murder such as this was clear evidence of involvement between the Mafia and the local Christian Democrats. It is suspected that Reina refused to make the necessary accommodations to the Mafia. Someone more amenable would have to be found. Cesare Terranova, a crusading judge who had devoted himself to the fight against the Mafia, was the next victim in the same year. He had single-mindedly pursued Luciano Liggio, whom he branded 'Public Enemy No. 1'. Like Giuliano, he realized that the only way to defeat the Mafia was to attack their money. He told his wife:

> If only I could have the power to investigate, to go into banks and investigate the finances of the people I know three months ago were pushing a cart and are now millionaires – then I could really do a lot.

It was Terranova's courageous stand against Liggio which sealed his fate. Signora Terranova recalls an occasion when her husband had gone to the Ucciardone prison to interrogate Liggio:

> He was told that Liggio was ill and couldn't come down. He realized that Liggio – which means Little King – the Little King of Corleone – couldn't accept the concept that he would come down to be interrogated by a magistrate. It had to be that the magistrate would go up and interrogate him. Just to make double certain, he asked the guard, 'Well, is Liggio in bed? Has he been in bed? Is he ill?' And the guard answered, 'No, actually, he's been out in the yard to take air in the courtyard up until ten minutes ago.'
>
> So at this point, of course, he insisted that Liggio be brought down. He said, 'I don't care how he's brought down but he's got to come down to be questioned.'
>
> So he sees Liggio arriving on a stretcher on which he is being brought down. The judge starts questioning him – going through the purely bureaucratic things, like 'What is your name?' And Liggio answers, 'I don't remember.' 'Who is your father?' 'I don't remember.' 'Who is your mother?' 'I don't remember.'
>
> So without batting an eyelid, the judge turns to the person who is taking all this down and says, 'Right, this man does not remember his name; he does not remember who his father was and he doesn't remember who his mother was.'

Terranova was insulting Liggio. He seemed to be implying that Liggio was admitting he was a bastard. Such was Liggio's rage that he was on the point of spitting at Terranova. He restrained himself, but did not forget: Judge Terranova was shot at point-blank range less than a hundred yards from his apartment.

As Buscetta has revealed, assassinations, especially those which produced 'illustrious corpses', could not be carried out independently by individual *mafiosi*. They had to be approved by the Commission:

> The Commission will then form the team that is to carry out the decision. They have the power to choose the executioners from any family without informing its boss; organizing the crime is, therefore, the exclusive province of the Commission and it is supposed to remain a secret from all the others; with the exception, of course, of the executioners themselves. In practice, however, it usually happens that a Commission member will inform his most trusted colleagues of the decision – but this has very little impact either on the planning or on the execution of the murder.

In the case of Terranova, however, Liggio himself was out for blood. He steamrollered the decision through the Commission, bypassing the members who would have opposed him. Buscetta is keen to stress the lack of 'propriety' in Liggio's haste to carry out murder. His lack of consultation with the other members of the board caused great resentment and would in the end help to precipitate the second Mafia wars. This is what Buscetta told Falcone about the murders of Reina and Terranova:

> I know for sure, because I heard it from Salvatore Inzerillo, that these murders were decided upon by the Palermo Commission, without any knowledge on the part of Inzerillo himself or of Stefano Bontate . . . These murders further widened the breach that already existed between Bontate and Inzerillo on the one side and the rest of the Commission on the other. In particular, Salvatore Inzerillo told me that the killing of Cesare Terranova had been committed on orders from Luciano Liggio. He didn't indicate the reasons, but it was quite clear that the motive for the killing was Terranova's legal activity against Liggio.

The police investigation into the murder of Terranova was pursued with about as much vigour as if it had been a traffic offence. Although Liggio was charged with the murder, the prosecution in the trial was hopelessly inadequate. As so often in Sicily, witnesses' memories miraculously faded once they appeared in court. Although the shooting had taken place in the centre of Palermo, no one had seen anything and no one had heard anything. The law of *omertà* was again invoked to shield the assassins.

The only forceful witness was the judge's widow. Signora Terranova confronted the supercilious Liggio with evidence about her husband's investigations, while he sat behind the bars which screened him from the courtroom. Dressed in a white polo-neck sweater, sporting a beard and allegedly suffering from one of his many ailments, Liggio cultivated the appearance and demeanour of an aggrieved businessman.

In an impromptu interview with a reporter, he proclaimed his innocence but spoke of how it was sometimes necessary to 'squeeze a lemon' – a casual reference to torture and murder in the pursuit of profit.

Signora Terranova's testimony was in vain. Personal tragedy degenerated into public farce, a familiar sequence in so many Mafia trials in Italy. Like many others who were killed by the Mafia, Terranova had threatened an individual and an organization which for years had enjoyed protection from powerful supporters. These supporters helped either because they were intimidated or because they knew they would be assured of money and power if they collaborated. In return, they would endeavour to guarantee immunity from the law. In some cases, outright corruption and inbred inertia ensured that the prosecution and trial of the Mafia was futile.

For Signora Terranova, the lack of reaction to her husband's killing made her all the more determined to attack the factors in Sicilian society and in Italy as a whole which had allowed the Mafia to thrive. 'Sicilians are born with resignation and also fear,' she says, and it is from these characteristics of the Sicilian mentality that the Mafia draws its life-blood. For both politicians and ordinary people, the easiest course is to let things remain as they are or to perfect the subtle art of appearing to do something whilst actually doing nothing, a political manœuvre designed to divert public pressure while protecting vested interests and the status quo. Above all, the Mafia could depend on the fear felt by the ordinary Sicilian, the potential witness who would suddenly suffer a loss of memory when called to testify.

Signora Terranova has now devoted herself to campaigning against the Mafia, encouraging other women to stand up to the mentality which exerts a stranglehold on Sicily. Out of her own tragedy and the suffering of so many others she has cultivated a powerful movement of hope. Today she sees encouraging signs in the street demonstrations and the anti-Mafia feelings that have developed in Sicily:

> It's exactly from those things that things will change –
> because it's the mentality that has to be changed. The
> children of today are the men of tomorrow. If you
> manage to change the mentality, to change the consent,
> to change the fear in which the Mafia can live – if you
> can change that, you can beat them.

Boris Giuliano's investigation into the Mafia's finances was taken over by a captain of the *carabinieri*, Emanuele Basile. He had been investigating links between the Mafia and Sicily's top bankers and financiers, some of whom were 'washing' millions of dollars of heroin money from the United States. By the early 1980s laundering money for the Mafia had become a major industry. There were more banks in Sicily than in any other part of Italy. In the town of Trapani in western Sicily, with a population of only 70,000, there were more banks than in Milan, Italy's financial capital. Between 1970 and 1980, banks in Sicily increased their turnover by 400 per cent. Even the smallest towns in the most remote parts of the Sicilian country-side had their own banks, while in Palermo they competed for customers on almost every street corner. It was an unedifying display of greed by the banking fraternity attracted like sharks to a city awash with money from a trade based on blood.

Although still deprived of the legal powers he needed to investigate bank accounts, Captain Basile became far too persistent for the Mafia Commission. On 1 May 1980 three gunmen put an end to him and his inquiries by shooting him on the street as he was returning home with his wife and young daughter. Within minutes the police picked up three Mafia soldiers for questioning. They had found two of them racing away in a car belonging to the third, who was arrested a few hundred yards away, trying to climb a high wire fence. He was 'searching for lemons', he explained to the police. The three men were already suspects in the murder of another police officer, and while none of them could account for their flight from the scene of the crime, they all gave identical alibis. They were, they said, returning from secret romantic liaisons with young married women. They could not possibly disclose their names as they were all 'Men of Honour'. One of them was from the Ciaculli family of Michele Greco, and the other two were from Inzerillo's family, the Passo di Rigano. It appears that Inzerillo and Bontate had opposed this killing, and the presence of two of Inzerillo's men suggests that they had been given the contract without his knowledge.

Inzerillo and Rosario Spatola were already being investigated and many arrest warrants had been issued against members of their organization. Inzerillo was so outraged by the warrants that he became almost deranged. Without consulting the Commission, he ordered the execution of the chief public prosecutor of Palermo, Gaetano Costa. On 6 August 1980, as the sixty-four-year-old prosecutor was preparing to abandon the heat of the city for his summer vacation, a young man approached him in the street, pulled out a .38 revolver from beneath the newspaper he was carrying and shot him five times at point-blank range.

Inzerillo's manic reaction was designed to show the Grecos and their allies on the Commission that he was as tough and ruthless as they were, but it was an act of pure insanity and it broke one of the fundamental rules of the Commission. His colleagues expressed shock at his petulance. Pippo Calò told Buscetta that Inzerillo had 'behaved like a child'.

By midsummer 1980 Salvatore Inzerillo and Stefano Bontate were almost totally isolated within the Commission. Michele

Greco and the Corleonesi, represented by Salvatore Riina, who loyally followed the wishes of Luciano Liggio, were virtually unassailable. They had the power of life or death over any individual in the island, and they exercised it with an utter ruthlessness. They reinforced their control by reorganizing the structure of power, subtly altering the commission system that Buscetta had helped to set up. Buscetta describes the effect this had:

> The new structure serves the purpose of enabling the Corleonesi and their allies to stick their noses into the affairs of other families and to dominate all the Mafia organizations. Just to give you an example, if a builder from one province is planning to undertake a big job in another province, it is the new structure that decides whether he should be allowed to do it or not.

The ceaseless organization of murder and crime was supported by an efficient bureaucracy. The new structure was known as the 'Interprovinciale'.

In 1979 a new killer had joined the Commission – as if they needed one. He has acquired a reputation as the most bloodthirsty psychopath that even the Mafia has ever seen. His name was Giuseppe 'Pino' Greco, known as 'Scarpazzedda', meaning 'Fleet of Foot'. He delighted in being present at Mafia executions. On one occasion he got so carried away that he chopped a man's arm off. He was a frequent visitor to a dingy basement room just outside the centre of Palermo. It was the Mafia's torture chamber, where victims would be garotted and their bodies either cut up or dissolved in acid. Michele Greco was the head of the Commission and his protégé Pino Greco, although not related, became head of the Ciaculli family. The Greco–Corleonesi faction was assuming all the positions of power, and Bontate and Inzerillo, fellow members of the Commission, found themselves increasingly isolated and humiliated. For example, to talk to Michele Greco they were forced to go first to Pino Greco, the newest and most junior member of the Commission. It was a calculated insult.

At the beginning of 1980, the Corleonesi, now fully in control, began to step up their challenge to the power of the state. In the process they transformed the Mafia into an organization which relied on the tactics of terrorism. The assassinations of public figures continued. They were meticulously planned, often with the benefit of inside knowledge of security arrangements and travel routes. As with the Red Brigades or any other terrorist group, the aim was to instil fear into the heart of the state and into the minds of those who fought the Mafia. All the major murders were planned and implemented with the full agreement of the Commission, although the votes at this stage could be fixed by the Greco–Corleonesi faction without fear of being overruled. The small measure of democracy which the Mafia had once adhered to was now replaced by a dictatorship. Michele Greco, his brother Salvatore 'the Senator' Greco, the psychopath Pino Greco, Salvatore Riina and Pippo Calò now had the power to eliminate their remaining enemies, both outside and inside the Mafia. The murder of public figures would eventually turn the whole of Italy against them. The vendettas being waged within their own ranks would mean nothing less than a new civil war.

9

The Second Mafia Wars

You are the only person who has enough influence
to be able to direct a counter-attack and lead a
revolt against the Corleonesi.

Gaetano Badalamenti to Tommaso Buscetta

At the end of 1979 Tommaso Buscetta was released from prison
on the Italian equivalent of parole. He went to live in Turin,
and took up his old trade of glass engraving once more. Although
he had to report to the local prison every night, he still managed
to make frequent trips to Palermo and Rome. The seven years
that he had spent in Ucciardone prison had greatly increased his
stature as a Man of Honour. He had been treated with tremendous respect. Fellow prisoners would actually bow in his presence or kiss his hand, and on one occasion his word was sufficient
to avert a potential riot.

The Mafia virtually control Ucciardone. Many inmates have
their food delivered from Palermo's finest restaurants, and carry
on their business and personal affairs almost uninterrupted.
When Buscetta's daughter Felicia was about to get married she
visited her father in prison. He arranged for her to see Pietro lo
Iacono, Stefano Bontate's deputy, who ran a shop selling fabrics
and trousseaus. Lo Iacono gave her a trousseau for her wedding
free of charge. Buscetta himself married, for the third time, in
1979, shortly before his release. Christina had been both loyal
and patient.

On his release Buscetta emerged into a different world. Sicily
and the Mafia had been radically changed by the profits from

the heroin trade. One kilo of morphine base could be bought for $6–9000 depending on the total quantity; once refined by the Mafia in one of their laboratories, the same kilo at 90 per cent purity would be worth $40–50,000. When sold in New York its wholesale price would be $200,000; its street value would be over $2 million. The Mafia would deal on average in shipments of between twenty and a hundred kilos, each transaction being worth between $4 and $20 million dollars.

Buscetta's family, the Porta Nuova, like all the Mafia families, was making enormous profits from the trade. Pippo Calò and its leading members such as Nunzio la Mattina had done especially well. La Mattina had been one of the principal cigarette smugglers and like most of his colleagues he had easily made the transition to narcotics.

In his confession Buscetta describes the changes that confronted him:

> After I returned to Palermo, I noticed that all the members of the Cosa Nostra were incredibly well off and Stefano Bontate told me that it was because of the drug trafficking. He agreed with me in thinking that the drug trafficking would lead to the collapse of Cosa Nostra. He said that at the beginning it had been Nunzio la Mattina's idea. They had begun to abandon tobacco smuggling around 1978, either because of the increased risks due to greater pressure from the police or because of internal arguments which had often caused important deals to fall through. La Mattina, who, as a smuggler, had access to the sources of production and of supply of the raw material for the production of heroin, wanted to try his luck and succeeded in convincing the more prominent members of Cosa Nostra.

Buscetta also reveals that the other Mafia families were all involved in the trade. They helped to finance the deals or bought the morphine base and refined it in Palermo's hidden laboratories. Buscetta noted with alarm that the eagerness for profits was breaking down the traditional divisions between families:

> I was perhaps the only Man of Honour in Palermo never to take part in the trafficking, both because, as I already said, I did see the extreme danger to the very survival of the Cosa Nostra and because, due, among other things, to my imprisonment, I was kept aside. Stefano Bontate also claimed not to be involved, but, to be honest, I cannot be sure what he says is true, as everyone kept their activities to themselves. Another Man of Honour who could not have taken part in narcotics trafficking was Gaetano Badalamenti, who, moreover, always told me that he kept himself apart from that business. This was not because Badalamenti did not want to participate but because, having been put out of commission, he would not have had any means to establish contacts with the Men of Honour who were controlling that traffic. However, precisely because of this, I do not know how closely Badalamenti's statements correspond to the truth. It should be said, however, that if he participated clandestinely in such activities, making contact with Men of Honour who should never have approached him, this means that, in effect, money corrupted everything and everyone, since that would have been a very serious violation.

Buscetta also named the suppliers of morphine base. He revealed that a man called Giuseppe 'Pippo' Bono was one of the major importers of Sicilian heroin in America. When the DEA and the other agencies put this new information together with other known sources of morphine base, particularly in Turkey, they began to see the network clearly for the first time. According to a secret DEA report a major supplier of morphine base from Turkey, much of it destined for the Pizza Connection, was the Yasar Musullulu organization.

Musullulu's real name is Avni Karadurmus, but under his alias he set up front companies in Zurich and conducted the

bulk of his business from there. He also sold arms to the Middle
East in substantial quantities and had contacts in Bulgaria, a
country whose government and intelligence agency has a long
history of connivance with the heroin traffic. It is now known
that some of the morphine base sold to the Mafia via Musullulu
was supplied from stocks seized by customs officials in Bulgaria.
Musullulu would guarantee delivery of morphine base, usually
in 500-kilo consignments, to an area within seventy nautical
miles of Sicily. He would dispatch his representative to Mazzara
del Vallo, a village near Trapani in Sicily, where Michele Greco's
refining laboratory was hidden. The morphine base would arrive
on a Turkish freighter and be transferred to a speedboat which
would in turn rendezvous with a fishing boat sent from a remote
part of the Sicilian coastline. One of the favoured transfer
points was the island of Marittima between Sicily and Sardinia.
Payment for each shipment would be made in Zurich. Mafia
cashiers would make regular flights to Switzerland to settle with
Musullulu. The two men he dealt with most frequently were
Nunzio la Mattina and Antonio Rotolo, known as 'Carlo'.

Early in 1983 Nunzio la Mattina was murdered. He had
arranged for $1.5 million to be 'stolen' en route to Switzerland.
Despite his claims that it really had been stolen, his fellow Men
of Honour decided not to afford him the benefit of the doubt
and he was duly eliminated. His place was taken by Rotolo,
who proved to be much more efficient and, perhaps noting the
fate of his predecessor, more than anxious to convince his
colleagues of his honesty. On his regular visits to Zurich, Rotolo
was always accompanied by 'six Sicilian-looking males' – who,
true to Sicilian tradition, remained silent throughout each meeting with Musullulu. Rotolo brought suitcases with him containing between $3 and $5 million in $50 and $100 bills. He
attended at least fifteen meetings of this nature, dealing in a
minimum of $45 million worth of morphine base. At a conserva-
tive estimate that was worth $500 million wholesale in New
York. Street price: an astronomical $5 billion.

It was a serious business.

Zurich, with its conservative façade and multitude of banks, was the perfect meeting place for the chief executives of the Mafia's heroin trade. Among the numerous banks there would always be some willing to receive the piles of small-denomination bills with few questions asked. Some banks would charge a commission for handling the bills. One of the respectable banking houses that became involved was Credit Suisse. The manager of one of their branches, Sergio Daffond, dealt directly with Cop Finance, one of the Swiss receiving companies for the proceeds of heroin sales from the New York 'Pizza Connection'.

Rotolo commuted back and forth to Zurich until April 1984. One of the last deals he did with Musullulu took place there in the spring of 1984. He arrived as usual in Switzerland with his escort and suitcases. This time he was paying the Turk $5.2 million for 500 kilos of morphine base. The Sicilians were actually in credit for $1.3 million and were buying the base at $13,000 a kilo. Shortly after the meeting Musullulu disappeared – taking with him over $6 million of Mafia money. He is now in hiding, although he is keen to get back to Turkey and is known to have offered a bribe of $750,000 to an official of the Turkish secret police for a safe passage back to his own country. Shortly after his flight from Switzerland he went to Bulgaria. There, in a bizarre incident, one of his henchmen set fire to him and he was badly burnt. Somehow he managed to survive the attack and is probably still in Bulgaria.

The fact that the Musullulu organization was only one of a number of major suppliers of morphine base to the Mafia laboratories in Italy gives some idea of the sheer scale of the trade. No wonder that, as Buscetta reveals, everybody wanted to get in on the act:

> All the Palermo families are involved in drug trafficking: every boss of the family sets it up and to some extent the Men of Honour of the family can take part in the traffic. In participating in the profits, those closest to the boss are favoured and they keep more of the money for their own use. The oldest and less enterprising take part to a lesser degree or are cut out of the profits altogether.

Anyone who took part in financing the purchase of a consignment of morphine base could choose either to take the heroin from the laboratories and arrange to sell it on his own initiative, or wait for it to be exported to the USA or elsewhere through the usual channels. The second choice brought bigger profits – but entailed running a financial risk and the possibility of seizure of the drugs during shipment.

When I arrived in Palermo, as well as this incredible amount of wealth, I also found a great deal of confusion among the various families and their Men of Honour, so that I soon realized that the principles that inspired the Cosa Nostra were definitely a thing of the past and that it would be best for me to leave Palermo as soon as possible, since I could no longer see myself in the organization that I had believed in since I was young.

As a veteran of one Mafia war, Buscetta knew only too well what 'confusion among the various families' could lead to. He was in a curious position. He was a leading member of the Porta Nuova family, whose boss, Pippo Calò, was allied to the Greco – Corleonesi faction. He was also a close friend of Gaetano Badalamenti, who had been thrown out of the Mafia by the Corleonesi. In addition he was the best friend of Stefano Bontate, who, along with Salvatore Inzerillo, was an increasingly bitter rival of the Grecos and the Corleonesi. His years in prison had meant that he had been detached from the beginning of the power struggle. He came out with his reputation enhanced. His prestige and neutrality gave him the opportunity to act as power-broker between the two opposing factions on the Commission. He could be seen as everyone's friend or as everyone's enemy. He was on a tightrope and it would require all his charm and skill to keep his balance.

Buscetta got permission from the supervising magistrate in Turin to visit Palermo. He stayed there, on and off, for a few months in a newly built apartment on Via Croce Rossa which he rented from his son Antonio. The restrictions of parole were becoming oppressive. He decided to stay in Palermo – as a fugitive once more.

His first contact in Palermo was Giuseppe Galeazzo, whom he had met in prison. Galeazzo approached him on behalf of the head of their family, Pippo Calò. A medium-sized man in late middle age with a moustache and a homburg hat, Calò looked more like a successful greengrocer than one of the most powerful post-war Mafia bosses in Italy. Yet appearances were not altogether deceptive. He had begun his career running a small butcher's shop in Palermo. He had diversified from the meat trade via cigarette smuggling and heroin to amass enormous wealth. Within his Porta Nuova family were some of Sicily's most successful heroin traffickers – Nunzio la Mattina, Tommaso Spadaro and Gerlando Alberti. Calò had also formed an alliance of several years' standing with Camorra clans from Naples, particularly with Michele Zaza and Antonio Bardellino, who became 'honorary' members of the Mafia. They had been useful collaborators in the cigarette smuggling business – now they moved into the infinitely more profitable business of heroin smuggling. Calò operated from a base in Rome, where he was known as 'Mario'. In one of his several apartments he kept millions of lire in cash and precious works of art which other *mafiosi* would sometimes buy from him. In his other apartments he would store heroin and explosives. His influence in Rome, especially his financial contacts, allowed him to act both as the Mafia's ambassador in the Italian capital and also as their chief accountant.

In Rome he had developed contacts with some of the leading gangsters and financiers, including men linked to Roberto Calvi, whose Banco Ambrosiano was used by the Mafia and by Michele Sindona to launder millions from the Mafia's narcotics trade. Calò also had 'business' interests in Sardinia with one of Calvi's associates, Luigi Faldetta, a wealthy building developer. Two men who were common to both worlds were Ernesto Diotallevi and Danilo Abbruciati, gang bosses of Rome's underworld. They were on good terms with Flavio Carboni, a millionaire property developer from Sardinia with an extensive network of friends ranging from government ministers to gangsters. Carboni was a leading member of P2 and close to the P2 grand master Licio Gelli. He was also a close friend of Roberto Calvi. When the Banco Ambrosiano became embroiled in a series of scandals involving the Vatican, during which it was discovered that Calvi had made a series of highly suspicious loans to Carboni for millions of dollars, there was an attempt to kill the deputy chairman of the bank, Roberto Rosone. The assailant was shot by a security guard. He turned out to be none other than Danilo Abbruciati, underworld associate of Carboni and Calò. As for Calvi, a few days after Carboni organized his secret flight to London, the banker was found hanging beneath London's Black-friars Bridge.

Through friends like these, the head of the Porta Nuova family had acquired power, influence and money. He had become a multi-millionaire while Buscetta had been languishing in prison. Buscetta was resentful because Calò had apparently done nothing to help his (Buscetta's) family, something a *capo* was obliged to do under the Mafia code.

When Buscetta abandoned his semi-parole in Turin, he re-sponded to Galeazzo's message and received word from Calò to contact him in Rome, which he did. Calò suggested that they forget about the past, saying that he had not realized how hard up Buscetta had been. Buscetta should stay in Italy, where they could make a lot of money together. The reason, he confided, was that the Mafia had the mayor of Palermo, Vito Ciancimino, in its pocket. Luciano Liggio's deputy, Salvatore Riina, who had taken over the leadership of the Corleone family after Liggio was imprisoned in 1974, had total control of the mayor. Calò explained that there would be another massive redevelopment of Palermo which would make a lot of money for everyone – and that Buscetta could share in this bonanza with Calò, without having to go through a *capodecina*. Buscetta would deal directly with Calò and no one else. It was an offer that most Men of Honour would not have refused.

In addition, Buscetta was offered a house in Rome so that his children could go to the best schools. The offer made, Calò turned to 'family' business. He told Buscetta that Stefano Bontate was behaving badly; he had formed an alliance with Salvatore Inzerillo against the rest of the Commission.

Back in Palermo Buscetta met Bontate and Inzerillo to hear their side of the story. The Grecos and the Corleonesi, they claimed, were undermining their power on the Commission. Bontate told Buscetta that for his own self-preservation he was planning to kill Riina. He claimed to have the support of an unaligned Commission member, Antonio Salamone, but he admitted that Salamone would not publicly declare his support for Bontate until after the event, at which point he promised to confirm in front of the Commission that Bontate had acted 'with right on his side'.

It worried Buscetta that Bontate would fall for such an empty promise. He warned him that to all intents and purposes it was a worthless agreement. Bontate was effectively on his own. Buscetta asked how he was going to kill Riina and Bontate replied that he was personally going to shoot him at a Commission meeting. Buscetta must have wondered about his sanity.

According to Bontate, Calò was now so completely dominated by Michele Greco that during meetings of the Commission in Palermo he no longer spoke at all, confining his contributions to an occasional nod of the head.

Now that he had heard both sides of the story, Buscetta knew that his friend was dangerously isolated. The tentative alliance with Salamone and the plot to shoot Riina seemed to be the manœuvres of a desperate man. Buscetta tried to reconcile the opposing factions with a round of 'peace talks'. Calò, Bontate, Inzerillo and himself would be the 'delegates'.

The talks took place, somewhat incongruously, in a motorway café, the Pavesi Autogrill at the end of the Naples–Rome motorway. The meeting was friendly and convivial. It did not last long, but the four *mafiosi* agreed to another round of talks before confronting the Commission. They wanted to prevent a complete break with the Corleonesi. Buscetta spent a few more days with Calò in Rome and then returned to Palermo.

His violation of parole seems not to have been taken very

seriously. He was able to move around with a minimum of anxiety – as he explains in his confession, it is a well-known fact that between 1.30 p.m. and 4.30 p.m. in Palermo it is impossible to find a policeman! Back in his native city, Inzerillo introduced Buscetta to Ignazio lo Presti, a successful builder. Lo Presti took him to see a villa complex he was constructing on the outskirts of the city, and offered him a villa at a massive discount, an offer Buscetta gratefully acknowledged but did not accept. They got on well, and lo Presti invited him to his house for dinner. When he got to know him quite well, lo Presti told Buscetta that he was a cousin of Nino Salvo, one of the most powerful and politically influential tycoons in Sicily. If Buscetta should ever have any problems with his parole he was just to tell lo Presti and his cousin would sort them out. Buscetta took him up on the offer. He became friends with Nino Salvo and his cousin Ignazio Salvo. They gave Buscetta the use of one of their seaside villas and chartered a plane to bring Christina and her family over from Paris for the Christmas celebrations of 1980.

Although Buscetta is understandably reticent on the subject, his sons had become involved with some of his criminal associates. Benedetto had already got mixed up with his father's dealings in New York and South America, and although there is little evidence that they committed any crimes, an incident involving Antonio occurred in the late summer of 1980 which gives some indication of the life they were leading.

Pippo Calò, who was still waiting for Buscetta to reply to his offer, told him that he had heard that Antonio was getting into trouble locally by paying for supermarket groceries with suspect cheques. Calò was annoyed, either because this was happening in an area controlled by the Porta Nuova family, or simply because petty crime of that nature was frowned on by senior *mafiosi*. In front of Buscetta he called Antonio 'a swindler'. Buscetta was surprised and angry. That same evening Antonio was summoned to see his father in the presence of Calò. Buscetta told his son in no uncertain terms what he thought of his behaviour. Antonio apologized but pleaded that he had been in such desperate financial straits that he had been forced to pawn his wife's jewellery. Calò seemed to relent. In a gesture of sympathy, the Mafia boss pulled out a wad of notes from his pocket and peeled off 10 million lire in 100,000 lire bills. He pressed the money on the grateful Antonio, saying that, as it was his birthday the following day, this was his present. Antonio went next day to the pawn shop in Palermo and paid 5,400,000 lire to retrieve the jewellery.

A few days later he was arrested as an accomplice in a kidnapping case: Calò's bills had been part of the ransom. When Buscetta found out he was furious. He confronted Calò, demanding to know how he could have done something as stupid as that. Calò attempted to justify himself with the excuse that he had been paid for a shipment of smuggled cigarettes and had no idea it was traceable ransom money. Buscetta did not believe Calò's story. He deduced that his *capo* had probably organized the kidnapping and then set up Antonio.

For Buscetta it was the last straw. He turned down Calò's offer and told him that he was now finally convinced that the best option for his family and himself was to leave Palermo and return to Brazil. Calò accepted Buscetta's decision and promised that he would pay for Antonio's defence. Buscetta remained in Palermo for the rest of 1980.

Before he left, his old friend Bontate threw a grand farewell dinner for him at his $500,000 villa. The house was protected by electronically controlled gates and closed-circuit television cameras monitored by soldiers from his family. The dinner was a grand affair with the finest Sicilian wines and local dishes. Among the guests were Antonio Salamone, Salvatore Inzerillo and Salvatore Contorno, one of the toughest and most loyal members of Bontate's Santa Maria de Gesù family.

In January 1981, equipped with a false passport, Buscetta took a car-ferry from Palermo and drove overland to Paris. From there he flew to Rio de Janeiro. Christina and the children travelled separately by air from Rome.

Once again, Buscetta had got out just in time. Three months

after arriving in Rio he read in the newspapers that Bontate had been murdered. It really had been a farewell dinner.

Sorrow at the death of a friend was tempered by the knowledge of what the cost of that friendship might now be. Buscetta arranged to visit Salamone, who was also in Brazil. Salamone was head of the San Giuseppe Iato family, which included some of the most important Italian and American operators of the Pizza Connection – Alfredo Bono, Giuseppe Ganci and Salamone himself. Salamone must have had some of the same misgivings as Buscetta. He was the man who had made the tentative alliance with Bontate to kill Salvatore Riina of the Corleone family.

The two met in San Pedro, Brazil. Salamone told Buscetta that he had already telephoned 'the Pope', Michele Greco, who claimed to know nothing about Bontate's murder. Salamone had also taken the precaution of contacting Inzerillo, who told him that he was in no doubt that the killing had been arranged by the Corleonesi and that Michele Greco's claim of ignorance was utter nonsense. Inzerillo was highly suspicious of Greco, but he was not too worried about his own safety. He was in the middle of a major heroin deal involving fifty kilos which he had obtained from Riina. He still owed Riina the money. No one, he was sure, was going to kill him until he'd paid up.

Inzerillo had told Salamone about the circumstances of Bontate's murder. Shortly before he was killed, his deputy, Pietro lo Iacono, the man who had provided a wedding dress for Buscetta's daughter, had been to see his boss. Bontate mentioned to lo Iacono that he was planning to go to his country house that same evening and stay the night there. It was his birthday. Armed with this information, lo Iacono left and alerted Giuseppe Lucchese, a soldier in Michele Greco's family who was waiting outside in a car. Lucchese relayed the message by walkie-talkie to the occupants of another car which lay in wait further up the road.

A few minutes later Bontate emerged from his house on Via Villagrazia and set off for his country retreat. He was preceded by an escort car driven by Stefano de Gregorio, his bodyguard.

When they reached the intersection of the Via della Regione Siciliana, the lights were just changing to red. De Gregorio sped on, failing to notice that his boss had been caught at the lights. Bontate was a sitting target. The killers opened fire. Although Bontate was armed, he never had a chance to use his gun. His car and his body were riddled with bullets from the automatic fire of a Kalashnikov assault rifle. He was mortally wounded but he still managed to steer the car for a few yards down the street. It crashed into a wall. De Gregorio got all the way to Bontate's country house before he realized that his boss had not caught up with him. He drove back six kilometres to the scene of the assassination. He took one look at the bloodstained body and knew that there was nothing he could do – except get out fast before the police arrived.

Bontate had become one of the most powerful Mafia bosses in Sicily at the age of twenty. On his forty-third birthday he was dead. 'The Falcon' had fallen prey to men more vicious than himself. Worse, he had been betrayed by his own family. The treachery of lo Iacono and the participation of one of Michele Greco's soldiers was clear evidence that the contract had been ordered by the Commission.

Bontate's funeral was poorly attended. The only two women who turned up wearing the customary black veils were the wives of Michele Greco and Tommaso Spadaro, Bontate's godfather. Another mourner was Salvatore Contorno. Although not well educated in the formal sense, Contorno was an intelligent and resourceful *mafioso* who was respected by his friends and feared by his enemies. He had a reputation as a 'man of courage', a euphemism for a Mafia soldier who has become an expert killer. His reputation had earned him the exotic title 'Coriolanus of the Forest'. His qualities, in particular his fierce and unquestioning loyalty, had been greatly appreciated by Bontate, who acknowledged him as one of the most important members of the Santa Maria di Gesù family. In recognition of his services, Bontate allowed him the privilege of dealing directly with him, instead of having to go through a *capodecina*. Contorno knew very well that Bontate was systematically being isolated within the

Commission. He knew that decisions to assassinate state officials were being reached without Bontate or Inzerillo being consulted. He had also formed a close friendship with his boss's great friend, Buscetta, a *mafioso* he admired almost to the point of worship.

The low turnout at Bontate's funeral confirmed his suspicions that his boss had been set up. One man whom Contorno felt he could still trust was Mimmo Teresi, the *sottocapo* of the Santa Maria di Gesù family. Teresi had been told by Michele Greco that he had nothing to fear and should continue as if nothing had happened. Teresi then had a secret meeting with Inzerillo at an iron warehouse in Palermo, on the Via della Regione Siciliana – the same street on which Bontate had been ambushed. The next time Teresi saw Michele Greco, 'the Pope' asked him why he had gone to the iron warehouse. Teresi realized that he was under surveillance by the Corleonesi. He admitted to Greco that he had met Inzerillo. Greco warned him not to meet Inzerillo again. He also told him that Pietro lo Iacono would now become the regent of the Santa Maria di Gesù family.

At this point Inzerillo still considered himself relatively safe. He still owed the money for the heroin that he had bought from Riina. Nevertheless, after the murder of Bontate, he took the precaution of buying himself a bullet-proof car – an Alfetta 2000.

From 1980 the Mafia's favourite assassination weapon was the Kalashnikov, a Russian-designed assault-rifle also known as the AK47. Regularly used by terrorists all over the world, its magazine holds thirty rounds of 7.62 mm calibre cartridges, short bullets with a steel-penetrating capacity. Set to automatic, it has a firing rate of a hundred shots per minute. At close range it will cut a man in half.

A few days after the murder of Bontate, the police had to deal with another shooting. It involved a mysterious attack on a jeweller's shop in the centre of Palermo. Who was behind it – and why – was a mystery. The display cases in Contino's shop had been sprayed with bullets, but nothing appeared to have been stolen. Buscetta has now solved the mystery. It was never intended to be a robbery. The man on the back of the motorcycle simply wanted to test the power of his Kalashnikov against the bullet-proof glass of the jewellery display case. The test was successful.

On 11 May 1981 Inzerillo was driven in his new bullet-proof car to a rendezvous with his mistress, who was installed in a block of flats on the Via Brunelleschi which had been constructed by one of his companies. As soon as he entered the house his driver, Giuseppe Montalto, signalled to a group of men parked across the road. When he came out of his mistress's apartment, Inzerillo was killed by a burst of rifle fire before he even had the chance to dive into his car. The murder weapon was the same Kalashnikov that had killed Bontate. Inzerillo's body was found with a loaded .357 Magnum in his pocket. His sense of security because of his heroin deal with Riina had proved to be false. To the Corleonesi the loss of a few hundred thousand dollars was a price well worth paying for the elimination of their most powerful enemy. In the event, they had not even had to shoot him through the bullet-proof glass. It was just too bad for Contino's jewellery shop that the experiment had been necessary.

As with Bontate, the Corleonesi had accomplished the murder of Inzerillo by ensuring his betrayal by one of his own family. They had now killed the two leaders of the opposition and installed their own men in their place. They then set out to dissuade those loyal to Bontate and Inzerillo from entertaining any thoughts of revenge. High on the list was Mimmo Teresi, who had ignored Greco's instructions and had arranged to meet Inzerillo at the exact spot where he was killed. His late arrival saved his life. Later, when he met Salvatore Contorno secretly and told him about his narrow escape, Contorno replied that Teresi was a 'dead man' and that he must not make any move which would make the situation worse.

In Brazil, Buscetta knew that he too could be a candidate for the Corleonesi death list. He was in considerable danger as both he and Antonio Salamone had known about Bontate's plan to kill Riina. Salamone, arriving back in Brazil from a conference with Greco, told Buscetta that the plot to kill Riina had been discovered though he did not know if Greco was aware that Buscetta and he had known about it. Even though they might not have committed themselves to taking part in the actual murder, the knowledge itself was more than enough to get them killed. Their anxiety was heightened when they heard that the Corleonesi were gunning for those still loyal to the Inzerillo–Bontate faction.

Mimmo Teresi and Salvatore Contorno were invited to a 'peace' meeting by Pietro lo Iacono. Contorno was suspicious and immediately sensed a trap. He decided not to attend and advised Teresi not to go either. Teresi was never seen again. It was the beginning of an orgy of bloodletting which claimed the lives of many of those who were thought to be supporters of Inzerillo and Bontate, or enemies of the Corleonesi. Presiding over the bloodbath was the psychopath Pino Greco.

Inzerillo's son, Giuseppe, was top of his list. Although Giuseppe was only seventeen years old, Pino Greco considered him a threat, having heard that the teenager had boasted, 'I will kill with my own hands that dog Salvatore Riina!' Pino Greco could not allow such open boasts to go unchallenged. He personally supervised the murder of Giuseppe Inzerillo. Before he killed him, he tortured him. As a final moment of horror, Greco cut his arm off and jeered at him, 'With this arm you will no longer be able to kill Toto Riina!'

The vendetta spread from Palermo to New York. Inzerillo's brother, Pietro, was discovered dead in the boot of a car with dollars stuffed in his mouth and his genitals cut off. These Mafia trademarks suggested that he might have been running around with the wife of another *mafioso* (a capital offence) and had been too greedy into the bargain.

Pino Greco next set out to hunt down Contorno, who was in hiding both from the police and the Corleonesi. But Greco's intelligence network passed word that Contorno was going to visit his parents. He moved swiftly to set up an ambush.

On 25 June 1981, at 7.30 in the evening, Contorno set off from his parents' apartment in the Via Ciaculli, driving his mother-in-law's Fiat 127. In the car with him was a cousin,

Giuseppe Faglietta, who had insisted on coming with him. His wife and son had left before him in a separate car. They drove down the Via Ciaculli and approached the overpass that leads to the Via Giafar. As they did so, Contorno saw someone he knew, Pino d'Angelo, driving in another Fiat 127. Contorno waved at him and let him pass. D'Angelo waved back, overtook and then started to slow down. Contorno was puzzled by that. He was now driving along the highest point of the overpass running parallel with the top floors of the apartment buildings by the roadside. Ahead and to the right, Contorno noticed another familiar face behind a top-floor window of a building beside the overpass. It was a man called Vincenzo Buffa. Contorno began to get alarmed. Alarm turned to fear when a few seconds later he saw a powerful motorbike racing towards him. The rider was Giuseppe Lucchese, one of the team which had killed Bontate. Another man was riding pillion.

It was Pino Greco.

The motorbike pulled in front of Contorno's car. Greco raised his Kalashnikov, took careful aim and opened fire, emptying a full magazine in Contorno's direction. Contorno threw himself against Faglietta to protect him. Miraculously, they survived the hail of bullets. Faglietta was hit in the cheek; Contorno was totally unscathed.

The motorcycle raced off down the road. Greco needed time to reload his magazine.

A few moments later, Contorno saw in his rear-view mirror that the motorbike was coming back at high speed. Reacting quickly, he stopped the car, pushed Faglietta out and crouched beneath the car headlights. In his hand was a .38 calibre revolver with five rounds. Greco opened fire again with the Kalashnikov and Contorno aimed carefully at his would-be executioner. He was sure that he hit Greco in the chest because the second burst of automatic fire went wild and Greco recoiled. Behind the motorbike was a Volkswagen Golf containing a back-up for the hit-team. Contorno recognized only one of them. Badly outnumbered and outgunned, he decided to make a run for it. Amazingly, both he and his cousin escaped.

Later, Contorno's cousin told him that he had seen Pino Greco on the beach in a swimsuit. His body showed no trace of any bullet wounds. He had been wearing a bullet-proof vest.

Contorno escaped with nothing more than a scratch from a splinter of glass and a shock of hair torn out by a bullet. He had had the narrowest of narrow escapes. He fled at once to Rome. There he thought of contacting Pippo Calò until he remembered that Bontate, shortly before he had been killed, had become increasingly uneasy about Calò's friendship and that Calò's visits to Bontate's house had noticeably diminished immediately before the murder. Contorno decided to lie low and let as few people as possible know where he was.

Soon after arriving in Rome, he received some disturbing news. His wife's uncle had been murdered. A bricklayer unfortunate enough to have been with him at the same time was also killed. Contorno was shocked. This was not some fellow member of the Bontate faction but a distant relative who was not connected with his Mafia activities. Contorno realized that the senseless killing could have only one purpose – to draw him out of hiding and turn everyone against him. There followed a series of brutal murders of his friends and relatives. Contorno continued to hide until he was arrested by the police. The arrest probably saved his life. He emerged as one of the few survivors of the Mafia war. He would follow Buscetta's example and write his own confessions. By the time they talked, both men had seen their families brutally murdered.

Buscetta was also lying low, in an apartment in Rio de Janeiro which had been bought by his wife, Christina. As ever, he maintains that he was not involved in any criminal activity during his second stay in Brazil, though there is evidence, based on intelligence reports and informants, that suggests otherwise. One theory is that he and Salamone were developing new heroin sources in South-East Asia and exporting the drug to America along the same South American routes as before. Interestingly, Carlo Zippo was again active during this period and was arrested in Italy in February 1983 on a charge of running a cocaine ring between Italy and South America. There are even eye-witness reports that Buscetta was spotted in Bangkok. Again he has denied them.

It is certainly true that the Mafia had developed close links with suppliers in Bangkok, especially as their own laboratories in Sicily were under increasing police pressure. The Mafia's main supplier in Thailand was Koh Bak Kin. On 24 May 1983, the Egyptian police discovered 233 kilos of pure heroin from Thailand on board a ship called the *Alexandros G* which had docked in the Suez canal. But even though the police had some success in closing down a few laboratories, they scarcely affected the overall production of heroin. Some of the laboratories were highly sophisticated, capable of refining a hundred kilos of morphine base per week. Others were fairly makeshift and could be moved quickly when danger threatened. The DEA estimated that in 1980 the Mafia was supplying at least 60 per cent of the heroin being smuggled through the eastern seaboard of the United States.

Partly because of increased pressure from the police in Italy, partly because of the growing trade in cocaine, much of the Mafia's trade in narcotics was now being run out of South America. Because so many Latin American countries had major cities with large Italian immigrant populations, it was an ideal location for Mafia activity. It was also easy to fly from South America to New York or back to Sicily. With false passports readily available and hardly any police surveillance, the *mafiosi* could move around undetected. Now that the French–Corsicans were out of the picture, it was a free market for the Sicilians. Also, the deadly conflict in Palermo could be more or less ignored in South America – there was no Commission to enforce loyalty and execute contracts.

Six months after the murder of his Mafia friends in Sicily, Buscetta was, literally, back on the ranch. Along with Christina's brother, Homero, and Valentin Machado, a close friend, he had acquired a 65,000-acre holding in the Pava province of Brazil, a remote area in the north-eastern part of the country near the mouth of the Amazon. With the help of his father-in-law he had acquired the land under a government scheme which granted large areas for development. If they were successful after a specified period of time, the developers would become the owners of the land. Buscetta and his partners planned a timber business. Another plan involved the planting of rubber trees. Where all the money came from to finance the machinery and other supplies needed for the ranch is something of a mystery. Buscetta claims that he was broke throughout this period.

In the autumn of 1981 Buscetta received some ominous news from Italy. Mariano Cavallaro, the brother of his first wife, Melchiorra, had been murdered in Turin. It looked as if Buscetta's worst fears were coming true, and that he was now implicated in the Sicilian power struggle. Desperate for news he called Pippo Calò, but Calò claimed to know very little about the killing. He tried to reassure Buscetta that it was just a local matter involving Turin and had no connection with events in Palermo. Calò invited Buscetta back to Palermo, offering to pay for the flight since Buscetta said he had no money. Calò would give the money to Salamone, who was in Palermo at the time. Whether Calò did give Salamone any money or not is unclear, but whatever happened, when Salamone returned to Brazil, he had a furious argument with Buscetta. He accused Buscetta of putting his life in danger by telling Calò that they had been associating with each other in Brazil. Buscetta told him he was talking nonsense but the argument created a rift between them. Salamone's experience also meant that Buscetta would now have to be very careful about trusting Calò.

Perhaps the invitation to return to Palermo was a trap. Although Buscetta had sufficient power to gather a small army of men loyal to him in Sicily, the murders of Bontate and Inzerillo had left him dangerously exposed. If Salamone feared for his life just because he had been near Buscetta that could only mean one thing. Buscetta himself was now seen as a significant threat to the Corleonesi.

Buscetta had no intention of going to Sicily. Instead he carried on with his new agricultural project. But there was to be no rural tranquillity. His Sicilian past caught up with him again when an old friend, who had also been a farmer in his time, appeared in Rio de Janeiro. It was Gaetano Badalamenti.

The visit was not entirely unexpected – Salamone had warned Buscetta that Badalamenti might contact him. This could clearly be extremely dangerous for both of them. Ever since he had been ousted from his position on the Commission and as head of the Cinisi family, Badalamenti had been a declared enemy of the Corleonesi. There was an open contract on his life which meant that any *mafioso* who came across him was under an obligation to kill him. Buscetta ignored the obligation and the warning. Badalamenti was a friend and he was curious to hear what he wanted. He suggested a hotel where Badalamenti might stay, the Regent Hotel in Belém, conveniently close to his ranch. Buscetta drove out to meet him.

Badalamenti was still a man of considerable stature. His message to Buscetta was simple:

> I am here to try and convince you to come back to Sicily because you are the only person who has enough influence to be able to direct a counter-attack and lead a revolt against the Corleonesi.

Buscetta was unmoved. As far as he was concerned the situation in Palermo was beyond redemption. Instead he tried to persuade Badalamenti that he would be better off in the lumber business. He wanted Badalamenti to believe that, like him, he could live safely on a ranch with all his family. Badalamenti knew it would be useless to try to persuade Buscetta on this occasion, so he gave up trying. The conversation turned to recent events in Palermo. Badalamenti blamed Salamone for really 'screwing things up' in trying to ensure the safety of his friends after the killing of Bontate and Inzerillo. Indeed, he went further, alleging that Salamone had only pretended to help them and actually betrayed them. Badalamenti added that he had contacted Inzerillo after Bontate's murder and offered his services for a counter-attack against the Corleonesi but that Inzerillo had turned him down.

Badalamenti was still immensely bitter towards Liggio for

engineering his banishment. In his conversation with Buscetta he recalled several incidents in which he had been infuriated and humiliated by Liggio. One that particularly rankled was an occasion when Liggio had organized the payment of a ransom on Badalamenti's territory. The Commission had ruled that there should be no more kidnappings in Sicily. It was a political decision because kidnapping created such resentment among the local population that it was damaging the Mafia's image. It also generated too much police activity. But Liggio carried on kidnapping in other parts of Italy, particularly in the north, and also arranged for a ransom to be paid near Cinisi, in Badalamenti's territory. This had resulted in a massive concentration of police in the area. Liggio had not only broken the Commission's ruling on kidnapping but had also committed a cardinal sin by operating in another boss's territory without prior consent. Badalamenti was furious at this calculated insult.

There were other incidents as well. Whenever they had met during Commission meetings, Liggio taunted Badalamenti, showing how much better educated he was and making fun of Badalamenti's grammatical errors when he spoke in front of the Commission.

Badalamenti confirmed that 'mopping up' operations by the Corleonesi were continuing. Amongst the victims was his cousin, Antonio Badalamenti, who had been installed as head of the Cinisi family after Gaetano was ousted. Another friend of Bontate and Inzerillo, Alfio Ferlito, the head of a family in Catania, eastern Sicily, had also been murdered by his sworn rival and a staunch ally of the Corleonesi, Benedetto 'Nitto' Santapaola.

Santapaola was involved in a bitter feud with Ferlito, who had been a close friend of Inzerillo. It was a friendship which caused great tension and suspicion between the two. When Ferlito was arrested Santapaola planned his revenge. On 16 June 1982 an armed escort of the *carabinieri* accompanied Ferlito as he was being transferred by car from prison in Enna to one in Trapani, but they were no match for the professional killers of the Corleonesi. Ferlito and his escort were wiped out in a carefully planned ambush – the latest victims of the Kalashnikov.

The contract was executed by the Corleonesi as a favour; since Santapaola was based in Catania, it was simpler and in everyone's interest for them to carry it out.

10

Operation Carlo Alberto

One of the first investigators to arrive at the scene of the Ferlito assassination was General Carlo Alberto Dalla Chiesa. Dalla Chiesa was Italy's foremost *carabinieri* General, a national figure of great prestige who had been largely responsible for the defeat of the Red Brigades during the seventies. In the spring of 1982, in a rare political initiative, the Italian government finally decided to respond to the public outcry at the killings in Sicily. Although no one was particularly upset about *mafiosi* shooting each other, the deaths of policemen, judges, politicians and journalists were beginning to sicken the public and the authorities in Rome. It was becoming increasingly difficult to pass the Mafia off as nothing more than 'a local problem'. Prime Minister Spadolini was also under political pressure – not least from Pio la Torre, the Regional Secretary of the Communist Party in Sicily. La Torre wrote to the Prime Minister in March 1982 to protest that the Mafia's 'multi-million-dollar drug production business, its international network and its penetration into politics, have transformed it into one of the most deadly serious dangers facing Italy today'. His outspoken attitude was too much for the Corleonesi. In particular, he was campaigning for a tough new law to investigate and seize the assets of the Mafia and their accomplices. On 30 April 1982, his car was ambushed in Palermo city centre. La Torre and his driver, Rosario Salvo, were shot and killed. When he arrived in Sicily, one of Dalla Chiesa's first official duties was to attend La Torre's funeral.

There was also diplomatic pressure from the United States government urging the Italians to act more decisively. Dalla

Chiesa's appointment was one of the results. He was made Prefect of the Republic of Sicily, empowered to coordinate the fight against the Mafia. He had served on a tour of duty in Sicily as a young colonel in charge of the *carabinieri* headquarters in Palermo, so he knew the terrain and the people, and he had given evidence to the Italian Parliament's Anti-Mafia Commission. Now aged sixty-two, he was Deputy National Commander of the *carabinieri*, a high-ranking position but essentially a desk job.

Support for his appointment also came from the Christian Democratic Party. The Party leader, Giulio Andreotti, advocated a tough initiative against organized crime and suggested the General was the man for the job. A previous Prefect of Palermo had been Mussolini's emissary Cesare Mori. Mori became known as 'the Iron Prefect', for his ruthlessness and brutality had been equal to that of the Mafia. When Spadolini offered Dalla Chiesa the job, he accepted on condition that he would be given special powers. Specifically, he demanded the political support to combat organized crime throughout Italy. 'Fighting the Mafia in the pastures of Palermo, and not in the rest of Italy, would simply be a waste of time,' he remarked.

The General knew that the Mafia was no longer just a Sicilian phenomenon. The tentacles of *la Piovra* (the Octopus) reached to the mainland and beyond. It had formed powerful alliances with other secret criminal societies such as the Camorra in Naples and it was well represented in Milan and Rome. Dalla Chiesa also knew that they were supported directly and indirectly by politicians. In a letter to the Prime Minister, he spelt out his demands:

Dear Professor,

I write to you with reference to our recent conversation. As much as I hate to take up some of your valuable time, I feel it my duty ... to bring to your attention the following points.

My possible appointment as Prefect, although indeed a great honour, would not convince me on its own to leave my present position. The terms of such an appointment as Prefect of Palermo cannot and must not include the fight against the Mafia as an 'implicit' function as this would give the impression that we do not know what the Mafia is, or what is meant by the expression 'Mafia'. This would also convince public opinion that the declared intention on our part to limit and fight the phenomenon in all its various manifestations is not a serious one.

The term 'organized crime' is not enough. It would also prove that the 'messages' sent to some newspapers by the most tainted political 'family' in Sicily have reached their objective.

Far from asking for exceptional laws or powers, it is necessary and honest that the person who is destined to fight a phenomenon of such dimensions should not only receive support from the press – which is not always authoritative or credible and liable to change sides – but that he should also enjoy an openly declared and legally endorsed support from the government. 'Openly declared' because the image of such an appointment must be commensurate with the importance of the task.

It must be 'codified' because, as experience teaches, all promises are forgotten, every reassuring statement – 'It shall be done', 'We shall do something about it' – is neutralized and everything is hushed up and limited as soon as certain interests are involved.

I would therefore like to ask you to intervene, in this very important part, not only of my career, but of my life as a loyal and faithful servant of the state, in a most qualified and confident manner, to ensure that this new appointment will be accepted with serenity, and with the most highly responsible attitude – that of true enthusiasm.

Behind the diplomatic extravagance of the language the General was asking the Prime Minister if he was really serious about defeating the Mafia, as serious, for instance, as the government had been about defeating the Red Brigades. He understood the Italian political skill of appearing to do something while actually doing nothing. He was not about to become the victim of another government public-relations exercise.

He also knew about Mafia infiltration of the political and business worlds both in Sicily and on the mainland. That was part of his testimony to the Anti-Mafia Commission. Before he left for Palermo, he warned the Interior Minister, Virgilio Rognoni, that if he were really going to attack the Mafia he would need to attack some of the most prominent members of the Christian Democratic Party in Sicily. Rognoni reassured Dalla Chiesa with the words: 'You are a general of the *carabinieri*, not of the Christian Democrats.'

Confident that political support would be forthcoming, Dalla Chiesa left for Sicily. In fact, Spadolini had referred the matter to the Italian Security Committee, which consisted of the Minister of the Interior, the heads of the two rival police forces (the *carabinieri* and the *pubblica sicurezza*), and the chiefs of the military and civilian intelligence services, the CISMI and the CISDE. These two agencies were riddled with members of Licio Gelli's P2. Emanuele de Francesco, head of the CISDE, was the only one to back Dalla Chiesa's request. The others voted against.

In the early summer of 1982, the General arrived in Palermo accompanied by the beautiful young woman he had recently married, his second wife, Emanuela de Settecarro.

He believed that the key to success would be the coordination of the various government agencies involved in the fight against organized crime. So the first thing he did was to make courtesy calls on all the officials whose support he would need. He met a curious response. When he mentioned the prospect of special powers the reaction was a mixture of scorn and contempt. Many told the General that he should leave things as they were. Others began a whispering campaign, largely about the Dalla Chiesas' marriage: 'Such an old man and yet such a young and pretty woman; surely it can't be right?'

Mario d'Acquisto, the Christian Democrat President of the Region, complained that he had not been consulted about the appointment. Salvo Lima, another senior Christian Democrat and a member of the European Parliament, publicly distanced himself from the appointment by declaring, 'The Christian Democrats of the island have not in any way contributed to the nomination of Carlo Alberto Dalla Chiesa as Prefect of Palermo.' Nello Martellucci, the Mayor of Palermo, grumbled that the city was full of honest people who did not need 'a general' to solve their problems.

The reaction to Dalla Chiesa's arrival in Palermo merely confirmed his suspicions that Sicily had become contaminated to its roots. He found himself confronted by the mentality that represents the essence of Mafia power – a way of thinking which permeates all levels of Italian society, from the corrupt policeman on the streets to the negligent prosecutor in the courts. At every level there would be someone who would benefit from the preservation of the status quo rather than radical change.

This corrupt conservatism acted like a shield behind which the most powerful *mafiosi* in Sicily could shelter. Dalla Chiesa tried to break it down – but no one would help him.

Describing the atmosphere which greeted him at the time, Dalla Chiesa recalled an episode from his earlier days in Sicily when he had been a colonel in the *carabinieri*. An officer from one of the Mafia towns of western Sicily, Palma de Montechiaro, was having difficulties with the local Mafia boss. He told Dalla Chiesa he had been threatened. Dalla Chiesa drove to the town in the late afternoon. It was the time of day, after the siesta, when people wander up and down the streets, gossiping, window-shopping and generally taking the air. Arm in arm with the officer, Dalla Chiesa strolled through the village. Several times they passed in front of the house where the Mafia boss lived. Everyone noticed. The message was clear – the officer had friends and was not alone. The Mafia boss laid off.

In the autumn of 1982, Dalla Chiesa said he desperately needed someone to do the same thing for him in Sicily: 'All I'm asking for is someone to take my arm and walk with me.' No one came forward. Isolated by his fellow countrymen, he turned to the Americans, asking them to increase the pressure on the Italian government to grant him the political support that he so desperately needed. His sense of isolation was heightened by his refusal to be drawn into the social life of Palermo's high society. He knew only too well how closely it was linked to the top Mafia families. There was even a certain cachet in being associated with *mafiosi*. Many members of Sicily's aristocracy were on first-name terms with people like Michele Greco, and when Queen Elizabeth II went on a royal visit to Sicily she was greeted by a delegation of the highest in the land. Among them was Prince Alessandro Vanni Cavello, a tall, immaculately dressed aristocrat wearing dark glasses. Cavello looked every inch a prince, but he was also a 'Man of Honour'.

Then there were men like the Salvo cousins, the island's government-appointed tax collectors, backers of the Christian Democratic Party and Sicily's most powerful businessmen. They too had been linked to the Mafia. Understandably, Dalla Chiesa wanted to put as much distance as possible between himself and such people. Life in Palermo was a lonely and difficult business. It was also highly dangerous.

For years the General had lived with the threat of assassination. His battle against the Red Brigades had put him in the front line of the war against terrorism. He had evolved a system of low-key security, varying his route to work and never becoming a creature of habit. His movements would never be predictable. The cardinal rule was to do the unexpected, like travelling in unmarked cars and arriving at restaurants unannounced, forsaking a heavily armed escort and cars with screaming sirens.

Dalla Chiesa soon began a secret investigation into the construction industry. It has been estimated that the Mafia controls four-fifths of the Sicilian building industry. It was a tremendous source of income and also a useful way of laundering billions of lire gained from the heroin trade. Dalla Chiesa believed that exposing the building industry would reveal the connections between the Mafia, the financiers and the politicians – the hitherto impenetrable 'Third Level'. The most lucrative building contracts were approved by the holders of high public office.

He focused on a deal which seemed to confirm all his suspicions. He began to investigate a contract worth L25 billion (nearly $20 million) that had been awarded to a firm run by Carmelo Costanza to build a convention centre in Palermo. One of the strange features of the deal was that Costanza was based on the other side of the island in Catania. Why should his firm have been chosen rather than one of the several based in Palermo?

The previous June, Dalla Chiesa had initiated a discreet investigation into the Salvo cousins. Six years earlier he had urged the Anti-Mafia Commission to scrutinize the Salvos' control of tax collection in Palermo. Nothing had been done and they continued to flourish. Now he had the power to act. He set up inquiries into three other building companies in Catania, including one run by Mario Rendo, a man closely connected to leading Christian Democrats like Salvo Lima, a member of the European Parliament. Rendo had used his political clout to campaign for the appointment of a friend, Luciano Cannarozzo, as head of police headquarters in Palermo. Cannarozzo was police chief of Catania. Rendo had also had discussions with Salvo Lima and Mario d'Acquisto about the possibility of setting up a printing firm for national newspapers in Catania – he thought it might result in more favourable press coverage.

One simple method of investigation Dalla Chiesa had found invaluable in his fight against the Red Brigades was the use of public records such as tax returns, property deeds and rental agreements. In Turin, they had helped him to find terrorist safe houses and 'people's prisons'. In Sicily he would use them to uncover the relationships between the Mafia, business and politics.

His investigation into Costanza's building firm began to pay dividends. The records revealed that Costanza had a business relationship with Benedetto Santapaola, the man who had authorized the murder of Alfio Ferlito. It was a significant discovery.

During the seventies the Catania families had relied on the

Mafia's traditional sources of income – gambling, protection rackets and smuggling. They operated independently of their cousins in Palermo. But the fact that building firms from Catania were now moving into the heart of Palermo suggested that an alliance had been formed between the families of Catania and Palermo. Although he may not have realized it at the time, Dalla Chiesa had touched a nerve – he had found a vital clue to the power base of the Corleonesi. Santapaola's men from Catania had indeed joined forces with their colleagues in Palermo. The Corleonesi controlled the heroin laboratories but they needed the smuggling channels which were controlled by the men from Catania. The alliance with the Corleonesi had brought Santapaola increased power and prosperity. It had also exacerbated the feud between Santapaola and Ferlito, ally of Bontate and Inzerillo. When Ferlito was arrested, Santapaola was desperately worried that he might avenge himself by talking to Dalla Chiesa. Indeed it is possible that Ferlito did provide the General with vital information about the Mafia's operations in Catania. The authorities certainly became concerned for his safety, hence his transfer from the prison in Enna to another in Trapani, and his assassination by the Corleonesi. The attack became known as the '*Strage della Circonvallazione*' – 'the Ringroad Massacre'.

When news of the killing reached the *carabinieri* headquarters, Dalla Chiesa was driven to the scene. Ballistic tests identified the use of the same Kalashnikov that had been used to kill Bontate and Inzerillo.

On the evening of 3 September 1982 the General set off with his wife to a restaurant at the Hotel la Torre in Palermo. He decided that they would take his wife's car, a tiny Fiat A112, which she had brought with them from Rome. In front there was an escort car with one lightly armed police agent, Domenico Russo. As they were driving along one of Palermo's main streets, the Via Isidoro Carini, a powerful motorbike carrying two men began to follow them. It drew alongside the small car. The man on the back raised his Kalashnikov and fired a full magazine into the driver, Emanuela Dalla Chiesa. The bullets tore into her face and body. The General threw himself across his wife to protect her, but he was too late. In the front car the bodyguard was shot in the head. He died in hospital a week later. The motorbike was followed by two back-up cars, a BMW 520 and a Fiat 132. As the BMW drew alongside, a man got out and fired another magazine into the bullet-riddled bodies of the General and his wife. It seemed that the Mafia had deliberately shot Signora Dalla Chiesa in the face as an added act of brutality before killing her husband. The General and his escort had been under surveillance from the moment they left his official residence. An eye-witness recalled seeing an additional motor-bike, a high-powered Honda. It followed the two cars and then alerted the eight-man execution squad. Other reports suggested that the team of professional assassins had been backed up by Mafia surveillance teams scattered throughout the city, using two-way radios to monitor the Dalla Chiesas' location. Thirty minutes after the shooting, a police patrol found the BMW, the Fiat and a Suzuki 750 cc motorbike. They had all been set on fire. The cars and the bike had been stolen earlier in the day.

All Italy went into a state of shock. The murders touched the conscience of the nation.

At the funeral of the General and his wife in Palermo the President of the Republic of Italy and members of the Italian Cabinet were jeered, booed and spat upon by the people of Sicily – not those who had so readily turned their back on the General, but the ordinary men and women who were all too aware of the terrible effect the Mafia had on their everyday lives, from the mutilated bodies that their children might see on the streets to the protection money they would have to pay if they had a small business. On a wall close to the spot where the killing had occurred someone wrote, 'Here dies all the hope of the honest people of Sicily.'

That poignant epitaph said more than all the fulsome tributes from the government that had sent the General to Sicily unpro-tected into the hands of the assassins.

Many, including the General's own son, Nando Dalla Chiesa, went much further. They alleged that there had been a political conspiracy which had first isolated Dalla Chiesa and then had

Right Lucky Luciano, head of the American Mafia, relaxing in Rome, 1949.
Below left Joe Bonanno, retired head of the Bonanno family, the New York Mafia family with the closest ties to Sicily and the heroin trade.
Below right The young Tommaso Buscetta, who met Luciano and Bonanno in Sicily in 1957.

THE PIZZA CONNECTION
Above The Raffeallo shipment: 82 kilos of pure heroin in 169 packets, 21 September 1971.
Inset Mike Fahy, the young US customs agent who discovered the heroin in the Ford Galaxie.
The shipment started the investigation that led to the "Pizza Connection".
Below Yasar Avni Karadurmus, alias "Musullulu" and "The Turk"; one of the world's biggest
suppliers of morphine base.

Pino Greco

Michele Greco

Luciano Liggio

THE LOSERS · Stefano Bontate (*inset*) His murder Palermo, 23 April 1981.

Salvatore Contorno

Gaetano Badalamenti

Salvatore Inzerillo

Right Benedetto Buscetta. Antonio and Benedetto, Tommaso Buscetta's two sons, disappeared in Sicily on 8 September 1982. They were never seen again, and are believed to have been murdered by the Corleonesi.

Left Tommaso Buscetta after his arrest in Brazil on 22 October 1983.

Tommaso Buscetta in court after his return to Rome, 15 July 1984. "The Godfather of Two Worlds" had decided to talk.

ILLUSTRIOUS CORPSES
Above The assassination of Judge Cesare Terranova, 25 September 1979, Palermo. Tommaso Buscetta has identified Luciano Liggio as one of the gunmen.
Below The assassination of General Dalla Chiesa and his wife, 3 September 1982, Palermo. The brutal killings shocked Italy and the world.

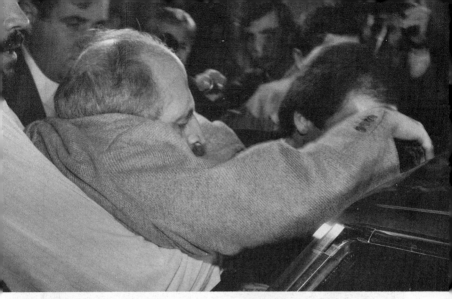

THE THIRD LEVEL

Above Following the confessions of Tommaso Buscetta, Italian police arrest Vito Ciancimino on 3 November 1984. Ciancimino was a powerful politician, a member of the Mafia, and a senior Christian Democrat.

Left Ignazio Salvo, the richest and most influential tycoon in Sicily. Denounced by Tommaso Buscetta and arrested 12 November 1984.

Right Nino Salvo, his cousin and partner in their business empire, which had included the tax collection office for Sicily.

Above The murder of Carmine Galante, who wanted to become head of the Bonanno family, 12 July 1979. Unsolved for six years, the investigation would play a major part in breaking the leadership of the American Mafia and the Sicilian control of the New York heroin trade.

Left Anthony "Fat Tony" Salerno, the head of the Genovese family in New York and "Boss of Bosses" on the Commission. Now serving 100 years in prison.

Right Anthony "Tony Ducks" Corallo, head of the Lucchese family. After Salerno, the most powerful member of the American Mafia Commission.

him killed. At the heart of the conspiracy were the vested interests of the Christian Democrats who needed votes in Sicily and hence the preservation of the status quo. Among those implicated by the General's son were the former Prime Minister Giulio Andreotti, Salvo Lima (who was subsequently interrogated by investigating magistrate Giovanni Falcone in the investigation into the assassination of the General and his wife) and Vito Ciancimino, the corrupt former Mayor of Palermo and a leading Christian Democrat friend of the Corleonesi. In November 1986, the Palermo court held a special session in Rome to hear the testimony of Andreotti during which he contradicted some of the assertions made by the General's son concerning the political circumstances of his appointment. The lawyer acting for the family has since initiated proceedings for perjury.

Others accused dismissed the allegations as the emotional outpourings of a young man who had tragically lost his father. But experts on the Mafia listened rather more carefully to Nando Dalla Chiesa. Father Pintacuda, a Jesuit priest who has devoted his life to the study of this manifestation of evil in Sicily, believes that:

> General Dalla Chiesa was sent to Palermo with the promise of special powers; he was not a prefect chosen at random by someone but was, in fact, one of the most remarkable men in Italy because he had succeeded in defeating terrorism. It was of the utmost importance that he should have been given special powers – such as the passing of the la Torre law to enable him to investigate the bank accounts of suspects – and the strongest support. Neither of these was given by the institutions of the state. He was also isolated within the *carabinieri* and, because of all this, I would say that his assassination was a state crime, rather than a real Mafia crime. The Mafia was involved, but Dalla Chiesa's death has much wider implications. I believe that General Dalla Chiesa was too dangerous a man for what I define as state or alternative power, not legitimate power. Presumably,

therefore, many people had an interest in the General's disappearance from the scene, either through forcing him to fail in his actions and thus discrediting him – or through killing him.

The special powers that Dalla Chiesa had been promised before he was sent to Palermo had never materialized. He told his son he was convinced that the special powers were being blocked by local representatives of the Christian Democratic Party. He believed the Andreotti and Fanfani factions within the party were directing the campaign against him. He told his son, 'They were in it up to their necks.'

The names he mentioned were Salvo Lima and Vito Cianci-mino.

Dalla Chiesa had been fatally isolated. The highest officials of the Italian government in Rome, either through neglect or because they were the accomplices or dupes of a more sinister conspiracy, had turned their backs on him. He had been sent to fight against overwhelming odds with the promise of reinforcements that never arrived.

He had of course been aware of the danger he was in. In an interview with Giorgio Bocca of *La Repubblica* on 10 August 1982, he referred to the murder of Piersanti Mattarella, the President of the Region who had been assassinated by the Mafia on 6 January 1980. Mattarella was the son of Bernardo Mattarella, the powerful Mafia-linked Christian Democrat from Castellamare del Golfo. Dalla Chiesa indicated that Matta-rella's son, who had also become a politician in the Christian Democratic Party, had been killed because he refused to make the same accommodations as his father had done with the Mafia. They had killed him to show others that there was no choice. Dalla Chiesa commented, 'I think I have understood the new rules of the game. The powerful are killed when there is a particular combination of circumstances. The fatal combination arises when a man becomes very dangerous *and* isolated. Then he can be killed.'

Pino Arlacchi, a member of the Anti-Mafia Commission,

supports the allegation of Nando Dalla Chiesa. He believes that the assassination of men of Dalla Chiesa's importance would not be carried out without authorization from a high political level. According to Arlacchi, Dalla Chiesa's isolation in Sicily was a clear signal to the Mafia that they could go ahead with their plans to kill him. The General was a threat not just to the Sicilian Mafia; he was also jeopardizing the political and economic élite on the mainland who had gained so much from the Mafia that they could not contemplate life without them.

Dalla Chiesa had signed his own death warrant by stating that he would end the political collusion which had flourished for so long. His investigations into Costanza and the Salvos demonstrated the direct threat that he posed to the Mafia's interests. Some notes found at the Villa Whitaker where he had been staying in Palermo (he did not trust the staff at the official residence) confirmed the tenor of his investigations. One hand-written note is particularly revealing:

> C. First FE and Santap, who is employed by C. and runs the hotel chain 'La Perla Jonica'. It employs the whole of the Mafia clan of Catania to get to PA.
> R. There has been a big scandal: they found a certain Cremona on a big building site with all the trucks stolen up North. Behind all this is Madonia, a *mafioso* from PA, an important contractor for R.

C. refers to Costanza, FE to Ferlito, PA is Palermo, Santap is Benedetto Santapaola and R. is the builder Rendo.

Dalla Chiesa had begun to unravel the alliance between the Corleonesi and the men from Catania, and their links with high finance and national politics. The arrogance of the Corleonesi was such that even the highest-ranking official of the Italian state was a legitimate target in protecting those links. And the killing of an innocent young woman as well, a crime which the old traditions of the Mafia would have forbidden, was nothing to the assassins. Where the terror of the Red Brigades had failed, the terror of the Mafia succeeded. The Corleonesi had even rung up a local newspaper a few days before and said, 'Operation Carlo Alberto is about to be completed.'

In the *carabinieri* investigation that followed, a curious episode occurred which cast further mystery over the assassination of Dalla Chiesa and his wife. It provides further support for Nando Dalla Chiesa's allegations of a wider and more sinister conspiracy.

The *carabinieri* claimed that they had found a key witness in a man called Spinoni. They said he described the attack in such a way as to provide convincing proof of his credibility. He also identified a picture of Benedetto Santapaola as one of the killers. Ballistics confirmed that the same weapons that had been used in 'the Ringroad Massacre' had been used to kill the General and his wife. Ten weeks after Spinoni made his statements, and after an official inspection of the assassination site, it was discovered that Spinoni's testimony was full of discrepancies. He was accused of perjury. Next it was discovered that the photograph of Santapaola which Spinoni had identified was in fact of somebody completely different, though it was clearly marked with Santapaola's name and address. The picture had been supplied by the *carabinieri* office in Trapani. The investigating squad there was led by Captain Melito. Some time later Captain Melito was arrested for collusion with Santapaola.

Who was 'running' Spinoni? Who invented his testimony and for what reasons? Why attract the attention of the investigating authorities to Santapaola when his involvement was already suggested by ballistic and circumstantial evidence? Most important of all, why did the *carabinieri* conduct such a superficial and incompetent investigation into the murder of the second most senior commander of their own police force? It was after all one of the most serious murders they had ever had to investigate. The questions remain unanswered, strengthening the suspicion that Dalla Chiesa and his wife were victims of a conspiracy which had wound itself deep inside the heart of the state.

In commenting on the investigation, Sicily's investigating magistrates remarked:

'Such behaviour is unacceptable, if not liable for prosecution.

'It was not an unknown robber who had been killed, but the ex-Vice General Commander of the Force, with his young wife and escort.'

New investigations directed by the forceful Giovanni Falcone and Paolo Borsallino were considerably more thorough. From secret testimony and their own painstaking inquiries, it is now possible to name some of the killers.

The driver of the motorbike was Mario Prestifilippo, a skilled rider of powerful bikes. When the newspapers had published reports that a young man with blond hair was being sought in connection with the attack, Prestifilippo dyed his hair. A fellow *mafioso* has pointed out that after the killing Prestifilippo's prestige was greatly enhanced within the Mafia. The other man on the bike is believed to have been Pino Greco.

The killing was ordered, planned and executed by the Commission. The members now charged include Michele Greco, Salvatore Greco, Salvatore Riina, Benedetto Santapaola, Rosario Riccobono, Bernardo Provenzano, Pippo Calò and Pino Greco. But there remained the suspicion of a wider conspiracy, as the magistrates themselves knew:

> It is important from the point of view of the proceedings to ascertain with the greatest accuracy if the Commission, with regard to those murders aimed at the elimination of government officials, is established on an independent basis, or whether it is connected to certain sections of society, with individuals who can themselves order or support the crimes at the highest levels of the Mafia, although they themselves represent the interests of different parties.

It was a frightening suggestion – that beyond the Commission lay another even more powerful group of individuals who could instruct the Commission according to their own interests. It sounds inconceivable until it is remembered that Italy is a country which has been tainted by an almost unimaginable number of conspiracies, some of them reaching into the Vatican and the highest levels of the state. The possibility of political involvement in the assassination of Dalla Chiesa is all too real.

In the long list of 'illustrious corpses', Dalla Chiesa and his wife became the most illustrious of them all. His spirit would return to haunt the *mafiosi* and the politicians who had connived at his death. The public outrage at the murders meant that the government could no longer stall. Wide-ranging powers to investigate bank accounts were finally approved, and a successor was appointed: Emanuele de Francesco, the head of Italy's civilian intelligence service, the CISDE.

It was the turning point in the fight against the Mafia: the Greco–Corleonesi killings represented the height of their power. Now there was nowhere to go but down.

11

Investigation in Brazil

If you've come to discuss my freedom, I'll start
with a million dollars. If you've come to question
me, I'll say nothing.

Tommaso Buscetta to the São Paulo Police

At the time of the killing of General Dalla Chiesa, September
1982, Gaetano Badalamenti was once more visiting Tommaso
Buscetta in Brazil. They met in the Regent Hotel, Belém. That
evening there was a report on Brazilian television news about
the killing. The two men sat in silence watching the bloody
pictures. When it was over, Badalamenti commented that the
murders were 'gross arrogance' on the part of the Corleonesi
and a foolish response to the General's anti-Mafia campaign.
He told Buscetta that soldiers from Santapaola's family in Catania had helped the Corleonesi to plan and execute the murders.
They were returning the favour for the Corleonesi assassination
of Alfio Ferlito. The advantage of using the Catania people was
that they could move around Palermo without being recognized.
He also told Buscetta that Mafia politicians had 'rid themselves'
of Dalla Chiesa because he had become 'too cumbersome'.

Buscetta was worried by the events in Sicily, but he could not
know how soon they would affect him personally. Eight days
after the assassination of Dalla Chiesa, on 11 September 1982,
Buscetta made a long-distance telephone call to Palermo to talk
to his son Antonio. Antonio had just been released from gaol
after serving his sentence for possession of the kidnap money

given to him by Pippo Calò. Antonio and Benedetto had started up a pizza business together called the Pizzeria New York in Palermo. They were running it in partnership with Giuseppe Genova, the husband of their sister Felicia.

The telephone in Palermo was answered by Antonio's wife, Yolanda. She was crying. Antonio, she said, had not been seen for three days and his brother, Benedetto, who had been with him, had also disappeared. Everyone knew what 'disappearance' meant in Sicily. It was called the *'lupara bianca'* – the 'white death', *lupara* being Sicilian for shotgun. It was very rare to discover a body after someone disappeared. For the relatives it would be a cruel torment, living in the constant fear that the victim was dead, while fervently hoping that he might still be alive.

Buscetta told Yolanda to contact the police in case his sons had been arrested. When he called her the next day, she said the police knew nothing.

Benedetto and Antonio Buscetta were never seen again.

A few days later, Badalamenti returned to Belén to see Buscetta. He came to offer his deepest sympathy. But he also saw his chance to goad him into action. Buscetta, he urged, should retaliate by killing Michele Greco's son, Giuseppe. Buscetta refused, saying that it would be a vicious reaction, especially as Giuseppe was a harmless young man who had nothing to do with the Mafia. When Badalamenti told him that Giuseppe was *'combinato'* – that he had taken his oath as a 'Man of Honour' – Buscetta still refused. Badalamenti insisted that he should return to Palermo to lead a revolt against the Corleonesi. Buscetta still refused. He calculated that if he did nothing the Corleonesi might let him and the rest of his family live in peace. He realized that the Corleonesi thought he had already formed an alliance in exile with Badalamenti to fight them, and that they had killed his sons in a pre-emptive strike. Although Badalamenti assured Buscetta that no one knew he had come to see him in Brazil, Buscetta is now fairly sure that he did tell others that he was going to Brazil to persuade him to return and fight the Corleonesi. He believes that the death of his sons was the direct result.

The next killing, in November 1982, was aimed at Badalamenti. The victim was Salvatore Badalamenti, the son of Gaetano's cousin Nino, who had taken over the leadership of the Cinisi family. Gaetano Badalamenti fought back during the bloody Christmas holiday of 1982. On Christmas Day a counter-attack was launched against the Corleonesi. The target was Pino Greco, the psychopath who had been behind most of the killings. Badalamenti and Giuseppe Romano, 'the American', set up an ambush but Greco escaped. Greco struck back with ferocious speed. Twenty-four hours later some customers walked into the Pizzeria New York in Palermo, which was still being run by Buscetta's son-in-law, Giuseppe Genova. Instead of ordering pizza, they shot Genova and two of his employees. All three victims were relatives of Buscetta.

Three days later, on 29 December, Vincenzo Buscetta, the brother to whom Tommaso had always been closest, was killed at his glass factory. His son Benedetto (Tommaso's nephew), a likeable young man who had never had anything to do with the Mafia, died with him.

Buscetta read about the death of his brother and his nephew in a newspaper. Within four months seven of his closest relatives had been murdered. He was devastated. He was also very frightened.

In February 1983, after the killings, Badalamenti returned yet again to Brazil in a further attempt to involve Buscetta. It was obvious, he said, that Buscetta's reluctance to fight was doing him no good. The brutal tactics of the Corleonesi continued to claim innocent lives. But then he made the mistake of telling Buscetta about the attempt to kill Pino Greco on the day before Giuseppe Genova had been killed. Buscetta knew at once that Badalamenti had organized the ambush. He was furious. Badalamenti had put him in great danger by trying to involve him.

Badalamenti may have deliberately implicated Buscetta to force him to return to Palermo to fight the Corleonesi. He might even have arranged the disappearance of Buscetta's sons himself – anything is possible in that Machiavellian world – although there is no direct evidence to support this. But, one way or another, Badalamenti had dragged Buscetta into the centre of the Mafia's civil war. And, as a consequence, Buscetta was now in the utmost danger.

On 8 February 1983 the Grecos struck again. In Fort Lauderdale, Florida, a suspicious car was discovered in the airport car park. There were two corpses in the boot: Giuseppe Romano and Giuseppe Tramontana, Buscetta's old friend from the drugrunning days of the seventies. They had both been shot. Romano had helped Badalamenti to ambush Pino Greco, and Tramontana may also have taken part in that attack or may just have been with the wrong person on the wrong day.

The killing power of the Corleonesi seemed limitless. To this day, the murders remain unsolved. So too does the extent of Buscetta's involvement.

A few days before their deaths, Tramontana and Romano visited Buscetta's only surviving son from his first marriage, Domenico, who had settled quietly in Florida where he was managing a pizzeria. Domenico has not been linked to his father's activities or to the Mafia wars, but Buscetta may have been passing messages through him. The murder of Romano and Tramontana lends some support to the theory that Buscetta *had* become involved in fighting the Corleonesi – it would certainly be characteristic of a powerful *mafioso* to try to avenge the death of the members of his family. Buscetta has denied any involvement, but then he is hardly likely to admit to conspiracy to murder. Probably the only person who knows, apart from Buscetta, is Badalamenti himself, and so far he has said nothing. Undoubtedly, the Grecos and the Corleonesi believed that Buscetta was actively plotting against them, and whether or not their suspicions were justified was of little consequence to them. Their ruthless calculation would have been the same. The fact that Buscetta was the most important friend of Stefano Bontate still alive, and could be decisive in rallying the remaining forces of opposition, was good enough reason for him to head their death list.

From February 1983 onwards Buscetta became involved with a group of individuals whom the Brazilian police believed were operating an international narcotics network. That he was mixing with them as well as spending time on his farm is not in doubt, but the exact nature of their activities remains unclear. The common denominator between them all was a company called Major Key. One of the main figures in the group was Paolo Staccioli, a restaurant owner in São Paulo, who described himself also as an employee of Major Key. His residence was paid for by the company. His restaurant, Paolo's Trattoria, was a popular meeting place for other Italians in São Paulo and it was there that he first met Buscetta in early 1983.

Staccioli introduced Buscetta to a young lawyer named Fabrizio Sansone. They got on well, and Sansone bought a share in Buscetta's farm on the Amazon. He arranged a number of cash transfers for the farm manager, and Major Key also financed the purchase of jeeps, chainsaws and other agricultural equipment for the farm. Sansone shared an apartment in São Paulo with Leonardo Badalamenti, Gaetano's son. He also had an apartment in Rio de Janeiro. One of his other services was to arrange the purchase of a car which Buscetta gave to his daughter, Alessandra, who was living with her mother in Rio in an apartment which was two floors below that of Antonio Bardellino, the Neapolitan gangster who had frequent dealings with the Porta Nuova family and was a known trafficker in cocaine.

Another of Buscetta's associates at this time was Alfredo 'Dino' Mortilli, a friend of Sansone's who described himself as a drawing teacher.

After the murder of so many of his relatives, Buscetta was understandably highly anxious about the safety of his wife and children. Christina's brother Homero had disappeared the previous August, and they both feared that he had become a victim of the Mafia war. So, in the autumn of 1983, they moved to São Paulo. Buscetta flew to Rio, went to Sansone's house and arranged to meet Christina and the children. He arranged that the two eldest and the youngest, Stefano, would sleep at Staccioli's house in São Paulo while the rest of the family would stay at Dino Mortilli's house. The Buscettas reached São Paulo on the Friday morning. They deposited the children at Staccioli's house, where they spent the day. In the evening Buscetta, Christina and the youngest child, Stefano, drove over to Mortilli's two-room apartment. The next morning, the three set off to take young Tommaso to school, where he had to go through the admission process. It was a journey they would never complete.

Unknown to Buscetta the Brazilian police had been investigating him and his colleagues for several months. They believed that he was at the centre of Brazil's burgeoning drug trade.

Just as in the early seventies Brazil had been a staging-post for the shipment of heroin to the United States, so ten years later it had become a major transit area for cocaine. Once again the United States, fighting an almost uncontrollable flood of drugs, had enlisted the support of as many friendly South American nations as it could. Since there was so much money generated by the trade, their cooperation was somewhat half-hearted, and often it had to be obtained by political pressure, arm twisting and the offering or withholding of substantial aid payments.

Brazil was ideally situated to play a major role in the cocaine traffic between South America, North America and Europe. It is a vast country with unpoliced frontiers adjoining the Andean drug-producing countries of Bolivia, Peru, Colombia and Paraguay. The Brazilian police suspected that the increased traffic from Brazil was being organized by the Mafia. Information from the Italian police and from the DEA supported the theory that Buscetta was at the centre of a new international network set up to streamline the manufacture, sale and distribution of cocaine in the same way that the Mafia had reorganized the heroin business in the 1970s.

The Brazilians' first break had come at the end of 1982, when Italian police officers flew to Rio de Janeiro in pursuit of two Mafia fugitives, Antonio Bardellino and Raffaello Scarnatto. The Italians had pinpointed them as key figures in a cocaine-smuggling operation between South America and Italy. Bardellino fled before they could arrest him, but they traced a car he had used to Aldo Alessandri, who had come to Brazil in 1954 and worked as a second-hand car salesman and tourist guide to the red-light district in Copacabana. When they searched Bardellino's apartment and followed up other leads, the Brazilians found that he and Alessandri were partners in a company called Ceico, set up in Rio to import and export fish. Documents recorded numerous shipments of worthless fish to Italy, and details of telephone calls all over the world. Transactions in fish were a known Mafia method for concealing shipments of narcotics. In another apartment registered to Bardellino's wife, Rita de Vita, the police found records of calls made to the Hotel Regent in Belém which Buscetta, Badalamenti and many of their mutual friends had used on many occasions. Ceico's telephone records also revealed frequent calls to and from the hotel.

As the police trawled through the documents the name of another company floated to the surface. It was Major Key with offices in São Paulo and Belém. When the Brazilian police went to the apartment registered in Rita de Vita's name in Rio, they took with them a dossier of photographs of organized-crime figures who had been known to use Brazil as a base for their operations. Among them were Buscetta and Michel Nicoli, who, of course, had been arrested by the Brazilians back in 1972. Curiously, the manager of the apartment block could not identify photos of Bardellino and Raffaello Scarnatto, but he immediately recognized the picture of Buscetta. He told the police that Buscetta had lived in an apartment two floors below Bardellino's until February 1983. He went on to say that a young woman called Christina now lived there with her children. Buscetta was known to him as 'Roberto Felice'.

The police immediately examined the telephone records for Christina's apartment. Once again they revealed copious calls to the Regent Hotel in Belém, Ceico, Major Key and several other numbers which tied in with those that the police had already found. The investigation revealed Buscetta's friends in São Paulo who were also connected with Bardellino – Paolo Staccioli, Giuseppe Bizzarro, Alfredo Mortilli and Fabrizio Sansone – as well as with the Major Key company. Christina was put under surveillance and before long she was spotted driving a Chevrolet. The police ran a check on all the Chevrolet dealers in Brazil and traced the car to a man called José Escobar. One of the dealers identified 'Escobar' from photographs as Buscetta. The guest records of the Hotel Regent showed that virtually all the suspects had been staying there including, of course, 'José Escobar', who had listed his occupation as rancher. By this stage the Rio police had found an informer, someone who was apparently involved with the supply of false passports, driving licences and birth certificates to fugitives in São Paulo and Rio. One driving licence which was recovered was falsely registered in the name of Otto Levy – the photograph showed the face of Homero Guimarães Jr., Christina's brother who was still missing. An investigation of Christina's bank records showed that 'Levy' had given her a large amount of money. A separate investigation discovered that he was in business with his father Homero Guimarães Sr. and that his father had transferred a huge ranch in northern Brazil to 'José Escobar' in the spring of 1982. The ranch was the one near Belém where the offices of Major Key and the Hotel Regent were located. The informant also told the police about Homero's disappearance, and they found out that in an attempt to trace him the father had sent several telegrams to hotels throughout Brazil and South America asking if the following people had been staying at their hotel within the last few months: 'José Escobar, Alfredo Mortilli, Otto Levy, Homero Guimarães.' In August 1983 the group got wind of the police investigation, and that some of Buscetta's ranch manager's associates had been questioned. Realizing that their investigation was now compromised, the police decided to arrest Buscetta – if they could find him.

On 9 September they saw a new car outside Christina's apartment. It was Buscetta's birthday present to his eighteen-year-old daughter, Alessandra. They traced the car back to 'Escobar', which meant that Buscetta was probably still in Brazil.

In São Paulo a separate investigation had been launched into Major Key and its mysterious employees. The company had been formed in 1979 and then bought in May 1981 by Giuseppe Fania and Lorenzo Garello, former employees of Fiat. Garello operated the major branch of the company from Belém. The company's representative in São Paulo was Fabrizio Sansone. The stated business of Major Key was the production of plasticized paper windbreakers used as promotional items for companies such as Kodak, Shell and Fiat. The company records revealed few significant business deals, except for a five-ton shipment to Paraguay which ended with Major Key filing a $359,000 insurance claim for 'lost material'. The records also list a three-kilo shipment of 'material' to New York City.

As in Rio, the São Paulo police had cultivated informers, both at the apartments of some of the suspects and within the Major Key offices. In their surveillance of Sansone they tracked a car which had previously been registered to Giuseppe Pagano, an associate of Ceico. Pagano had sold the car to Sansone. A surveillance team also observed Aldo Alessandri, one of the partners of Ceico, drive up to Sansone's apartment for a meeting. In the course of watching Mortilli, they observed a meeting at his apartment which consisted entirely of a group of young women. The police suspected they were being groomed as cocaine couriers.

Back in Rio the police were tipped off that Christina had left her apartment and loaded her car with six suitcases. They knew this could be the break they needed, and notified their colleagues in São Paulo. If they left her alone she might lead them to Buscetta, the principal target of their operation.

It was the climax of an exhausting investigation. For more than five months Pedro Luiz Berwanger had been hunting Buscetta. He led a team of six agents in a special Mafia unit within the Brazilian Federal Police narcotics squad, which had been set up to investigate the Mafia takeover of cocaine and heroin smuggling operations in Brazil. They had an outstanding warrant against Buscetta for the crime of being an illegal alien. They planned first to arrest him and then identify the full extent of his narcotics network.

Buscetta, though, proved highly elusive until the small hours of 22 October 1983. Berwanger's surveillance agents were desperately tired. Many hours earlier they had heard that Christina was leaving Rio. They watched Staccioli's apartment in São Paulo all night hoping that Buscetta would turn up. Their hopes were raised when they spotted an American Ford Landau, registered to one of the people connected to Buscetta's network, parked outside the building. But Buscetta did not appear. He and Christina had gone to Mortilli's apartment, as Staccioli's apartment was occupied on this particular night. The surveillance team thought they might have lost the trail.

At 5.00 a.m. the cause seemed lost. The police abandoned their surveillance and returned, dispirited, to their hotel. Moments after they arrived, a call came through from an informant. He was ringing from a payphone. Buscetta, he said, was at Mortilli's. Suddenly morale was high again – the team raced off to Mortilli's apartment. There they saw a Volkswagen saloon with Belém plates from the state of Minas Gerais. It was another vehicle used by the Buscetta group. It also happened to be the one being used that night by Buscetta.

'We fixed one of the tyres so he would have to get out and change the flat,' one of the police agents later revealed. 'He came out of the apartment with his wife and son Tommasinho. It was around 7.00 a.m. on a Saturday and it was raining and they were taking the boy to school to register him for classes. He started the car and went about a hundred yards. At that point one of our agents passed him in his car to check the identity. Buscetta pulled over to change the wheel and was getting out of the car when we got him.'

There was no shoot-out, no machine-guns, no car chase. The plan worked perfectly.

Even before they identified themselves, Buscetta instinctively knew that the casually dressed, unshaven and exhausted-looking men who quickly surrounded him were neither street thieves nor a Sicilian hit team but plain-clothes Brazilian policemen. Inside the car Christina panicked, thinking that they were thieves. She screamed and started to take off her gold watch. One of the armed officers said, 'Shut up, Christina!' His manner and the fact that he knew her name calmed her down. She realized it was probably the police.

In a quiet suburban street on a wet autumn weekend in São Paulo, Brazil, a middle-aged man was arrested while driving his wife and kids to school.

It was an incongruous end to the criminal career of one of Sicily's most feared *mafiosi*.

For Buscetta it was the end of a long period as a fugitive. He had begun his second stay in Brazil living quite openly in the luxurious apartment he shared with Christina in the Barra de Trijuca suburb near the beach in Rio de Janeiro, but he had been forced to go underground in the summer of 1982 when the war had intensified against his family in Sicily. At that stage he would meet Christina at the houses of Italian friends in Rio or São Paulo. Even then they were not frightened to show their faces among the large Italian community. They went to São Paulo's night clubs and Italian cantinas, where Buscetta, a great lover of Brazilian night life, would sometimes sing with the guitar players in a fine baritone voice.

The arrest set in motion a carefully planned operation to close in on the other members of the gang before they knew what was happening. The previous week, Pedro Berwanger had flown from Rio to São Paulo to confer with Romeo Tuma, the city's police chief. They agreed that the arrests would be a joint operation and that they would aim to capture as many of Buscetta's gang as possible at the same time.

The agents who had arrested Buscetta drove him back the few hundred yards to Mortilli's apartment to keep him 'under wraps' while the next phase of the operation was launched. A young Brazilian detective was left in the room with him. He says that Buscetta's first words to him were, 'If you've come to discuss my freedom, I'll start with a million dollars. If you've come to question me, I'll say nothing.' Buscetta's version is characteristically different. He maintains, innocently, that the conversation began with the policeman saying, 'One million dollars will set you free.' Buscetta claims that he replied, 'All I can come up with is a thousand dollars.'

Whatever the truth of that exchange, Buscetta's arrest had left behind some very worried people. His original host, Paolo

Staccioli, could not understand why he had not heard from either Buscetta or Christina. He drove over to Mortilli's apartment in the Ford Landau to see what had happened and walked straight into the police trap. Giuseppe Bizzarro, arriving soon after, parked his battered Volkswagen outside the apartment building. But he became suspicious, or perhaps he was tipped off by the hall porter. He fled back to Staccioli's house in the Morumbi suburb, where he walked straight into another police team and was arrested. He was so surprised that he did not even have time to pull the .38 he always carried with him.

The police team's next target was the head office of Major Key, in the small town of Belém, near Buscetta's ranch in Minas Gerais, the conservative heartland state of Brazil. Berwanger did not believe that Major Key's fantastic profits had been earned from the sale of plasticized paper windbreakers. He was convinced they came from drugs and that Major Key was the front company for the money-laundering activities of Badalamenti, Buscetta and Bardellino's fish company. All he needed was the documents to prove it.

The police went to pick up Major Key's two directors, Giuseppe Fania and Lorenzo Garello. In São Paulo, another patrol raced downtown to Avenida Angelica, where Fabrizio Sansone ran the small local office for Major Key. In it he had kept records of numerous air tickets, many of which had been bought for Buscetta and Christina in the company's name. Major Key had also supplied them with the use of several cars. The police removed boxfuls of documents, air tickets and banking records, and arrested Sansone at his apartment. Sirens screaming, they headed back to the São Paulo headquarters with their six captives. They were pleased with their day's work. They were convinced they had smashed a major Mafia narcotics ring.

In Rio de Janeiro they arrested Buscetta's ranch manager. At the same time they sent a plain-clothes patrol to the apartment of Homero Guimarães Sr., Christina's father. When they arrived they warned the doorman not to tell Guimarães that they were policemen. The doorman ignored the warning and told Guimarães over the intercom that there was a group of suspicious-looking individuals on their way up to see him.

When they got to the door, Guimarães told his maid to open it. He saw the plain-clothed policemen with their guns drawn. Apparently thinking he was about to be attacked, he opened fire on them, shooting one of them in the leg. The policemen returned the fire, and he was hit by at least seven bullets. Miraculously, he survived. The police found nothing in the apartment.

It was a bizarre climax to the operation. The only violence had come from an elderly citizen, a friend of a former Brazilian President, whose son-in-law was a member of the Sicilian Mafia. The net had been drawn in – but on what?

As the police went through Major Key's records, they discovered that the company was capitalized at only $6000 but it was worth close to $1 million. Apart from the Paraguay and New York transactions, there was no record of any real business activity. Leonardo Badalamenti, who had been using the alias Ricardo Vitale, had been about to open another branch in Curitiba, Brazil. Vincenzo Randazzo, Gaetano Badalamenti's nephew, who used the alias 'Faro Lupo', was planning to open another office in New York. The records showed that company employees had been travelling all over Brazil and to Paris, Rome, Milan, Caracas and Zurich. All these places featured in the Mafia's international narcotics trade.

The investigation in Brazil was at an end. The evidence was collated and handed over to the United States Drug Enforcement Administration. The DEA has a vast back-up system with undercover agents and informers all over the world. It also has access to FBI files, and its own central computerized Drugs Intelligence files, so it was no surprise that further details were revealed in a DEA report in December 1983.

One of the most interesting of those details came from a cross-check on 'Faro Lupo', who was on file as an associate and relative of Baladamenti. The FBI had picked up his trail in New York City on 5 October 1983, just a few weeks before the Brazilians broke up the Badalamenti–Buscetta organization. He was staying in New York at the Hotel Roosevelt, where he had met Salvatore Mazzurco, a key figure in the Pizza Connection case. Mazzurco was being watched because he had been identified as a principal figure in the heroin ring run by Salvatore 'the Baker' Catalano, the Sicilian underboss of the Bonanno family.

Antonio Bardellino had some interesting connections as well. The DEA identified him as the right-hand man of Carlo Zippo, the central figure of the French–Italian–American heroin ring which Buscetta and Pino Catania had run in the late sixties and early seventies. Zippo had been arrested in February 1983 in Italy and charged, along with twenty other *mafiosi*, with controlling a cocaine-smuggling operation between South America and Italy.

The DEA's computers continued to throw up new connections. Giuseppe Bizzarro was identified as a fugitive from another indictment in Italy which had named 176 *mafiosi*, charged with conspiracy to smuggle narcotics. He had been using the alias Carlos Fattori Lanza, under which name travel records and bank accounts surfaced in Caracas, Venezuela. It was also noted that he had received a telephone call from the Los Angeles house of the Camorra boss, Michele Zaza, at the same time that the Sicilian Mafia boss, Antonio Salamone, was visiting Zaza.

The receiving company for Ceico's fish shipments was identified as Lo Squalo, another fish company, located in Naples. A further intelligence trawl showed that a car registered to Lo Squalo had been observed in France at a meeting of major organized crime figures. The DEA's big mainframe computer, known as NADDIS, was working overtime.

Leonardo Badalamenti, Gaetano's son, turned out to have the phone number of a Carlos Lauricella, whom NADDIS identified as a suspected heroin trafficker. Several other numbers found in his possession were similarly interesting. The computer indicated numerous connections with South-East Asian heroin traffickers.

As for Gaetano Badalamenti, the Americans noted that he, his wife and his two sons had travelled to Paris in July 1983, the date of an organized crime summit in France.

The December 1983 DEA report concluded:

Buscetta, around 1981, was allegedly involved in a consortium of organized crime figures who were attempting to develop South-East Asian sources of supply for heroin. Buscetta and Badalamenti have aligned forces in South America in an effort to conduct illegal narcotics trafficking activities.

It appears that several of the individuals in Buscetta's group travel to or from Belém. Because of Belém's prime location and frequent flights available to Europe, it is suspected that Buscetta's nearby ranch, which is located on the Amazon river, offers a prime spot for transporting or manufacturing illegal products, such as cocaine. Initial analysis of the telephone numbers, names, companies, etc., found in possession of or at the locations associated with the eleven arrestees, has revealed numerous 'hits' in DEA's NADDIS system regarding cocaine and heroin trafficking.

The analysis was based on the most sophisticated processing of raw intelligence that the Americans could contrive. They believed that a large heroin and cocaine network was being put in place or was already functioning.

The central figure in the network, Tommaso Buscetta, maintains that he was not involved in any illegal activities during his second stay in Brazil. His claim is neither confirmed nor refuted by the evidence. In front of a jury, he would be presumed innocent until proven guilty.

Either Buscetta is one of the most maligned members of the Mafia, whose reputation as the 'Prince of Cocaine' and one of the world's biggest narcotics traffickers has unfairly haunted him through police files all over the world, or he is such a clever operator, able to cover his tracks with such skill, that he has concealed all the hard evidence that would have implicated him. Even today DEA agents and law enforcement officers in Italy are unable to support their suspicions. But of course, since he decided to talk, their interest in proving him guilty has seriously diminished: all they really want now from him are names.

12

The Enigma of Tommaso Buscetta

On my name weigh legends and fantasies, but also gross slanders. There is no proof of anything. I am a man like other men who hasn't done anything secret or mysterious to hide or defend. I have my loves, my life, my family and my children who are all in America. I'm not a *mafioso*. I have never been one, and no one can prove anything against me.

Tommaso Buscetta, interviewed in *Il Mattino*, 20 November 1973

The crucial period of investigation which followed the arrest of Buscetta and his gang was hindered by a fierce bureaucratic rivalry between the Brazilian police in São Paulo and the Special Organized Crime Unit in Rio de Janeiro.

Berwanger and his team owed much of their success to their low-key approach. After Buscetta's arrest they wanted to develop further leads in Rio, in particular the trail of Antonio Bardellino. They had also received reports that Gaetano Badalamenti had been sighted in Santa Cruz de la Sierra, one of Bolivia's main cocaine centres. To their dismay, the mass of publicity generated by Buscetta's arrest destroyed the potential for further action.

The credit for Buscetta's capture fell not to Berwanger but to Romeo Tuma, São Paulo's politically adroit and publicity-conscious police chief. (His career reached a climax in June 1985 when he presided over the discovery of the remains of Josef

Mengele, the notorious Nazi war criminal.) The story was presented to the press in such a way as to exclude any reference to Berwanger's special unit, and in the official police records their role was played down in favour of Paulo Gustavo de Magalhães, an ambitious young protégé of Tuma who soon afterwards became head of the Federal Drug Squad. Although the follow-up investigation failed to produce the hard evidence needed to convince the courts, in view of Buscetta's later decision to cooperate, Magalhães and the Brazilian police are at least partly justified in their satisfaction with their work. As Magalhães says:

> Our objective was achieved. Look how many *mafiosi*
> were put away as a result. It took them years to get Al
> Capone. They finally bagged him on tax evasion charges,
> whilst here in Brazil we got our man for illegal re-entry,
> use of false documents. It comes to the same thing in the
> end.

According to Magalhães, Buscetta lived like a king in gaol:

> It was a great honour for the other members of the group
> to be handcuffed together with him! . . . They used to
> kiss his hands in the morning, and when they were being
> moved, he always got into the police van first. He kept
> up the routine of discipline, always giving orders to the
> others.

At night in the cell, the other members of the group slept around Buscetta in a protective ring. It was rumoured that rival *mafiosi* were already suspicious that he might break *omertà*.

The Brazilians were convinced that the group had been organizing a massive cocaine-smuggling operation with Major Key at the centre providing support services, principally travel arrangements and money laundering. But Article 14 of Brazil's criminal code relating to drug offences requires more than circumstantial evidence for a conviction, and hard evidence was elusive. 'This type of crime is very tough to investigate,' Magalhães admitted, 'because these people would never have touched the drugs themselves and certainly never used them. It's very tough to prove in court.'

When the police presented their evidence to Sylvia Steiner, a young federal prosecutor who was standing in for a colleague on vacation, she warned them that it would not stand up in a court of law. 'Our judicial system is very demanding in terms of proof for cases under the drugs law and the police could offer no proof in their testimony,' she commented.

'Judges here tend to be too demanding,' says Magalhães. 'They've got an exaggerated tendency to show that they won't be influenced by what the police or the press would like them to think.'

Magalhães' inadequate evidence, accompanied by vague promises that the American and Italian police would provide definitive proof, failed to satisfy Steiner even though she had no doubt that the Italians were involved in organized crime:

> They all had a very high lifestyle that was completely inconsistent with their stated activities. It was evident that their money came from illegal activities but it was never proven what they were. I never saw any documents proving the legality of Buscetta's earnings. One of the versions that the police put forward was that they hadn't yet started drug trafficking. The police had a huge map on the wall of the São Paulo headquarters linking up the members through telephone contacts: but it never went anywhere. I think the police rather rushed into the arrest without getting everything ready before they picked him up.

The law in Brazil requires the police to complete their case and present evidence to the state prosecutor within five days of arrest, after which they must request special detention. 'The police turned up with their charges on the fifth and last day and the magistrate told Superintendent Tuma there simply wasn't enough proof,' Steiner recalls. Nevertheless, Buscetta and the other Italians stayed in prison because of the false-document charges, which allowed the police fifteen days to complete their case. And by this stage, the Brazilian Justice Minister, Ibrahim Abi Ackel, had intervened, ordering special detention at the request of the authorities in Italy and the United States, as both countries were keen to extradite Buscetta.

The police were relieved when the case was transferred from the critical Sylvia Steiner to a more senior federal prosecutor, João Carlos da Rocha Mattos. Today Mattos is a judge, but in 1983 he had just moved from his job as an investigator with the federal police to become a state prosecutor. He had a reputation as a tough operator, and both Tuma and Magalhães regarded him as 'one of the boys', who could be relied upon to support them against the sort of nitpicking judge who would have too enthusiastic a desire for objective proof. Mattos took over the case from Steiner in early November 1983 and spent a weekend studying the evidence. He recalls that:

> The police were euphoric that I had been chosen – and they had high expectations that I would present a formal charge under the drugs law – even though they hadn't got any concrete proofs against Buscetta. Two or three of the agents working on the case came to visit me. They were accompanied by an official from the US Consulate and a special attorney [Charles Rose] from New York. They were very friendly and told me the case was considered very important in the US and that I should give it special attention. You couldn't say there were any threats or pressure from the Americans. It was a very informal conversation in which they admitted that most of the information they'd got about Buscetta, such as telephone taps, wouldn't stand up in a US court of law.

Whatever the evidence or lack of it, those who knew the realities of the Mafia were in no doubt about the potential value of Buscetta. If he talked, his knowledge would be immensely useful in investigating the Mafia's civil wars and the heroin traffic between Sicily and America. The Italians were keen to interrogate him, but protocol demanded that the Brazilians must first be allowed to present their case. The police were so confident that the judicial authorities would collaborate in a conviction of Buscetta's organization that they failed to comply with a number of legal procedures. They failed to present their prisoners within the stipulated time, or to request authorization to hold them for another two weeks pending inquiries. This created a real danger that Buscetta might once again slip out of everyone's grasp.

Mattos, however, was sticking to the rule book:

> I made a declaration that there wasn't sufficient evidence to charge Buscetta and that the case should go back to the police for further investigation. But there was a clear case against Giuseppe Bizzarro and Leonardo Badalamenti for use of false documents, and against Buscetta for illegal entry. I suggested that the case be split up into four separate accusations because there wasn't sufficient evidence to prove a conspiracy amongst the accused.
>
> You can't claim that just because foreigners of the same nationality get together there's a 'conspiracy to traffic drugs'.

Mattos' refusal to charge the defendants with narcotics trafficking was greeted by the local press as a victory for the Mafia. The police made it quite clear that they were very disappointed with his decision, but the former policeman is unrepentant:

> I couldn't go along with their fantasy and press charges which would later have been thrown out of court by the judge. You could never say that they were innocent, but there just wasn't any proof of a crime or the formation of a conspiracy to traffic. If the gang really existed, then the police rushed into an arrest without getting sufficient evidence together even to press charges.

Romeo Tuma has admitted that the police had difficulties:

> We had serious problems in detaining him because the judicial authorities here thought there was nothing to pin on him for drug trafficking. But the US and the

Italians immediately sent important officials to testify here. His presence was the first indication we had of the international Mafia in Brazil. We became aware of the importance of Buscetta only when the US and the Italians started requesting his extradition. But there was the problem of proof. He was the leader and so you would never find any direct contact with drugs.

Even after Tuma had established regular contact with Giovanni Falcone, Italy's chief anti-Mafia prosecutor, he still could not produce conclusive evidence to nail Buscetta:

I think we aborted Buscetta's operation as he hadn't yet finished setting up the infrastructure – he was still in the phase of setting up a legal façade and normalizing his right to remain in the country. What's important for us is that we didn't wait for him to commit serious crimes in order to catch him after the event. Once you know someone is planning a crime you try to preempt it, as the evil is much greater afterwards. I don't believe that Buscetta would have come to Brazil just to rest up – as some have maintained. What's important is that he didn't succeed in his aims and his imprisonment has been for the general good. No one's going to finish off the Mafia but from what we understand the results [of his testimony] have been exceptional.

No one was more delighted with the shortcomings of the case than Flavio Augusto Marx, Buscetta's Brazilian lawyer. A flamboyant figure who is an accomplished painter as well as a lawyer, Marx spends most of his time helping São Paulo's wealthy businessmen to register the Mercedes Benz cars they bring across the border from Paraguay. He remains convinced that the police had virtually nothing on his client:

I challenge Romeo Tuma to prove there was ever a Brazilian connection. The basic point is that Maria Christina [Buscetta's wife] was pressuring him to stay away from crime. The thing he did wrong was to enter

Brazil illegally. He didn't have any other illegal activities and was emotionally and psychologically downcast because of what had happened to his family in Sicily.

Buscetta once said to me, 'I'll always be suspected of being an active member of the Mafia because of my past – no one entertains the possibility of rehabilitation.' But I'm convinced he had already left the Mafia when he came to Brazil. They killed his family in Italy to make him come back.

Despite his eccentricity, Marx is renowned in Brazilian legal circles as a tough opponent, and he immediately put the police on the defensive by challenging them with a writ of habeas corpus. As a result the Justice Minister Ibrahim Abi Ackel was obliged to go to the Supreme Court to request Buscetta's continued detention. Marx also defended Fabrizio Sansone and succeeded in getting him out of gaol under laws which permit first-time offenders to answer charges while at liberty.

With the press firmly on Tuma's side, Marx fought a losing battle to convince public opinion that Buscetta had been the victim of dubious police tactics. He arranged an interview for the *Globo* newspaper of Rio on 25 October 1983, in which Buscetta attributed the accusations against him to a conspiracy between the police and the press:

It was you people who created this image which does not correspond to the person I am. I want to stay in Brazil and live here with my children, who are Brazilian citizens.

The only gang I had in Brazil was my family.

Buscetta was disgusted by Tuma. He believed that he had used his arrest to build up his own image.

In 1972 Buscetta had been tortured by the Brazilian police; now he felt that they were crucifying him with adverse publicity and wild allegations. He joked with Marx about the calibre of his supposed gang of *mafiosi* whom the police had portrayed as an élite team run by the 'Godfather of Two Worlds'. In the police version Aldo Alessandri carried out the same functions in Rio de Janeiro as Fabrizio Sansone in São Paulo – arranging cars and financing for the Buscettas. According to Buscetta, Alessandri was 'nothing more than a doddering old pimp who made a living by taking Italian tourists to sex shows in Rio's red-light district'. Staccioli was a failed restaurateur who had been evicted from his house for failing to pay his rent, and Armando Almendares, a Cuban-born American from Tampa, Florida, was a homosexual hustler. 'Buscetta used to joke with me that these three imbeciles were his "Mafia",' Marx recalled. 'He thought the whole thing was ridiculous!'

Buscetta did not mention Sansone, Salamone, the Badalamentis or Bardellino, who were certainly not on the police files in Europe and the United States for being imbeciles.

If the Brazilians were in a quandary over what to do with Buscetta, the Italians and the Americans had a more concrete case against him. He was wanted in Italy for breaking parole and in America for the heroin-trafficking case involving Giuseppe Catania and Michel Nicoli. Both countries demanded his extradition.

Meanwhile he languished in prison. Soon after his arrest he had been pictured laughing and joking, indulging his celebrity status with a posse of reporters and photographers, but now the months in prison were beginning to wear him down. He was due to be transferred to another gaol in Brasilia in early 1984 to await eventual extradition either to America or back to Italy. As neither prospect appealed to him an escape attempt was organized before he had to move. One of the police officers claims:

> He'd arranged the whole thing. A hole had been dug through the ceiling of the bathroom and a car was to be waiting outside to take him to Rio de Janeiro to hide out in an apartment – but the man in the apartment was one of our agents and gave us valuable new information about a second group looking after Buscetta's interests after the first group had been arrested.

The escape route was discovered and the attempt foiled. Buscetta's account is slightly different and, of course, entirely innocent:

> It is true that there was an escape plan – which I had nothing to do with – while I was in the prison at São Paulo. Around Christmas of 1983, some of the Brazilian prisoners told me that they had made a hole in the plaster ceiling of the bathroom and asked me to escape with them. I asked them if they had money and if there was someone waiting for them outside the prison. Since they answered 'No' to both questions I convinced them – with a great deal of effort – to abandon an attempt that was doomed to failure. In May 1984 I was transferred to Brasilia and I believe that it was the result of manœuvring by the other prisoners who thought that my presence was an obstacle to their plans for escape. In fact a few days after I was transferred from São Paulo to Brasilia they escaped from São Paulo prison, using the hole that I had made them conceal and disguise.

With the possibility of escape now out of the question, the prospect of extradition to Italy was looming like a death sentence. Buscetta was under no illusions that, once he was back in the Ucciardone or any other prison in Italy, the Corleonesi could arrange his murder with little difficulty. He would be a sitting target. Christina had made several visits to the US Embassy, desperate to contact anyone who could arrange a passage for her husband to the much safer United States. The messages were never passed to the right channels. Meanwhile Charles Rose telephoned Giovanni Falcone to give him some news: the United States were going to withdraw their extradition request. In return the Italians would withdraw their extradition request on another international fugitive whom the Americans were anxious to interview. It was a fair exchange. The other fugitive was Gaetano Badalamenti, who had been arrested in Madrid in April 1984.

Buscetta became increasingly anxious, not so much for himself as for his family. Furthermore, he knew that the terrible vengeance exacted on his sons and relatives in Sicily could easily be directed against Christina and their children if she followed him back to Sicily. His surviving family would be plunged straight back into the Mafia wars with no means of protection – and little hope of survival.

'He was in despair at having to go through everything again. These people are normal and they have their weaknesses too,' comments Marx.

Giovanni Falcone, his young team of bodyguards and some of Italy's most senior police investigators flew to Brazil to make the final arrangements for bringing Buscetta back home. For Buscetta, the 'Man of Honour', there seemed to be only one way out. On 7 July 1984, a week before he was due to be flown back to Italy, Brazilian police officials took him by armed convoy to the capital's Instituto Medico Legale for a thorough medical check-up. After his nine months in captivity they wanted to be sure that he was being handed over to the Italians in sound medical condition. As he was being driven from the federal police headquarters to the IML, he was concealing a small phial of strychnine which he had managed to keep with him ever since his arrest. When they arrived he crushed the glass phial between his teeth and swallowed the bitter-tasting liquid. The poison was quick-acting. The Sicilian prisoner began to go purple in the face and then fell to the floor, gasping. He was rushed into intensive care. The embarrassed Brazilians faced the humiliation of losing one of the most valuable Mafia prisoners in captivity.

Fortunately, the prompt action of a police doctor saved Buscetta's life. A stomach-pump minimized the effect of the strychnine, but he remained in a coma. According to Buscetta, his attempted suicide

> was not an act of weakness or a mental breakdown or fear of being threatened by those who had so savagely and unjustly attacked innocent members of my family. Rather, it was an act of love towards my wife and children because I thought that, if I was out of the way,

it would make their life much less complicated than it would certainly be if I was imprisoned in Italy. It wasn't out of desperation, or through being mentally unbalanced, rather it was a carefully calculated act of love towards those who are my sole reason for living.

With diligent nursing, Buscetta emerged from the coma and convalesced in the hospital for a week. Still shaky, and now under even more intense security, he was driven to the airport. With a blanket wrapped around his shoulders, he looked frail and vulnerable as he was helped up the steps of the Alitalia 747 jet which would fly him to Rome.

His narrow escape from death had given him a new perspective on life:

When I finally came out of the coma ... I understood that such a solution, that of dying, would not have been enough. Something more was required – to destroy the present reality of the Mafia.

To destroy the Mafia: this is for me so important that I haven't hesitated to accept all the risks that this entails, including those to which the members of my family will be exposed.

Sitting beside Buscetta on the long flight back to Italy was Gianni de Gennaro, one of the leading police protagonists in the war against the Mafia in Sicily. Buscetta still felt very ill from the after-effects of the poison and was uncertain that he would survive. This narrow escape from death confirmed something he had been feeling for a long time:

To start with, during my detention in Brazil, a desire began to take root to shed the burden which was crushing me; and then the final moment came on the aircraft taking me to Italy. Among the police officers was Gianni de Gennaro; during that anguished flight, when it wasn't yet clear to me whether I would be able to survive, I began to talk, to open up to him. De Gennaro, with his way of reasoning, made me understand that the moment had arrived to tell the truth. He and his colleagues did not put pressure on me, as had been the case in the past. They showed me the true face of the policeman who believes in his work.

On 15 July 1984, Rome's Fiumicino airport was surrounded by an impenetrable security ring worthy of a visiting head of state. Armed police and *carabinieri* with sub-machine-guns and flak jackets patrolled the airport and its perimeter.

Tommaso Buscetta had come home to talk.

13

The 'Third Level'

As long as certain political or business circles linked to the Mafia continue to find it easy to get support and protection in the political world in general, it will be extremely difficult for the magistrates to investigate. We hope, therefore, that this connivance, this protection which is provided for political reasons, will cease.

Examining magistrate Paolo Borsallino

For a man who lives every moment of his life unsure that he will survive to enjoy the next, Giovanni Falcone is remarkably good-humoured. A permanent and slightly mischievous smile seems to be visible beneath his dark beard. That smile conceals the reality of a man living in a constant state of siege. So many of his fellow magistrates have been murdered that his survival remains something of a miracle. He and five other magistrates are bonded together by the threat of death and the will to continue the work of their murdered colleagues. Their method of team work helps to protect them: their knowledge is shared, so the Mafia would have to kill all of them to damage their investigations.

Falcone is the most heavily protected man in Italy. He is escorted everywhere by a dedicated team of young bodyguards armed with high-velocity rapid-fire light machine-guns. They wear flak jackets, crash helmets and visors. Falcone is driven in a bullet-proof, bomb-proof Alfa Romeo in armed convoy at high speed through the heavy Palermo traffic. The drivers are as expert as the bodyguards. Overhead a helicopter scans the route ahead for potential trouble. The inhabitants of the city centre are now so accustomed to the daily ritual that they can detect which magistrate is on the move by the sirens they hear and the number of escort cars they see. Falcone has the most. Although part of a team, Falcone has the reputation as the leading magistrate in the fight against the Mafia. A recently married man, whose private life is severely restricted by his security, he has perhaps taken on a greater burden than his colleagues.

On all of them the physical and mental toll is devastating. They shrug it off, but most of them smoke incessantly, suffer from exhaustion and live in an atmosphere of oppressive security which adds to the pressure and cuts them off from the everyday realities of life. To go out and have a meal at a restaurant is a major security problem. They cannot even venture down the street to buy a newspaper. Virtually all the things which people take for granted have become impossible. One magistrate admitted that he occasionally gives his escort the slip so that he can get out for a walk alone.

The terrible price they have paid in their personal lives has had a measure of compensation in their public success. Inheriting the cases of their murdered colleagues, Falcone and the other examining magistrates have compiled the most exhaustive dossiers and indictments ever prepared against the Sicilian Mafia. And it was a major breakthrough in that war when Tommaso Buscetta agreed to testify.

The bunker in Rome's Rebibia prison was originally built to house captured members of the Red Brigades terrorist group. It is the ultimate in maximum security. There, from 16 July to 12 September 1984, Buscetta talked to Falcone. His statements covered 700 pages. At the end of sixty days of intensive questioning his conversations with the Italian prosecutor added up to the most valuable confession of a high-ranking *mafioso* that the world had ever heard. He identified and corroborated the names of members of the Mafia who had ordered and carried out many of the brutal 'illustrious corpses' killings. He detailed the principal figures in the heroin trade, the buyers, receivers and suppliers of morphine base. He outlined the background to the Mafia wars. He identified the leadership of the Sicilian Mafia over a thirty-year period and the composition of the Commission. He described the territorial demarcations agreed by the different families, and he supplied an exhaustive list of all the people whom he knew to be members of the Mafia. That list ran into hundreds of names.

The magistrates were reassured to discover that many of the facts they thought they knew and many of the theories they were working on were corroborated in detail by Buscetta. And although some of his statements about the Mafia command structure were familiar, he now revealed to them the strict degree of accountability and control that existed at different levels of the Mafia. Paolo Borsallino, one of the team of magistrates working alongside Falcone, was impressed:

> Buscetta allowed us to see this organization from the inside, that is, to acquaint ourselves with the rules that the various Mafia members undertake on oath and on pain of death. Before it was as if we were looking at a building from the outside ... we knew it existed and that it had a certain structure and certain dimensions. Buscetta has allowed us to see it from the inside, room by room.

Within weeks the police were ready to act on Buscetta's evidence. In naming hundreds of individuals who were members of Mafia families he provided the authorities with a valuable intelligence base, from which the *carabinieri* constructed detailed charts known as the 'order of battle'. In Italy, unlike America, membership of the Mafia is itself a criminal offence.

Before dawn on 29 September 1984, 'Operation San Michele' began. It was the largest round-up of *mafiosi* since the days of Mussolini. Armed with 366 arrest warrants, the police sealed off the streets of Palermo. They pulled dozens of *mafiosi* out of bed, herded them into police vans and brought them back to police headquarters in chains. Helicopters kept watch overhead and armoured cars patrolled the streets.

The operation was hailed as a great success, not least because of its propaganda value. The show of strength, dutifully reported by the press and filmed for television, gave the positive impression that the police had the Mafia on the run. Although that might not quite have been the case, the balance was beginning to change. Most importantly, the police now had the initiative instead of being constantly on the defensive.

One month later a second blitz was launched. More Mafia soldiers and some of their bosses were herded up, handcuffed in full view of a battery of television cameras, and led into the police headquarters to be charged.

By the end of 1984, largely as a result of Buscetta's testimony, the police and the *carabinieri* had issued warrants for more than 500 of his former associates. They ranged from ordinary soldiers through to the top members of the Commission. Michele Greco, 'The Pope', his brother Salvatore Greco, 'the Senator', and Pino Greco, were on the run. At last the supremacy of the Corleonesi had been seriously threatened.

Most important of all, the magistrates and the police now began to move against the 'Third Level', the politicians and businessmen whose connivance had protected men like Michele Greco for so long.

When the Palermo Flying Squad, their sirens screaming, screeched up to the house of a senior Christian Democrat, he thought it must be official business. As a former mayor of Palermo and one of the most important men on the island of Sicily, Vito Ciancimino was accustomed to dealing with senior policemen and government officials at every level. And he was untouchable. He was after all one of those who had spoken out courageously against the Mafia many times.

When the police told him that he was under arrest, the 'respectable' politician simply collapsed. He fainted into the arms of a surprised detective and had to be half-carried down the stairs to the convoy of police cars, where the press and television recorded his fall from grace. The Italian press, particularly the crusading Palermo newspaper *L'Ora*, had campaigned against Ciancimino's blatant corruption for more than a decade. Now the photographers and reporters were there to witness the moment of his collapse.

Ciancimino, dazed and shocked, sprawled in the back of the police car. The patrol cars sped off, transporting their illustrious passenger into political oblivion and the prospect of prison.

For years Ciancimino had been a staunch political ally of Giulio Andreotti, leader of the Christian Democrats and a former Prime Minister. Neither Andreotti nor any of his other powerful friends would help the half-dazed politician now. After thirty years of political service to the Christian Democrats and the Mafia, he was to be thrown to the wolves.

Ciancimino's collapse was not feigned. He was so utterly astonished that the political support which had kept him out of prison for so long had disappeared that he literally passed out. It was a graphic illustration of how protected such men felt while they were still 'in favour'. For decades men like Ciancimino had been beyond the law, and though report after report, including the testimony of General Dalla Chiesa, had implicated him in a variety of corrupt deals benefiting the Mafia at the expense of the people of Sicily, nothing had ever been done. The shock of discovering that the protection had been withdrawn was overwhelming. It was the end of an extraordinarily long and dishonest political career.

Vito Ciancimino was born in Corleone on 2 April 1924. His father had emigrated to New York in 1910, returning to Corleone to start a barber's shop. Local people remember the young Vito lending a hand.

From an early age he had the right family connections. His uncle ran a shop selling arms and ammunition, in Corleone a more worthwhile trade than being a grocer! His cousin married Cirò Maiuri, a close friend of Dr Michele Navarra, the head of the Corleone family in the fifties until Luciano Liggio killed him and took over. Maiuri's son was killed in the aftermath of the power struggle between supporters of Navarra and Liggio.

Ciancimino's fortunes took off when he left Corleone for

Palermo. He started in the construction industry, getting hold of a concession for contracts with the state railway company. He was helped by Bernardo Mattarella, Under-Secretary to the Minister of Transport and a man with powerful friends in the Mafia, for whom he had performed a variety of favours. In return the Mafia had ensured the delivery of thousands of votes for Mattarella, and political support from Sicily was smiled upon in Rome. It was hardly surprising that Mattarella should have voted against the formation of the Italian Parliament's first Anti-Mafia Commission.

Mattarella was one of the generation of post-war Mafia politicians who carried the interests of his clients with him when he went to Rome to become a senior member of the government. He was aided by Giovanni Gioia, who had become Secretary of the Christian Democratic Party in Palermo and an ally of the Fanfani faction. (Italian political parties have been split by so many internal disagreements that most of them are divided into factions whose shifting alliances frequently change the balance of power; hence the regular changes of government in Italy since the war.) Mattarella belonged to the faction headed by Aldo Moro, while his fellow Sicilian Christian Democrats, Giovanni Gioia and Vito Ciancimino, gave their allegiance first to Fanfani and later to Andreotti.

With help from Mattarella, Ciancimino went into business. One of his first partners was Carmelo la Barba, the brother of a convicted *mafioso*, Giovanni la Barba. It was a lucrative association and Ciancimino soon prospered. He could now afford to turn his attention full-time to politics. He served his political apprenticeship on Mattarella's staff in Rome. When he returned to Palermo he was rewarded with an appointment as commissioner for the Christian Democratic Party, a post which he held for sixteen years. When his friend Salvo Lima became the mayor of Palermo, Ciancimino succeeded him as the alderman of public works. It was a job he held from July 1959 to June 1964. The position does not sound too important until you remember that public-works contracts in Palermo are literally a matter of life and death. At the beginning of 1985 one of Sicily's leading businessmen, Roberto Parisi, was shot dead in his car, along with his driver, allegedly after a dispute with the Mafia over a percentage of the street-lighting contract in Palermo which was held by one of Parisi's companies.

There are more street lights in Palermo than in any other city in Italy.

Ciancimino held public office during the prosperous years of the sixties, when *mafiosi* emerged overnight as millionaires. Speculation in new buildings was almost guaranteed to make you rich. The alderman of public works took an intense personal interest in local construction projects – and made himself a fortune.

In July 1962, within a month of the announcement by the President of Sicily approving a new town-planning scheme, which promised another bonanza for Mafia-controlled building companies, a new company was formed called ISEP (Instituto Sovvenzioni e Prestiti). It soon increased its share capital from L1 million to L200 million. Guiding the company into profitable areas of business was Signora Ciancimino, who held 10 per cent of the shares. (With its customary understatement, the Anti-Mafia Commission report in 1976 noted, 'Ciancimino's wife has found herself in the company of some quite undesirable characters.') The company then changed its name to COFISI (Compagnia Finanziaria Siciliana). Also on the board were high-ranking members of the Mafia, 'businessmen' like Angelo di Carlo, a powerful *mafioso* from Corleone. Other Mafia shareholders were Nino Sorci from Palermo and Frank Garofalò, formerly Joe Bonanno's deputy and a veteran of the Hotel delle Palme summit of October 1957. He had retired to Sicily in 1956 and decided to put some of his 'retirement pay' into COFISI. As well as being able to offer advice on some of the more technical aspects of planning permission, COFISI paid handsome dividends and fringe benefits to their Mafia associates.

Ciancimino has aged considerably since his arrest. The investigation into the favours he performed for his friends from Corleone is continuing. His lawyers in Palermo are dismissive of the charges against him, pointing to the lack of substance and mere technicality of 'currency infringements' with which he has been charged. A more serious charge which has emerged from the investigation, and one which the lawyers do not mention, is that he was a fully 'made' member of the Corleonesi family under the leadership of Salvatore Riina. As well as easing their way through building contracts, Ciancimino performed a variety of other services for his Mafia boss. He laundered five million Canadian dollars through Montreal for the Greco family, illicit money which was almost certainly 'black money' from the heroin trade. The money was washed into real-estate deals in Canada. Ciancimino's contact in Montreal had been Michel Pozza, financial adviser to Montreal's leading Mafia family, the Cotronis. As well as smuggling narcotics between Mexico, Canada and the USA, Vincent Cotroni's family specialized in financial frauds, mainly stolen securities and share certificates. Pozza, a stockbroker by trade, was a useful contact. His deals on the financial markets meant that he could place the 'hot' shares and he was in an ideal position to help launder the Mafia's profits. Pozza had been introduced to Ciancimino through a mutual friend from the Bonanno family and had spent some time in 1979 as Ciancimino's guest at the picturesque seaside resort of Mondello, ten miles outside Palermo.

Pozza was one of the distinguished guests at a wedding reception for Giuseppe Bono, at the Hotel Pierre in New York City in 1981, which yielded investigators a wealth of photographs of the leading Sicilian and American *mafiosi* involved in the heroin business, including the leading participants in the Pizza Connection. Ever since Carmine Galante's operations in Montreal, the relations between the Bonanno and the Cotroni families had been extremely close. Vincent Cotroni was listed as a ranking member in the Bonanno family, and Giuseppe Cotroni had been the receiver for Galante's heroin shipments.

Michel Pozza was shot dead outside his home on 28 September 1982. A number of documents linking him to the Sicilian Mafia were discovered in his car and at his house. His death was part of a power struggle within the Cotroni family. The family had been run by Vincent Cotroni until he died of cancer. When his brother Frank Cotroni, who was involved in heroin and cocaine smuggling between Mexico, Canada and America, was imprisoned for heroin trafficking, the reins of power were seized by Nicholas Rizzutto, who headed the Sicilian faction within the Cotroni family. Pozza was reporting to Rizzutto and a few days before his murder had been observed meeting one of Rizzutto's lieutenants.

Among the documents retrieved from Pozza's attaché case was a list of telephone numbers and addresses in Palermo. There was also a credit note for five million Canadian dollars ($US 2.6 million) drawn on current account number 1189638, Canadian Imperial Bank of Commerce, Montreal. The account was registered to Sergio and Giovanni Ciancimino, Vito's two sons. The money had been transferred from Cimasol Anstalt Inc. in Vaduz, Liechtenstein, a financial centre well known for its discretion. Jean Pozza, Michel's brother, was listed as one of the Cimasol company directors. Ciancimino's sons had been used as couriers because he was afraid of air travel.

Vito Ciancimino's arrest and the charges that have been brought against him by the Sicilian magistrates represent a significant victory in the war against the Mafia. Pino Arlacchi, until recently the consultant to Italy's current Anti-Mafia Commission, has no doubt about how Ciancimino was able to survive for so long:

> Because Ciancimino was a political figure, his position produced a fairly important number of votes for his party in western Sicily. Ciancimino, and not only Ciancimino, other people belonging to the same lobby, had been the dominant political élite in western Sicily for more than twenty years – so at a central level in Rome nobody could easily challenge their power in Palermo because they represented their own part of the dominant political system.

Paolo Borsallino, one of the magistrates who are directing the Mafia investigation, acknowledges that the delay in attacking the 'Third Level' has made their task more difficult:

The parliamentary Anti-Mafia Commission report of ten years ago contained very precious information that unfortunately was ignored for a decade. We have found ourselves facing an enormous investigation precisely because of this ten-year void, which was caused by a variety of factors; this is one of the reasons why some of the accusations in the Anti-Mafia report have not been followed up.

But one has to be clear on this point: we mustn't deceive ourselves into thinking that only the magistrates can succeed in shedding light on the connivance between the political world and the Mafia. As long as certain political or business circles linked to the Mafia continue to find it easy to get support and protection in the political world in general, it will be extremely difficult for the magistrates to investigate. We hope, therefore, that this connivance, this protection which is provided for political reasons, will cease.

The Ciancimino case is ample proof of all this. In fact, when hard evidence enabled us to reach Ciancimino and order his arrest, he was in a state of political isolation such as he had never experienced before. Practically until the eve of his arrest, he had continued to enjoy protection in political circles. Once this stopped, it became much easier for us to find witnesses, evidence and the documents that nailed him.

Falcone, Borsallino and their colleagues still receive only sporadic support from Rome. They are under constant threat. Every morning Borsallino arrives for work at Palermo's central court, the Tribunale, a massive building in the Fascist style favoured during Mussolini's rule. He is driven straight to the entrance at breakneck speed in a bullet-proof car preceded by an armed escort wearing flak jackets and protective helmets. As they hurtle through the streets their guns are already drawn and aimed out of the car windows.

The guards are extremely young – partly because their reaction time is faster and partly because the pressure of bodyguard duty is immense, even though the shifts are short so as to reduce the strain which would otherwise slow their reflexes. Young men are also less likely to be married with families.

The strain on Borsallino and his fellow magistrates is hard to imagine. Their pride, courage and independence is a true testimony to the fierce qualities of the Sicilian character which have been so denigrated by the charade of principles paraded by the 'Men of Honour'.

After the arrest of Ciancimino, the magistrates struck again at the 'Third Level'. Two of Sicily's most prominent businessmen and well-known backers of the Christian Democrats were arrested — the Salvo cousins from Salemi. Although Buscetta originally denied that he knew anything about the Salvos, he did eventually admit that they were friends and, better still, that he had been the 'guest of honour' at one of their seaside villas at the end of 1980 when he was in hiding in Sicily. It was the evidence of collusion that the magistrates needed.

As with Ciancimino, rumours, reports and accusations had bounced off the Salvos for several years without affecting their business interests and political connections. They had built multi-million-dollar fortunes from the sinecures they held as Sicily's official tax collectors. The money had gone into construction, real estate, finance, agriculture and vineyards. Their wealth and power was fabulous and, like Ciancimino, they were untouchable. Yet the investigations set in motion by General Dalla Chiesa had not been in vain. They were supported by the work of the senior investigating magistrate in Palermo, Rocco Chinnici, whose official title was Consigliere Istruttore. In 1983 he had finished preparing a comprehensive indictment against Michele Greco and the leading members of the Corleonesi. It was also reported that arrest warrants against the Salvo cousins were imminent. His investigations were interrupted on the morning of 28 July 1983 as he emerged from his apartment block surrounded by the cordon of security guards who had been assigned to protect him. A car parked outside the apartment block was packed with 50 pounds of TNT. Triggered by a remote detonator, it blew up three bodyguards, the receptionist from the apartment and Chinnici himself. Little remained of their bodies and the surrounding cars were reduced to twisted scrap metal. Warrants for the murder were immediately served against Michele Greco and his brother Salvatore Greco, 'the Senator'. Although tried in his absence, Michele Greco was found guilty and then acquitted on appeal. Another trial appealing against the acquittal is to be held in Catania in early 1987. His lawyer is confident of another acquittal. For the other magistrates, particularly Falcone, who admired and worked closely with Chinnici, the brutal assassination was a devastating blow. They resolved in future to work even more closely as a team so as to reduce the vulnerability of any one magistrate and to carry on the work that Chinnici had been responsible for. They were given invaluable assistance within the year when Tommaso Buscetta began to detail his exhaustive list of friends and acquaintances, including those he had known as members of the 'Third Level', particularly the Salvos.

In the autumn of 1984 the testimony of their former house guest helped to precipitate the Salvos' downfall. On 12 November at 9.30 a.m. a heavily armed *carabinieri* patrol arrived at 3 Via Vittorio Veneto and took the lift up to the luxurious attic apartment of Ignazio Salvo. The door was opened by his wife, who told them that her husband had just left. After a quick search of the apartment they went down to the ground-floor office of SFIS, one of the Salvos' many financial companies. Ignazio Salvo, wearing a brown and green suit, a brown woollen tie and an ivory white shirt, and looking very much the suave Italian businessman, answered their call. The *carabinieri* asked him to accompany them. Salvo, known as 'The Diplomat' because of his unruffled appearance and his ability to smooth things over, said calmly, 'I would like to tell my wife.'

'She has already been told,' he was informed.

His diplomatic skills were no longer any use to him. From then on he did not say another word. He was taken to the *carabinieri* headquarters in the Via Carini, where he was presented with a warrant for his arrest and subjected to the indignity of being photographed for police records. More accustomed to scanning balance sheets detailing million-dollar investments, he read the warrant without emotion. He asked again to be allowed to talk to his wife and to have his personal belongings delivered.

At 11.30 a.m. Salvo emerged from the headquarters under heavy escort. He was guided through a gauntlet of photographers and reporters who besieged him with questions which went unanswered. Impassive, the richest financier in Sicily got into a waiting Alfetta and was driven off with the screaming sirens so beloved by Italian police drivers.

The same morning, his cousin Nino Salvo was arrested as he was getting into his BMW to go to work. Normally witty and talkative, he remained silent as he was taken to police headquarters and charged. At 3 p.m. the cousins were driven under armed guard to Punta Raisi airport and held in temporary custody at the small customs shed which stands on the edge of the runway. The airport was surrounded by armed *carabinieri*. Fifteen minutes later the Salvos boarded a DC9 and took off for Rome. On arrival they were taken to Rome's maximum security Rebibia prison – the same prison in which Tommaso Buscetta, their accuser, had made his extensive statements to Giovanni Falcone.

Thirty years of unchallenged financial and political power had been wiped out in six hours. Nino Salvo had once announced, 'We are the most important financial group in Sicily – our liquidity is unlimited.' It was a statement of fact rather than an idle boast. Now the empire had crumbled.

Under the new laws that had been passed in the wake of the assassination of General Dalla Chiesa, the magistrates were able to confiscate all the assets of accused *mafiosi*. The burden of proving that the assets were legitimate rested firmly on the accused. The state now claimed that the Salvos' financial empire had been built on the proceeds of criminal activities, that it had been financed with laundered money, mainly from the heroin trade. Their businesses were put in the hands of two official receivers.

The principal companies involved were Finanziaria Immobiliare SPA and Finanziaria Immobiliare, both investment companies. The first belonged to Nino Salvo and had been established in 1966. Its holdings included the beautiful 1200-acre Acate estate in Sicily's Ragusa province and the 520-acre estate of Misilbesi in the province of Agrigento. To finance the estates, Nino Salvo had used some of the income derived from Sicily's tax offices, together with substantial regional loans at favourable rates of interest. Acate supported a vineyard of 400,000 vines and a wine cooperative, and had built the region's first covered citrus grove. The other company, Finanziaria Immobiliare, was controlled by Ignazio Salvo. The assets included a 320-acre vineyard just outside Palermo, the Cannavata farm on the lake of Scanzano and other plots of land in the Trapani area.

One of the most impressive of the Salvos' companies was EnoSicilia. It comprised twenty-four wine producers' cooperatives and produced three million hecto-litres of new wine a year (approximately sixty-six million gallons). EnoSicilia accounted for a quarter of the total wine production of Sicily. The company had also benefited from a series of loans at favourable interest rates, in particular one for L50,000 million for the promotion of wine sales in countries such as the Soviet Union.

Only in Sicily, it would seem, could the tax office itself become a Mafia front. But that's where the Salvos' wealth began. They ran two tax-collecting companies called Satris and Sigert, which provided an almost inexhaustible source of income until the system of collection was transferred to a syndicate of banks. But by that time the Salvos' commercial conglomerate was already set up. Their interests included construction companies like Sedim, Semate (maritime and land services) and SIAP (Italian Society for Public Contracts). Among the registered shareholders were the Salvos' wives, children and son-in-law.

All of these companies went into the hands of the receivers, as did Nino Salvo's yacht, a Mercedes 280, a number of flats and plots of land in Trapani and their birthplace, Salemi.

Under Falcone's interrogation, the Salvos have offered the time-honoured excuse that, like all honest businessmen in Sicily, they could not avoid coming into contact with the Mafia and on occasion being forced to deal with them. 'Man of Honour in the Salemi family? No – I am a victim of the Mafia,' was Nino Salvo's first reply to Falcone's accusation.

Falcone also questioned the Salvos about a mysterious episode in their relations with the top *mafiosi* which revolved around the kidnapping of Nino Salvo's father-in-law, Luigi Corleo. This is what Nino Salvo had to say:

> Until 1975, that is until the kidnapping of my father-in-law, Luigi Corleo, I believed that I had established a peaceful, if uncomfortable, coexistence with the Mafia, believing wrongly that it would be all right if you behaved yourself and avoided problems with anybody.

But all this changed when his father-in-law was kidnapped:

> I decided to turn to Stefano Bontate, whose very high position in the Mafia was known to everyone – and for whom I had even done small favours in the past which had given me certain 'guarantees' in my vast circle of friends. Stefano Bontate gave me his word that he had nothing to do with the kidnapping, but that he would be interested in helping me. I had already received a telephone call in January 1976 which had asked me for a ransom of L5000 million.
>
> It was the intervention of Bontate that, after a series of discussions with the kidnappers, reduced the ransom to L2500 million. At least that is what Bontate told me and I can neither confirm nor deny that the boss was possibly involved in the kidnapping.

Salvo implied that Bontate had been responsible for his father-in-law's kidnapping. It is an accusation fiercely denied by Salvatore Contorno, Bontate's faithful lieutenant, who has said, 'It's easy to blame everything on the dead.' In fact the kidnapping was probably organized by the Corleonesi.

Nino Salvo told Falcone, 'I had to deliver the sum requested directly to Bontate, who told me that he had assumed the responsibility for delivering it directly to the kidnappers.' The ransom money was to be collected in Milan. An associate of Salvo's picked up the cash from the Commercial Bank of Milan and delivered it to Salvo's Palermo office in the Via Ariosto. Salvo then called Bontate and gave him the 2500 million at Villagrazia: 'Bontate was in the company of a big Mafia personality whose name I don't want to give because I'm afraid for the safety of my family.'

Despite Bontate's intervention, Luigi Corleo was never seen again. Salvo told Falcone, 'I found out from Stefano Bontate, after paying the ransom, that my father-in-law was no longer alive, but you have to keep a good face in bad fortune.'

The magistrates in Milan thought the ransom story might have been a ruse to export money from the country and thereby avoid Italy's strict currency controls. Salvo denied this and said that from that moment on he was 'obliged' to return favours to Bontate. He claimed that when Bontate approached him with a request to accommodate Tommaso Buscetta, he complied: 'I obviously had to.' Salvo denied ever having met Buscetta, despite the fact that Buscetta had lived for a time at one of the Salvos' seaside villas in Casteldaccia. Falcone and Borsallino did not believe him. They pointed out that he was on first-name terms with Buscetta and that the Salvo cousins had expressed the hope that Buscetta would return to Palermo in the middle of the Mafia war, after the murders of Bontate and Inzerillo.

Although the magistrates told Salvo that they had wiretaps to prove this, he refused to change his story. 'The truth is what I've said,' he insisted. 'Put me in front of Tommaso Buscetta. Yes, I want a meeting with my accuser.'

As for Ignazio Salvo: 'Tommaso Buscetta? And who is he?' he said disingenuously. 'I've never seen Buscetta and I never knew that he was a guest of Nino Salvo towards the end of 1980. I also don't know that my cousin ever gave over his villa to Stefano Bontate in 1980.'

He also denied all knowledge of Stefano Bontate: 'I don't know if my cousin, Nino, was a friend of Stefano Bontate or if he knew him. As far as I'm concerned, I can say that looking at the photos of Bontate in the papers after his death, it seemed to me that his face was vaguely familiar, but I couldn't say if I had seen him under some circumstances.'

'And Buscetta, have you ever met him?' asked the magistrates. 'From the statement of Tommaso Buscetta, it has come out that you and your cousin went to see him in the villa at Casteldaccia.'

'It's not true, it can't be true,' replied Ignazio Salvo. 'Talk to Buscetta again.'

Skilful interrogation by the magistrates uncovered a series of contradictions between the two cousins. They might have been good businessmen but they were not very good liars.

Among the wiretaps on the Salvos was one from Ignazio lo Presti's phone in Palermo. Lo Presti was the builder friend of Inzerillo, who in turn had introduced Lo Presti to Buscetta. They subsequently became close friends. Lo Presti's wife, Maria Corleo, was the first cousin of Nino Salvo's wife.

Soon after the murder of Inzerillo, Ignazio Salvo telephoned lo Presti several times, using the alias 'Giuseppe'. His explanation was that lo Presti owed him money and, since he thought the phone might be tapped, he used the alias to avoid embarrassment.

As for lo Presti, he disappeared in the summer of 1981, a victim of the '*lupara bianca*', a fate that had befallen many of the friends of Inzerillo and Bontate in the aftermath of their murders. His wife, Maria, remembers Buscetta as 'a man about fifty, tall and dark, without a beard or a moustache, rather corpulent and a flashy dresser'. He was using the name 'Roberto', and had come to the Lo Prestis' house with another man and stayed for dinner. Signora Lo Presti did not like them. One of the things that annoyed her about 'Roberto' was that all through dinner he talked constantly about making massive real-estate investments in Venezuela. He apparently asked her husband if he would be willing to move out there with his entire family. She also recalled an international telephone call she got from 'Roberto' later on, asking her husband to make a telephone appointment for the next day with someone called Santino. Maria had asked Ignazio, 'Who is this Santino?' 'The brother of Salvatore Inzerillo, the boss assassinated a month ago,' Lo Presti explained to his wife.

Unable to find Santino, Lo Presti took the call from Buscetta, telling him that 'Nino' had also disappeared. According to a statement made by Maria Corleo to Falcone, 'The Nino of whom my husband spoke on various calls is certainly Nino Salvo.'

The Salvos, through Bontate and Inzerillo, were dangerously associated with the losing faction. Their relations with Buscetta put them in an even more precarious position. All this would have been recognized by the Corleonesi, who probably arranged the disappearance of lo Presti. He had been too close to Inzerillo and was mediating between the Salvos and Buscetta. They, like Badalamenti, had been trying to persuade Buscetta to return to Palermo. The Salvos must have calculated that his influence would have been enough to guarantee them protection. In the event, they escaped the fate of the other victims of the Mafia war – not least because of the exalted position they occupied within the 'Third Level'.

One of the reasons the Grecos and the Corleonesi would have resisted attacking the Salvos was their tremendous political influence. They gave generously to the Christian Democratic Party and knew Salvatore Lima extremely well. They were the people who had given him a bullet-proof car as a present.

No doubt Lima was able to represent Sicily's best interests at the European Parliament and the Salvos' extensive agricultural holdings would in turn have benefited from the range of EEC Common Agricultural Policy statutes which have been so helpful to the winegrowers of Sicily. In addition, Lima's son, Marcello, secured a job with their tax collection company, Satris.

The Grecos would have been foolish not to realize that a direct blow against the Salvos could have rebounded on them very quickly. In any case, even if they wanted to bring Buscetta back to Sicily, the Salvos were too astute as businessmen to put all their money into such a high-risk venture.

On 19 December 1980, before the height of the Mafia war, Nino Salvo arranged a bank draft through the Banca Commerciale in favour of Salvatore "the Senator" Greco. The amount was L300 million. He later arranged a further loan and on both occasions front names were used to disguise the lender and the receiver.

If the loans were an insurance policy, they paid off.

The investigation into the Mafia connections of the Salvos is continuing. That they were at the centre of the different worlds of high finance, organized crime and political power is indisputable. The fact that they survived unscathed and unchallenged for so long is testimony enough to their power and influence.

The Salvos were also accused of involvement in the murder of Chinnici. The cousins dismissed the allegations. They were, they said, victims of a political conspiracy coordinated by the Italian Communist Party.

At the end of 1985 Nino Salvo died of cancer in a clinic in Switzerland. His cousin still awaits trial.

14

The Pizza Trail

Assistant US attorney Louis Freeh asked me numerous times, 'Do we want the heroin or do we want Badalamenti?' I said, 'Louis, anybody can get heroin. Get a shot at Badalamenti.'

Mike Fahy, US customs special agent

Late one night in December 1984 at an American Air Force base near New York City a plane from Madrid touched down. It carried the man who had once been the '*capo di tutti capi*' of the Sicilian Mafia, Gaetano Badalamenti. It was nine months since Badalamenti and his nephew, Pietro Alfano, had been arrested in Madrid – months in which the men who now waited at the Air Force base had had plenty of time to anticipate the moment when the man they regarded as the biggest heroin trafficker in the world would arrive on American soil to stand trial for his actions. Among the welcoming party was Mike Fahy, special agent with the US customs service, a man who had devoted a large part of his professional life to the fight against drug traffic and Badalamenti in particular. He was there to enjoy the most important arrest of his career.

That night he had his first opportunity to talk to Badalamenti. What was the special agent's reaction when he met the man he had been chasing for so long?

'He scared the shit out of me.'

Mike Fahy is not the kind of man who scares easily. In his late thirties, dark-haired and six foot tall, he has that well-fed look of the fit American male. His office is in the World Trade Center at the bottom of Manhattan Island, flanked by the Hudson and the East River. His expertise is in smuggling and everywhere he looks he sees new ways of bringing illicit cargo into New York and taking it out. Hundreds of craft ply the waterways around the city. Light aircraft, civil airliners and helicopters fly to and fro constantly. Fahy says that New York City is probably the hardest place in the world to do surveillance; he could add that it's probably the hardest border to police for narcotics and money smuggling.

On 21 September 1971, thirteen years before Badalamenti's arrest, Mike Fahy was at the New York docks. He was part of a team of customs agents waiting for the Italian cruise ship *Raffaello* to dock. Some of the agents were responsible for the routine processing of passengers, but sixteen of them, including Fahy, were waiting to search for something far more serious — a large shipment of heroin.

It was Fahy who found it — hidden in the door of a 1970 Ford Galaxy. He had tried the left rear window and found that it would not wind down. When he looked into the gap between the door and the window he saw something white. Concealed in the door and under the rear seat were 169 packages containing eighty-two kilos of 99 per cent pure heroin. It was one of the biggest hauls the US customs have ever made.

For Fahy, who was on release to customs while completing a course at Boston University, it was a great coup. In his office there is an old photograph which tells the story. It shows a much younger Fahy squatting beside the rear panel of the car. He says, 'Unfortunately, any monkey could have found it, let's be honest with you. I just happened to get lucky and be there at the time.' But the look of satisfaction in the photograph is still on his face today as he considers how he finally caught up with the Sicilians who took over the drug trade from the traffickers of the French Connection.

'That particular car was Badalamenti's car,' says Fahy. 'It took fourteen years to find out where it was going.'

It was Buscetta who eventually confirmed the car's owner and destination. In his 1985 debriefing by DEA agents, he recalled that when he was in prison with Badalamenti, shortly after his first extradition from Brazil in 1972, he heard that Badalamenti had organized the car, the shipment and distribution of the drugs in New York.

Having found the heroin, the US customs made what they call a 'controlled delivery'. With the help of the courier who had come over with the car, whom they had little difficulty in persuading to change sides, they arrested a number of New York *mafiosi*.

The man who was to collect the heroin-laden car was Frank Rappa, a relative of Carlo Gambino. For the next forty-eight hours Rappa was trailed closely. Driving a Buick, he followed the Ford to a rest area near Deer Park Avenue where the cars were to be switched. Before Rappa had a chance to take the Ford he found himself surrounded by police and customs agents. One agent later recalled:

> It was wild. There we were in this rest area, about ten of us, with this guy in handcuffs saying it's all a mistake. The helicopter is hovering overhead, and up comes this Long Island Parkway cop with his car lights flashing, and our panel truck right behind him. The guys in the truck had gotten lost and got onto the parkway by mistake. Trucks aren't allowed there so this cop had pulled them over to give them a ticket. Now he's giving them an escort to the scene. Everybody is slowing down to see what's happening. The traffic is backed up for miles!

Despite the chaos it was a successful operation, although they were unable to track the men at the top who had financed the shipment. That Ford and its load was only the beginning of a trail that finally ended in Courtroom 506 in October 1985.

The most significant aspect of the seizure was the mass of evidence it yielded on many of the *mafiosi* who a decade later would emerge as the principal figures in the Pizza Connection. It produced clues which pointed to Badalamenti in Sicily and several of his relatives in the Detroit area, though there was not enough evidence to arrest them. US customs also came across a number of Italians all connected by the pizza business. The common denominators were Louis and Michael Piancone.

Louis Piancone was the founder and president of Roma Foods of South Plainfields, New Jersey. He loaned substantial start-up money for pizza shops in Pennsylvania and New Jersey. Roma was the exclusive East Coast distributor for Grande Cheese Company, a Wisconsin firm linked to Joe Bonanno. Louis Piancone ran his business in partnership with his brother Michael until 1967, when Michael went independent. An associate of the Gambino family, Michael Piancone became a major pizza shop supplier and franchiser in Pennsylvania and New Jersey. Some of his pizzerias employed illegal immigrants from Sicily, many of whom were undoubtedly brought over the Canadian border by the organization in which Zippo and Buscetta had been implicated. Several Piancone Pizza Palaces were operated by the Sollena brothers, suspected heroin traffickers who were also Gambino family associates and – as police would find out later – nephews of Badalamenti. Another was run by Buscetta's friend, Filippo Casamento, who in 1973 would use it as a front for narcotics smuggling. Frank Rappa also ran a Piancone Pizza Palace.

In 1972 the US government, alarmed that America was becoming the most attractive market in the world for drugs, formed the Drug Enforcement Administration. The control and prevention of narcotics abuse was taken out of the hands of US customs, although they would still have responsibility for seizures at airports, ports and borders. Mike Fahy and his colleagues turned their attention to the illicit movement of the large sums of cash associated with the drugs trade. It was a field that at first sight lacked the excitement and publicity of major seizures, but ultimately would provide the evidence to close in on the men at the top. It might be more glamorous to discover bags of heroin hidden in a car, but it was highly unlikely that any major drug baron would be sitting in the front seat.

'What we found,' says Mike Fahy, 'is that the main organizers of an enterprise were closer to the money than they were to the narcotics.'

The next time Mike Fahy came across Badalamenti was in 1978, after the police arrested a woman called Joanne Adiego in Marlton, New Jersey, on a charge of carrying counterfeit currency. When they searched her they found $18,000 in real money in her handbag and another $33,000 in her car. She was also carrying three cashiers' cheques, which are similar to British bankers' drafts. Two were for $9000 and the other was for $7000. Further investigation revealed that Joanne Adiego, her boyfriend Salvatore Sollena and his brother Matteo Sollena had previously bought forty-eight cashiers' cheques for a total of $330,000. The significance of this was not lost on the FBI and customs. Cashiers' cheques for less than $10,000 do not have to be reported by the bank. The implication was clear – the cashiers' cheques were being used to launder one-third of a million dollars, doubtless obtained from drug dealing. Investigation of the Sollena brothers connected them with Badalamenti and the Ford Galaxy shipment of 1971. The $330,000 had been transferred to the account of a Francesco Giglia in a Palermo bank. Signor Giglia did not exist. The police were convinced that the money had been sent to a consortium of Palermo-based heroin dealers.

Their next discovery came in 1979, when they learnt that over the past two years more than $4 million had been shipped from New Jersey to Palermo. The Italian police obtained documents revealing that $1 million alone had been sent by Frank Castronovo, a small-time pizza man in New York. The money was used by Salvatore Inzerillo for a property deal.

Then came Boris Giuliano's interception of the suitcase containing $497,000 at Punta Raisi airport in June 1979. This was the shipment wrapped in pizza aprons that were traced to Salvatore Sollena's New Jersey pizzeria. The Pizza Connection was beginning to take shape.

By 1980 Fahy had built up an intelligence database that became invaluable. Today he describes it as 'my bible for the last five years'. Much of the later information confirmed the original intelligence gained from the *Raffaello* seizure. In Fahy's 'bible' were the names of the men who were taking over the narcotics smuggling industry and turning it into a multi-billion-dollar business. Ultimately it would be the dollar trail, not the deadly white powder, that would be traced around the world and lead to the downfall of the Sicilians.

It was decided at the beginning of 1980 to combine the resources of the DEA, the US customs, the FBI and various police forces. Their investigation into the Pizza Connection uncovered for the first time the full extent of Sicilian Mafia control of the heroin trade on the East Coast of the United States. It also gave a new insight into the relationship between the Mafia in Sicily and America. It was a relationship that revolved entirely around the heroin trade. The Sicilians had the supply and the Americans had the demand. Although many of the people involved were brought together by Mafia connections, a good many of them were also related within their own families and, almost without exception, they were Sicilian. Buscetta's confessions contributed invaluable information about the patterns of operation of the heroin trade across the Atlantic. While the Sicilian and American Mafia worked together, the management of the enterprise fell largely to Sicilian immigrants who lived in America.

By the beginning of 1980 Sicily had become the world's major centre for the refining of heroin and the major supplier to the world's largest market, the United States. As Buscetta confirmed to Giovanni Falcone, the production of heroin from morphine base and its subsequent sale to the United States was now the principal source of income for the Sicilian Mafia. And an increasing amount was being sold for domestic consumption in Italy. In the past, the Mafia had a self-imposed ban on pushing the drug in their own country, but the fantastic profits of the trade soon undermined whatever shaky principles the 'Honoured Society' might once have had.

The uninterrupted supply required by the New York operators depended on their close connections with the leading Mafia families of Sicily. In particular they relied on the Mafia's major importers of morphine base, which was refined in laboratories either in Sicily or Milan.

In New York the two families with the closest blood ties to Sicily, the Gambino and Bonanno families, were also the most active in the heroin trade. In the case of the Gambino family, relatives from Sicily settled in New York in the late seventies to receive shipments from Rosario Spatola and Salvatore Inzerillo, who were also related to the Gambinos. Following the murder of Inzerillo by the Corleonesi in 1981 and the arrest of Spatola and the Gambinos, the New York Connection was dominated by the Bonanno family. At the top was Sal 'the Baker' Catalano, who headed what amounted to a Sicilian subsidiary operating in New York with the approval of the American Mafia. Although Catalano was a high-ranking member of a New York family, he was also a Sicilian immigrant, and could not have survived as a top organizer in the narcotics trade in New York City without the permission of his own family boss, Phil 'Rusty' Rastelli. He also needed the tacit agreement of the ruling Commission, made up of the heads of the five New York families – although Rastelli's membership was in dispute due to his family's heavy involvement in the 'junk business'.

With the loyal assistance of his broad-shouldered lieutenant, Giuseppe Ganci, whose size had earned him the nicknames 'the Fat One' and 'the Buffalo', Catalano presided over the billion-dollar business from his humble bakery in New York City. According to one of the investigators who watched his rise to the top, his bakery was one of the finest in Queens. A few blocks away was the Al Dente pizzeria, a less salubrious establishment which was jointly operated by Catalano and Ganci. It was one of the many businesses acquired by the pizza men and used as fronts for their heroin deals. From the payphone outside on the pavement calls would be made and received from all over the world to facilitate the payment and delivery of hundreds of kilos of high-purity heroin.

Those payphone calls were just a few of the thousands of calls meticulously logged by the FBI. The pizza men were obviously worried that their home and business phones were tapped, as indeed they were. Yet, astonishingly, they disclosed the numbers of the payphones they intended to use on their own tapped phones. The FBI simply tapped the payphones too.

The FBI listened for over three years to the biggest series of wiretaps ever instituted in a single investigation. All the conversations were in code. On the face of it the Catalano ring was running one of the most diverse and lucrative alternative businesses ever devised by man. They were dealing in 'shirts', '100% cotton shirts', '20% acrylic shirts', 'shoes', 'plants', 'base material', 'tomatoes', 'cheese', 'sardines', 'ovens' and 'pants', among many other commodities. Even more surprising, these goods were normally priced in a few dollars or even in cents.

If they were genuine business calls, how did these modest goods realize such staggering sums of money? Could even a successful trade in sardines give you such an enormous financial problem that you had to take suitcases stuffed with money to several major banks and ship your cash out to foreign countries? Common sense said 'no', though the FBI had to admit that, as most of the Sicilians were indeed involved in the pizza business in America, some of their conversations must inevitably be about legitimate transactions. After months of intercepts they began to sense when heroin deals were about to be made. The raw intelligence from the wiretaps was backed up by twenty-four-hour surveillance on the pizza men's movements. The more coded their conversations and the more clandestine their movements, the more likely it was that they were going to arrange a transaction involving a large amount of heroin or money or often both at once.

As the transcripts mounted up and the intelligence was pooled, reviewed and 'massaged', the FBI, DEA and US customs realized that Gaetano Badalamenti was one of the principal suppliers. He appeared to be operating out of South America. The man in charge of American sales and distribution, who also kept a distinctly low profile, was the swarthy baker from Queens. When his profile was observed he had a powerful, frightening presence. He did not seem like your friendly neighbourhood baker.

Despite the vast turnover of his empire, Catalano lived un-ostentatiously. A square face, close-cropped dark hair, narrow eyes and a bull-like neck give him an imposing physique which compensates for his lack of height. Although he dressed and behaved in a manner befitting the powerful Sicilian 'Man of Honour' that he was, his subdued lifestyle was in marked contrast to that of many of his American counterparts, the brash New York *mafiosi* with limited intelligence and unlimited money, who liked to be seen driving fast cars in the company of fast women.

Salvatore Catalano was in his mid-forties at the height of the Pizza Connection. He had become a permanent US resident in 1966 and lived in an unimposing suburban house in Queens, an area of low-key respectability. The house itself was registered in the name of his sister Vita and his brother Domenico Catalano. Salvatore Catalano paid them $300 a month rent. This arrangement would be very useful if anyone tried to confiscate the property under American law. For a high-ranking *mafioso*, Catalano also had the advantage of a remarkably clean record – one conviction for a firearms offence in 1975. According to his defence lawyer, he is, of course, an exemplary citizen, whose life has been a testament to the work ethic of the immigrant. He began his life of honest toil working for his brother Domenico as the manager of the Coloseo Gift Shoppe on Knickerbocker Avenue in Brooklyn. From there he moved on to the Jamaica Pizza Corporation in Queens. After that he founded the Catalano Brothers bakery with his brothers Domenico and Vito and his sister Vita, later expanding through the purchase of the Al Dente pizzeria across the road in partnership with Giuseppe Ganci.

Catalano was a senior member of the Bonanno family, but most of his other associates, including Ganci, were 'made' members of families in Sicily. He was the principal link between the Cosa Nostra in both countries, and the fact that he and his lieutenants were Sicilians was significant. The operation was essentially controlled by the Sicilian rather than the American Mafia. The New York Commission had approved the operation, although they would pay lip service to the traditional Mafia disclaimers about never being involved in something as dishonourable as the narcotics trade. They were elderly men who looked back with nostalgia to the traditions of their ancestors in Sicily, but the members of their own families were mostly second- or third- generation Italian—Americans who were uninterested in or even scornful of the old values. A significant cultural shift had taken place, and some bosses had become anxious that the traditions of the 'Honoured Society' were being degraded by the brasher values of the modern American school of gangsterism. Some had gone so far as to recruit illegal immigrants from Sicily in an attempt to redress the balance and renew the old values.

Catalano had maintained close contact with the Cinisi family, headed by Nino Badalamenti and including among its members a number of Badalamenti relatives. Their home town, Cinisi, is a small, desolate seaside village to the east of Palermo which is dominated by a spectacular sheer cliff which rises into mist and clouds. At weekends the village is a restless mass of Sicilians strolling up the main streets, boys and girls eyeing each other, families out for gossip and street talk and old men drinking in darkened rooms. The Badalamentis have lived in Cinisi for generations – one of the main streets bears their name. Traditionally, the Cinisi family has jurisdiction over Punta Raisi airport, a few kilometres away from the town. Control of the airport helped Badalamenti to control the heroin traffic. Some of his relatives emigrated to the Mid-West of America in the sixties, and over the next twenty years acted as his 'point men' for the distribution of heroin. They in turn would liaise between Badalamenti and Catalano in New York.

By the end of 1982 the Corleonesi had consolidated their victory in the Mafia war, successfully murdering many of Badalamenti's relatives, including Nino Badalamenti himself. Nevertheless, Gaetano Badalamenti continued to organize narcotics deals for the Pizza Connection even though there was a contract on his life.

A second family Catalano knew well was the Borgetto family. Its members included Salvatore Lamberti, a Catalano associate and 'businessman' who was running a company in New York with the appropriate title Pronto Interior Demolition, and Giuseppe Soresi, who acted as the contact man between the heroin laboratories of Sicily and Milan and the New York customers headed by Catalano.

The third family Catalano worked with was San Giuseppe Iato, headed by Antonio Salamone, the man who had been a tentative ally of Inzerillo and Bontate before they were both murdered. Salamone had moved at the same time as Buscetta to Brazil, where they had continued to see a lot of each other. Other members included Giuseppe Ganci and Alfredo Bono, Giuseppe Bono's brother.

The fourth and most important family was the Bolognetta, headed by Giuseppe Bono, now identified by Buscetta as the principal supplier of heroin to the United States. Bono was a 'Man of Honour' of great wealth and prestige. He presided over considerable investments in Milan, Palermo and New York. Dressed in a dark suit and wearing glasses, he looked every inch the powerful businessman. As a 'Man of Honour' he received enormous deference from his underlings — even his brother, Alfredo, felt humbled in his presence, and would kiss his hand as a mark of respect.

In the autumn of 1980, the friends, relatives and associates of the American–Sicilian heroin trade were united, almost in their entirety, by a family celebration. The occasion was the magnificent wedding reception held for Giuseppe Bono and his bride at New York's luxurious Hotel Pierre. Tables were laden with a plentiful supply of champagne and the finest Italian food that New York could offer, an orchestra serenaded the guests and huge black limousines disgorged dark-suited guests under the hotel's elegant striped canopy. It made the wedding scene in the film *The Godfather* seem like a small-town affair.

It was also a red-letter day for the FBI. Car numbers were taken and a guest list drawn up which confirmed Giuseppe Bono's status as a high-ranking *mafioso*, a man of great importance not only in Sicily but also in New York, New Jersey and Canada. Among the guests of honour were Salvatore Catalano;

Giuseppe Ganci; Alfredo Bono; Gaetano 'Tommy' Mazzara, one of Catalano's associates; Nick Rizzutto, the leader of the Sicilian faction in the Cotroni family; Michel Pozza, financial adviser to the Cotroni family and one of the principal money-launderers for the Mafia in Sicily, notably through his connections with Vito Ciancimino; Filippo Casamento, owner of Eagle Cheese and a friend of Buscetta; Salvatore Inzerillo (who would be assassinated by the Corleonesi in 1981); Pietro Inzerillo, a receiver in America for much of the heroin sent by his brother from Sicily (he was later found murdered in the boot of a car in New Jersey); Tom Gambino and Erasmo Gambino, both relatives of the late Carlo Gambino, former 'boss of all bosses' in America.

Also at the reception were Antonio Virgilio and Luigi Monti, the two principal Mafia financiers from Milan who had invested the Mafia's heroin profits in some of the city's finest hotels. They had also acquired the exclusive Hotel Majestic in Rome's Via Veneto, the city's equivalent of Fifth Avenue.

Most of these rich and 'respectable' New York businessmen were about to have their worlds turned upside down.

The first detailed checks on Catalano and his lieutenant, Ganci, were pen register devices, which allowed the FBI to record the telephone numbers the men phoned though not to record the conversations. The people Catalano and Ganci were talking to were traced and watched. When the DEA ran the names through the computer, several of the suspects were found to have convictions for drug trafficking. At that point the FBI had enough evidence to apply to a judge for a Title Three Affidavit, the official name for an authorized wiretap. They settled down to listen to Ganci's calls. From then on the FBI and the other authorities seemed to be omniscient. Every time a telephone rang, they were listening; every time a car drove off, they would follow; every time a bag or suitcase changed hands, they were watching.

At the same time another investigation, parallel but unconnected, was going on in Philadelphia. Frank Storey, one of the FBI's supervising officers, tells what happened:

About two or three months into the Title Three surveillance, there was an investigation down in Philadelphia being conducted by FBI/DEA which did not directly relate to the New York investigation. But we had a person down there named Dominic Mannino, who ran a pizzeria on Roosevelt Boulevard in Philadelphia. A DEA undercover agent had been talking with Mannino about other related things, and one day he asked him if he knew where he could purchase heroin, he wanted to buy some heroin. It was a kind of flyer. He had no idea that this pizza operator had any kind of contacts at all. He was involved with some drug activity, but it was at a low level. It was not heroin. Mannino said 'Yes' – he knew a person in New York that he could secure heroin from and sell it to the undercover agent. The next day Mannino contacted Ganci – and of course we [the agents in New York] were listening – and asked Ganci for some heroin that he wanted to sell. We immediately alerted our Philadelphia office, 'Who was Dominic Mannino, etc.?' – and they told us they had him under investigation.

It was an extraordinary coincidence. For the first time the investigating team were able to prove that Ganci did indeed have heroin for sale. Mannino came up to New York, collected the heroin and paid Ganci the money that the undercover agent had given him. All along the way he was under surveillance. With this solid evidence, the FBI felt confident enough to continue an investigation that was becoming very expensive in terms of time, manpower and resources. According to Storey, Mannino's 'buy' was a 'key break in the case'.

Another undercover operation was to prove equally significant. Once again the location was Philadelphia.

In May 1983 an undercover DEA agent established a business relationship with Benito Zito, another heroin dealer. The agent was introduced to Zito by a person the records describe as 'a confidential source of the DEA'. Such was Zito's trust that on one occasion he joked, 'If the people who supply me ever suspected that I had dealt with a federal agent, they would snuff me.' Ironically, he never suspected that the man he was talking to was exactly that.

In June the agent set up a deal with Zito. On 18 June the wire-tap on Ganci's phone recorded a call from Zito saying that he was ready to 'close the contract', and two days later Zito arrived in New York and met Ganci, Frank Castronovo, Gaetano Mazzara, Salvatore Mazzurco and Salvatore Lamberti.

Mazzara and Castronovo ran the Roma restaurant in Menlo Park, New Jersey. Mazzurco and Lamberti were in the demolition business – with Lamberti's brother Giuseppe they ran Pronto Interior Demolition in a back-street area of Queens. The company had its own fleet of trucks, each with the company's name on its side in blue and white. One of its activities was garbage collection, an enterprise that was virtually controlled by organized crime.

On 27 June Zito told the DEA agent that the deal was on, but that he needed the money up-front – $110,000 for half a kilo. On the telephone Ganci told Zito to give him a day's warning before coming to collect the goods. He also said he should take a look at 'the lease for the pizzeria'. He went on to say that the 'pizzeria is "good"', meaning that the quality of the heroin was high.

The next day Zito tried to telephone Ganci again but he was out. He spoke to Ganci's wife instead, who gave him the number for the Al Dente pizzeria. Zito eventually got through and said, 'I've got the package.' The DEA agent had paid him.

Ganci's next move provided the listeners from the FBI, DEA and the US customs with valuable information about his associates. He made several calls in an attempt to reach Frank Castronovo. The investigators knew from their records that Castronovo had been involved in siphoning heroin money from America to Sicily. That money was payment to the Inzerillo family for one of their heroin consignments which had arrived in New York a few years earlier. Ganci was also desperately anxious to get in touch with Mazzara, Castronovo's partner.

He could not reach him either. Ganci rang Zito back and said, 'I can't get hold of anyone!'

He told a disappointed Zito that he would call him again.

Later that evening, after visiting Catalano, Ganci telephoned Zito again and confirmed that there would be no deal that night. Zito, who had been by the phone all day, anxious to complete the deal as he was holding over $100,000 in cash, was becoming just a touch impatient: 'I was very available tonight,' he complained. 'I was ready to come down.'

He offered to come down later that night, but Ganci assured him that there was no chance of the deal coming together. Later Ganci was observed in the company of Cesare Bonventre, a member of the Bonanno family and one of Catalano's Sicilian crew. Bonventre was a flash young Sicilian–American who drove a black Ferrari. He was looking for promotion in the Bonanno family and had served his apprenticeship as Carmine Galante's bodyguard until Galante was gunned down in a Brooklyn restaurant. (Bonventre later became overambitious. His body was discovered chopped into small pieces inside a fifty-five-gallon oil drum.) Ganci went over to the café that Bonventre ran called Café Cesare. They discussed the Zito deal – Ganci was probably asking him if he could supply the half-kilo. Bonventre was unable to help.

The next morning, 29 June 1983, Ganci drove over to Catalano's bakery in Queens and once again telephoned Castronovo. He was still not at home. He had better luck with Mazzara, whom he now managed to reach at the Roma restaurant. Ganci told him that he was at home but had 'to go again to do another thing'. Mazzara agreed that Ganci had 'things to do at the pizzeria', and urged Ganci to 'do it first, this way you have time to go to work'. Ganci asked Mazzara to come with him as he had 'to straighten this out here'.

At lunchtime Mazzara arrived at Ganci's house. Although he did not know it, he was still being watched by the FBI. He went into the house and then came out to his car and took a rolled-up brown package from the passenger side. He took the package into Ganci's house and emerged without it a short while later.

The heroin had been delivered. Early that afternoon Zito called Ganci and arranged to drive to New York. Ganci then left for Catalano's house.

When Zito arrived at Ganci's house in Queens nearly three hours later, he was clutching a brown paper bag. Ganci came out to meet him and they chatted together by the garage. They then exchanged packages, Ganci handing over the package that Mazzara had delivered to him earlier that day. That evening, when he arrived back in Philadelphia, Zito arranged to meet his customer. He handed over the half-kilo to the DEA agent. When the DEA chemists checked it, it was found to be 'of very high purity'. Back in New York Mazzurco, a small, grey-haired middle-aged man with a ready smile, arrived for a meeting with Ganci. To the observation team it looked as if Mazzurco had come to collect the money Zito had given Ganci for the heroin.

Two weeks later the DEA agent in Philadelphia received authorization to make another undercover buy – this time the deal would be for a whole kilo. The DEA hoped that it might lead them to other suppliers associated with Catalano and his group. Zito – who referred to the undercover agent as 'the American with money' – went through the same procedure, although this time there was a lot more cash involved. He told him that his source in New York required a few days' notice before he could get the deal together. Zito explained that he was going to have to charge 'the American' $5000 for his service. In fact, Zito bought the kilo from his New York suppliers for $215,000 and charged the agent $245,000. On 3 August 1983, when the deal finally came together, Zito would make $30,000 – a substantial commission for a day's work. Zito felt no compunction about ripping off the American. If he had been a fellow Sicilian, Zito would have thought twice. When he handed over the parcel containing the heroin to the DEA man, he joked, 'Hope you enjoy the shirts!' The agent pretended to look puzzled and Zito, much to his delight, explained that they used the word 'shirts' as a code word for heroin. It was further confirmation for the diligent interpreters of the conversations picked up by FBI wiretaps.

When the DEA analysed the package in their laboratory they discovered that it was 82 per cent pure. The high quality showed that the New York distributors were obtaining their supplies directly from the laboratories in Italy. The DEA ran regular tests on heroin seized from street pushers and they knew that by the time the drug reached the street-corner salesmen, who were usually addicts themselves, the purity level was reduced on average to 3 or 4 per cent – the rest would be milk powder or quinine or some other substance used to dilute or 'cut' the drug and increase the seller's profits. The heroin would go through four or five different dealers before it reached the street, and each one would cut it along the way, hence the massive price differential between the wholesale and retail prices. The one kilo which had cost Zito $215,000 would eventually be worth anything between two and five million, depending on how many hands it had passed through. Heroin between 80 and 90 per cent purity indicated, almost without exception, that the buyer was very close to a laboratory source.

These undercover deals in Philadelphia were crucial to the investigation. They confirmed the customs agents' belief that the millions of dollars being laundered were related to heroin. The telephone calls and meetings watched by the surveillance teams identified the key members of the Pizza Connection, and the involvement of Zito and Mannino showed that the enterprise was not just confined to New York. The structure resembled a pyramid, with more people becoming involved in an increasingly minor respect towards the bottom of the triangle. At its pinnacle was the swarthy baker, Catalano, who took great care not to be seen with parcels of heroin or dollar bills in his hands. Throughout their surveillance and telephone intercepts, the agents picked up least information about the man they knew was the most important. It was one of the Mafia's methods of operation: the more important you are, the less exposed you become to the day-to-day operations you ultimately control. The man at the top invariably runs the least risk and reaps the greatest reward. It is one of the reasons why, until very recently, the highest-ranking members of the Mafia in New York have been so successful in keeping out of prison.

Significantly, Catalano himself was seldom heard on the telephone; most of his instructions were communicated verbally to Ganci. As Catalano's lieutenant, Ganci's principal function was to make the dozens of payphone calls from New York to co-conspirators in the United States and Mafia suppliers overseas. When problems arose Catalano would call a 'sit-down', a meeting of the pizza men, to resolve them.

One of the problems was Ganci's health. Standing on cold street corners in the New York winter was damaging his already weak lungs. As his health began to deteriorate, he was forced to delegate some of the calls to Giuseppe and Salvatore Lamberti, who in turn were assisted by the diminutive Mazzurco. Every transaction involved many telephone calls, usually from payphones. They used codes as a security precaution to refer to individual payphones in their network. Every call the leg-men made involved the FBI, US customs and the DEA in hours spent tracing and monitoring and then translating the Sicilian dialect into something which even in English was almost incomprehensible. One of Buscetta's contributions to the preparation for the trial was to help decipher the weird language used to negotiate the heroin deals. It was a tedious, expensive and time-consuming task; the Mafia were constantly on the phone, partly because the nature of their business demanded a lot of organization, made even more complex by their inability to speak openly, and partly because, being Sicilians, they loved to talk. A log from the FBI's records (opposite) showed the amount of work created for investigators in just a few hours.

DATE	TIME (Central Standard Time)	FROM	TO
11/12/83	10.14 p.m.	[815] 732 2774 Pietro Alfano	[608] 868 4872 Emmanuele Palazzolo
12/12/83	6.32 a.m.	[608] 868 4295 Palazzolo	[039] 91 66415 (Sicily)
12/12/83	6.35 a.m.	[608] 868 4295 Palazzolo	[039] 91 665162 (Sicily)
12/12/83	6.59 a.m.	[608] 868 4295 Palazzolo	[815] 732 2774 Alfano
12/12/83	7.04 a.m.	[608] 868 4295 Palazzolo	[815] 732 2774 Alfano
12/12/83	1.10 p.m.	[608] 868 4295 Palazzolo	[212] 389 8200 Pronto Interior Demolition

The law enforcement agencies were now committing massive resources to the Pizza Connection. One critical factor was a new agreement between the FBI and the DEA to cooperate in major narcotics cases – previously the Bureau did not have any jurisdiction over narcotics investigations. As the result of an agreement worked out by former US Attorney General William French-Smith in 1981 and 1982, the full resources of the FBI became available in the fight against drugs for the first time. The FBI's great strength is physical and electronic surveillance. It began the biggest operation it had ever undertaken. More than 1000 telephone calls were intercepted, monitored, transcribed and translated and at least 100 surveillance operations were carried out in Brooklyn, Queens, Manhattan, Newark and Philadelphia. Often the surveillance would continue in other cities and other countries. The combination of FBI involvement and the 1982

Mutual Assistance Treaty between the Italian and United States governments gave the investigation impetus and a spirit of unprecedented cooperation. After four years, in April 1984, it would culminate in a devastating indictment of organized crime and drug trafficking and result in one of the most complex conspiracy trials ever to come before a United States jury.

15

Black Money

It is the most significant case involving heroin trafficking by traditional organized crime that has ever been developed by the government. The five-year total importation is at least 1650 pounds of heroin – 330 pounds of heroin a year for the past five years. Its street level value is $1650 million.

William French-Smith,
United States Attorney General,
9 April 1984

If the hundreds of pages of Sicilian dialogue intercepted by the FBI told a cryptic story, the billion-dollar deposits made by the world's largest heroin distribution ring spoke volumes. Louis Freeh, the former FBI agent who was the assistant US attorney coordinating the investigation, was in no doubt about the importance of the money trail. 'Follow the money' had become the motto and the tactic seemed to be paying off. The trail spread all over the world.

It was the sheer scale of the profits that caused the pizza men problems. The more you examine the Pizza Connection case, the more obvious it becomes that they were the victims of their own criminal success. Because their commodity was heroin and other proscribed drugs, they were forced to deal in cash. Just as they had to operate on payphones, so they had to handle vast sums of money in the small-denomination bills which originally came from the junkie on the street corner. In the early days the procedure was relatively simple. They would pack a couple of suitcases with half a million dollars and take them to Switzerland. Soon, however, they had too much cash to handle. In 1980 they recruited a man called Salvatore Amendolito whose job it was to go to Castronovo's pizzeria each week, meet Giuseppe Ganci and walk out lugging bags or boxes filled with money. At first Amendolito would run round the banks of New York exchanging the dollar bills for cashiers' cheques in the names of false payees in amounts under $10,000. The money would then be sent to Switzerland. This method was also defeated by the piles of small-denomination bills. As the prosecution would later remark in their opening address to the jury in Federal Courtroom 506, 'The conspirators were making so much money that there weren't enough banks in New York or hours in the day for Amendolito to be able to change all the cash he had to launder.'

Towards the end of 1980 the pizza men asked him to move $9 million. It was more than one man could handle. But Amendolito was nothing if not resourceful. He began to charter private jets from New York companies to freight the money to Bermuda, the offshore tax haven renowned for its discretion. The planes were met by security vans from the Bank of Butterfield, the British colony's most prestigious bank. Bags and cases crammed full of dollar bills were driven into town and unloaded directly into the bank vaults. Once deposited in Bermuda, the money would be wired to accounts in Switzerland.

But the problem of sheer volume persisted. In New York, Amendolito hired a man called Philip Matassa just to carry the cash from Castronovo's restaurant to Ganci's house in Queens. Yet even with Matassa's help the flood of dollars was still overwhelming. So they tried a new tack. They simply shifted the money direct to Switzerland in suitcases. They organized what the Swiss call a 'transport'. A team of couriers would do nothing but fly to America, pick up two suitcases from Ganci or his aides and fly right back to Switzerland. They were lucky if they got to stay in the Sheraton Hotel for one night.

The New York–Zurich crossing was made with astonishing frequency, but there was still too much money for them to cope with. To make matters worse, it became obvious that there was a degree of 'leakage'. With so much money around it was inevitable that someone would dip their fingers in the till. At one point a whole suitcase went missing. This motivated Ganci to fire Amendolito and hire a new team. Now the pizza men decided to move their money using the traditional methods employed by international corporations. They would draw on the services of the major financial institutions.

The art deco façade of the Waldorf Astoria Hotel at 301 Park Avenue symbolizes its status as one of the most distinguished buildings in Manhattan. The gold lettering of the hotel's name reflects style and wealth. The large American flag flying over the main entrance is a reminder of the renowned guests who have passed through its doors, from presidents to film stars. Inside, the vast reception area and the panelled walls are dimly lit. The Waldorf exudes opulence. It is redolent of traditional New York money, in marked contrast to some of its flashy steel-and-glass rivals. Liveried footmen usher the guests through revolving doors into taxis or luxury limousines. It is a busy thoroughfare for those who can afford it – the world's richest and most powerful men and women.

In the spring of 1982 a Swiss financier, Franco Della Torre, was staying in one of the hotel's best rooms. He picked up the phone and called for a bank security guard. On the floor of his suite lay the reason for his anxiety – a collection of gym bags and attaché cases containing more than $1 million in small-denomination bills.

When the guard arrived the two men picked up the cases, took the lift to reception and walked through the revolving doors. A liveried footman hailed a yellow cab. It was a fifteen-minute ride downtown to the head office of Merrill Lynch, the giant securities and banking conglomerate. It was one of several trips made over a three-year period. The cash was dutifully counted by a teller and deposited in an account the Swiss financier had opened under the name Traex.

Further downtown in Battery Park Plaza was another of Wall Street's international finance companies, E. F. Hutton. There the Swiss businessman had opened further accounts under the names

Traex and Acacias Development Corporation. The security guard was perfectly used to handling a million dollars, but he had never before seen it in $5, $10 and $20 bills stuffed into gym bags. He reported the bizarre transaction to the FBI. They already knew about the activities of Franco Della Torre. Over the next eight weeks Mike Fahy at US customs traced a series of multi-million-dollar deposits made by Della Torre in New York. This is a sample of what he discovered:

DATE	ACCOUNT	AMOUNT	BANK
24/3/1982	Traex S.A. 11908122	$1,000,110	Merrill Lynch
25/3/1982	Traex S.A. 11908122	$1,310,000	Merrill Lynch
26/3/1982	Traex S.A. 11908122	$689,910	Merrill Lynch
22/4/1982	Traex S.A. 11908122	$499,960	Merrill Lynch
23/4/1982	Traex S.A. 11908122	$1,408,455	Merrill Lynch
27/4/1982	Traex S.A. E0794031	$653,000	E. F. Hutton
6/5/1982	Traex S.A. E0794031	$715,000	E. F. Hutton
7/5/1982	Traex S.A. E0794031	$400,095	E. F. Hutton
24/5/1982	Traex S.A. E0794031	$1,301,296	E. F. Hutton

In less than six months, together with other deposits, Della Torre banked more than $20 million.

Della Torre had several finance companies in Switzerland which he used to launder and recycle the 'black money'. As he commuted first class between Switzerland and America at the Mafia's expense, he could reflect on a highly successful career. He had gained his first experience of the world of high finance as a cashier with a Swiss credit institution. From there, he had worked his way up to become director of a Lugano finance company called Finagest. Now, at the age of thirty-nine, he was about to set up another company called Consultfin.

US customs and the FBI, who were 'stringing wire all over New York City', had compiled a list of his acquaintances in New York. Pen register devices on his telephone revealed that he was talking to Filippo Salamone, who in turn was in regular contact with Ganci.

Traex had been set up by another Swiss entrepreneur, Enrico Rossini, who had formed the company when he was only twenty-four years old. It now employed a staff of ten and dealt openly in property, raw materials, forward trading and real estate, and clandestinely in 'black money'. 'We do everything the banks do but we stay open longer to fit in with the money exchanges in the USA and are more flexible than the large banks,' boasted Rossini when asked by a journalist about the key to his success. He omitted to mention that part of that flexibility lay in the company's readiness to receive cash from the narcotics trade without asking questions. He has since denied all knowledge of the source of the money he handled:

> I a *mafioso*? I only dealt with one customer who was recommended to me by somebody at the deposit house in Chiasso. One day a currency dealer rang me, he has a customer for me, Franco Della Torre. When his people brought suitcases full of dollar notes into my office and counted them on the money counting machines, I asked the dealer again and was told that Della Torre is in order. The bank took those without hesitation.

When the police began to put pressure on the Swiss dealers who were handling money for the Pizza Connection, Rossini began to have doubts about Della Torre. Although many of the respectable Swiss banks are careful about who they do business with and are now more cooperative with international investigators, they admit that, if they turn someone away, he will not have to walk very far to find someone else who will accept him.

The incentives are enormous. Working on a commission of 5 per cent, Della Torre earned at least $1 million for six months' work. Some of the other Swiss dealers made even more by using the Mafia's huge supply of cash to do side deals on the commodities, shares and currency markets. Della Torre's activities came to an end when the Americans told the Swiss where his deposits came from. Della Torre swore that he had been entrusted with the accounts by two Lebanese gentlemen who were dealing in cigarettes in the Middle East. 'They were small notes because they were paid direct from the daily takings of the tobacco kiosks,' was his disingenuous explanation. When the investigators pressed him he could not remember the names and addresses of the eccentric tobacco traders from the Lebanon who had entrusted him with more than $20 million. He has now spent several months in prison and faces further charges.

Enrico Rossini was equally affronted by the suspicious attitude of the Swiss authorities, reacting with an air of injured pride: 'Traex is a serious finance business – and I have been treated like a criminal. It's a scandal.'

Lugano, with its beautiful lakes and mild climate, had always been a popular resort for the rich and aristocratic members of Swiss and Italian society.

In the 1980s it was the favoured banking centre for the Sicilian Mafia. So much black money was pouring through the quiet town that one prosecutor was seriously alarmed that it could undermine whole sections of the Swiss economy. A network of money movers and couriers all worked from Lugano – with at least three companies involved in the Pizza Connection. Just thirty miles from Milan, Lugano is an immensely convenient location for the financial transactions of the Sicilian Mafia. In the past many of the same people had laundered money from the tobacco trade. One of them had even gone into partnership with a *mafioso* to open a counterfeit Marlboro cigarette factory which produced an identical cigarette, even down to the carton. Tobacco money was soon replaced by the richer rewards of heroin.

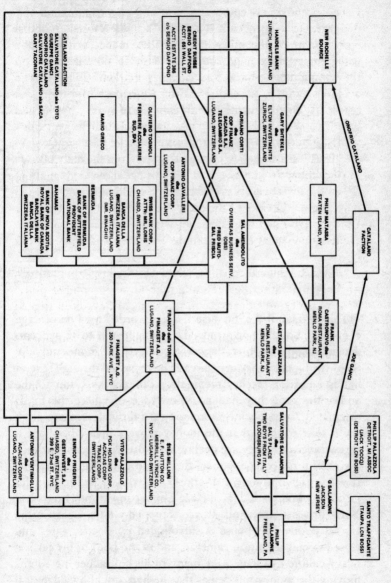

The international route for some of the $1,600,000,000 heroin money from the 'Pizza Connection'.

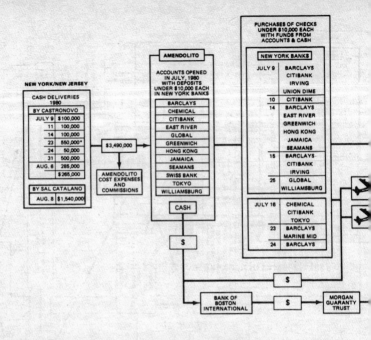

NEW YORK/NEW JERSEY

CASH DELIVERIES 1980	
BY CASTRONOVO	
JULY 9	$100,000
11	100,000
14	100,000
23	550,000*
24	50,000
31	500,000
AUG. 6	285,000
	$265,000

BY SAL CATALANO	
AUG. 8	$1,540,000

$3,490,000

AMENDOLITO COST EXPENSES AND COMMISSIONS

AMENDOLITO

ACCOUNTS OPENED IN JULY, 1980 WITH DEPOSITS UNDER $10,000 EACH IN NEW YORK BANKS

BARCLAYS
CHEMICAL
CITIBANK
EAST RIVER
GLOBAL
GREENWICH
HONG KONG
JAMAICA
SEAMANS
SWISS BANK
TOKYO
WILLIAMSBURG

CASH

$

PURCHASES OF CHECKS UNDER $10,000 EACH WITH FUNDS FROM ACCOUNTS & CASH

NEW YORK BANKS

JULY 9	BARCLAYS
	CITIBANK
	IRVING
	UNION DIME
10	CITIBANK
14	BARCLAYS
	EAST RIVER
	GREENWICH
	HONG KONG
	JAMAICA
	SEAMANS
15	BARCLAYS
	CITIBANK
	IRVING
25	GLOBAL
	WILLIAMSBURG

JULY 16	CHEMICAL
	CITIBANK
	TOKYO
23	BARCLAYS
	MARINE MID
24	BARCLAYS

$

$

BANK OF BOSTON INTERNATIONAL

$

MORGAN GUARANTY TRUST

The services of the 'financiers' are rewarded by a percentage commission of the money moved, ranging from 1 to 10 per cent, depending on how 'hot', dangerous or dirty the money actually is. As the black money may already have passed through several hands before it reaches them, they can always claim to the authorities that they had no knowledge of where the funds originated. Consequently laundering is a difficult crime to prosecute. The truth is that the money movers invariably have a shrewd idea that they are dealing with drug proceeds, but they are careful never to ask their clients too many questions. The rewards are enormous. Adriano Corti, who helped to transfer just over a million dollars of Pizza Connection money from New York, drives a large Rolls Royce equipped with a sophisticated car telephone. His house is surrounded by electric gates and closed-circuit television cameras, and in the boot of his car is a heavy-calibre handgun. Like many of his colleagues, he admits moving the money but denies that he had any knowledge of it being drug money. He has fought a vigorous defence against the charges.

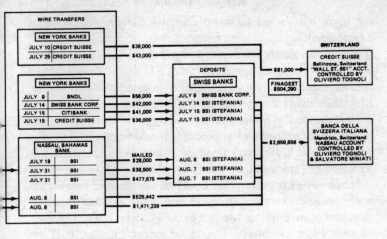

Five weeks of narcotics money laundering.

Several Swiss banks were also ready to take the million-dollar deposits – some with few questions asked. Credit Suisse, in Bellinzona, had a number of accounts used for the Pizza Connection. The accounts were handled by one of their officers: Sergio Daffond. He was particularly helpful to the clients of the Pizza Connection. An account named Wall Street 651 was the recipient for millions of dollars from the heroin sales in New York. Yet the nominee holder for the account was Olivero Tognoli, a highly respectable industrialist from Brescia, Italy, whose family was in the steel business. Much of their work was done in Sicily and among Olivero Tognoli's contacts were some of the leading Mafia bosses of the time. Tognoli was a member of the Third Level. As an industrialist and financier with Mafia connections, he provided the heroin network with a ready-made and respectable front for their Swiss deposits. Daffond himself was entertained by some of his clients in Sicily, where he was introduced to Leonardo Greco, the head of the Bagheria family and a key Sicilian contact of the Pizza Connection. Today he has left the bank but as yet faces no criminal charges. Tognoli has disappeared.

The Pizza Connection began and ended in Switzerland, where the Turk Musullulu's company, Oden AG in Zurich, completed the international circle of crime and money. It was there that Musullulu made the arrangements for the shipping of the morphine base to the Mafia heroin refineries in Sicily, and it was there that the million-dollar proceeds would be returned by wire transfer from Wall Street or, more mundanely, crammed into suitcases and smuggled by air.

In the five-year period that the Pizza Connection functioned, the operators carried an estimated $1.6 billion in small-denomination bills to the banks in grocery bags, suitcases, cartons and pizza boxes. One agent calculated that, if all the notes were stacked in one big pile, they would weigh eight metric tons.

The most respectable finance houses on Wall Street and the best banking facilities that the offshore tax havens could offer accepted the Mafia's heroin money with few questions asked. The role of the banks was all too familiar to the investigators, as Rudy Giuliani explains:

> If you just consider the fact that heroin trafficking is international in scope and in the multi-million-dollar range, it could not happen at the level at which it goes on unless financial institutions played a large role in assisting it. You could not transfer this kind of money in the old-fashioned way.

Giuliani had begun his career specializing in narcotics prosecutions, but the scale of this one was unique:

> It is probably the most significant case that we have ever brought in the United States because it exposes in the broadest possible ways the international organizational structure of a heroin-importing operation – and it exposes it at a very high level. In other words, the people at the very top who are making the multi-millions of dollars in profit from this trade.

To their intense annoyance the federal authorities found that the Swiss banks cooperated more willingly than some of their own institutions. When a Grand Jury subpoena was served on E. F. Hutton, the bank's response was to alert Della Torre's associate in Switzerland, Vito Palazzolo. Giuliani and his men were furious. It looked as if the entire investigation would collapse. Catalano and his team were already 'surveillance conscious', and if Palazzolo tipped them off it could mean years of wasted effort, as well as the likelihood that the top men, who were within their grasp, would get away.

'We got blown out of the water by E. F. Hutton,' says Mike Fahy, while Giuliani recalls with some bitterness:

> We really had two different financial institutions that we were dealing with – Merrill Lynch and E. F. Hutton. Now, we went to both of them and asked both of them to withhold for a period of time notifying particular customers about our subpoenas and our interest in information. Merrill Lynch voluntarily agreed to cooperate with us and did not disclose to their customers and did not jeopardize our investigations. So it could have gone forward.
>
> E. F. Hutton made exactly the opposite decision and did disclose. It's something that was within their legal discretion to do. We're not saying that they committed a crime. If they did, we would have charged them with a crime. But it's something that they also had the discretion not to disclose and they put what we would regard as their narrow financial interests ahead of the broad public interest.

When Giuliani says, 'If they did, we would have charged them with a crime,' – he means it. No doubt he personally went through every financial statute he could find for a felony he could pin on E. F. Hutton for what he regarded as their self-serving decision.

As it happened, Hutton's indiscretion does not seem to have harmed the investigation unduly. Although the pizza men heard of the FBI inquiries and although a number of them suspected they were under surveillance, their attitude was to regard it as nothing more than an occupational hazard. They carried on trading.

The Pizza Connection investigation came to a climax when the 'Men of Honour' fell out among themselves. They relied on three principal sources for their supply of heroin, all of them linked to Catalano. The first and most important was Gaetano Badalamenti, who had operated from Cinisi between 1978 and 1980. When he fled to Brazil he continued his operations through his nephew Pietro Alfano. Alfano lived in Oregon, Illinois. He took orders from Badalamenti over the street payphone and passed them on to New York, in particular to Mazzurco and the Lambertis. On occasion the New York contingent talked directly to Badalamenti, who went under the code name 'Uncle'. The other suppliers were Leonardo Greco in Bagheria in Sicily, and Giuseppe Soresi in Partinico. 'Peppino' Soresi, known as 'the doctor from far away', was a member of the Borgetto family, as was Salvatore Lamberti, who was based in New York. Greco had supplied heroin in 1980 but in 1981 he switched to smuggling huge sums of money from America through Switzerland to Italy. Soresi took over the main supplies from Sicily in 1983 and 1984.

In early October 1983 Catalano's New York henchmen were conducting negotiations for large shipments of heroin with both Soresi in Sicily and Alfano in the Mid-West. Badalamenti was respected and feared by other *mafiosi* but his nephew was regarded as something of a fool by Catalano's men. Alfano's usual contact was Mazzurco, while Soresi, who was taken a lot more seriously, liaised with Giuseppe Lamberti, who was backed by soldiers in the Bonanno family.

At the same time as they were negotiating with their main suppliers for the first big heroin shipments of 1984, Mazzurco was beginning to make arrangements to import several luxury cars from Europe. Mike Fahy in the US customs knew very well from the heroin-packed car that had come over on the *Raffaello* back in 1971 that automobiles were ideal for the movement of

drugs. He began to search the surveillance reports and telephone intercepts for clues to the imminent arrival of another
big shipment. He discovered that there had been a series of
highly secret meetings between Ganci and Catalano, on one
occasion on a New York dockside, strolling along beside the
QE2.

While he was organizing the car shipment, Mazzurco was also
planning to meet Soresi and it looked as if the meeting would
take place in Rome. But there was a problem. One of Badalamenti's men was already holding some narcotics for delivery to
Ganci but wanted payment up-front. So far it had not been
made. Ganci was stalling. He did not want to commit himself.
He thought he might have a better source of supply in Soresi,
and was urgently awaiting news from Sicily.

Eventually Soresi did call him at the payphone outside the Al
Dente pizzeria. He told Ganci that there was a problem with the
'manufacture' and that someone would have to come over
immediately or he would lose all his 'skilled workers'. It looked
as if Soresi was having trouble with the laboratory where the
heroin was being refined. He probably needed the money to pay
in advance for a skilled chemist. It was decided that Giuseppe
Lamberti rather than Mazzurco should go out to meet him and
at the same time organize the shipment of the cars.

By now Catalano's network was under twenty-four-hour surveillance. Although US customs, the DEA and the New York
City Police Department were also monitoring the pizza men, it
was the FBI surveillance division who were most involved. These
highly trained men and women can adopt a variety of disguises,
from mail delivery clerks, cab drivers and street sweepers to
courting couples and even mothers with prams. They were
backed up by the latest technology – miniature video cameras,
directional microphones, microwave listening devices which can
detect sound vibrations through glass, and tracking devices,
transponders which can be attached to cars so that they can be
followed at a safe distance. The greatest hazard they face is
getting 'burned' – noticed by the suspects they are following.
Frank Storey from the FBI recalls one particular incident:

We were following Salvatore Mazzurco and he had just picked up three kilos of heroin, we believe, from Ganci – because there had been an earlier conversation about 'three shirts' – 'I'll be over', etc. – and he came over a short time after. We had thought about following him to see where he was going to deliver the heroin – but he took such evasive tactics that if we had stayed with him he would have burned us – we would have burned him. So we decided to pull off. Those things happen very frequently.

With so many agencies involved there was bound to be a degree of inter-service rivalry, but it seems to have been kept to a minimum. They agreed on a division of tasks. For example, when a suspect was followed by the FBI to an airport where it looked as if he might be taking an international flight, they would alert US customs as far in advance as possible so that they could take over from the moment the suspect entered their area of control. Consequently, when Lamberti and Mazzurco turned up at JFK airport to take an Alitalia flight to Rome, the FBI surveillance team radioed ahead to the customs agents and Mike Fahy's team went into action.

The plan was to do an 'outbound' – a clandestine inspection of luggage and belongings as they were on their way to the plane's cargo hold. Fahy recalls:

We do the outbound. We find a lot of documentation in [Lamberti's] luggage. This time we photographed it. I bring on a portable photocopying machine, we plug it in, we copy everything he's got in his suitcases. We then pass him on to the Italians. We notify the FBI and customs in Rome, our people in Rome, they start the surveillance. But it gets screwed up because they miss him – they were only there for a couple of hours and then they go on to Luxembourg.

Now in Luxembourg we have authorized surveillances by the authorities there and we find out when they're coming back. Instead of coming back through Italy, they

go in through London. So we get there [JFK], I put my
team out at the airport. Lo and behold they come in
through British Airways [terminal]. My guys do their
little thing before the luggage comes into the customs
area, we photograph everything again.

The documents revealed that they had bought seven cars.

Ten days later Lamberti made another trip and met Soresi on
a remote hillside in Cinisi in Sicily. All the indications were
that a major heroin shipment was imminent. Meanwhile Pietro
Alfano had been calling Mazzurco to complain that he had not
heard anything from New York for three weeks. Mazzurco, who
was waiting to hear the outcome of negotiations with Soresi,
was forced to be non-committal. He and Ganci still hoped to
deal with Soresi. So he gave Alfano the brush-off. But it trans-
pired that Soresi and his suppliers in Sicily were annoyed with
New York about a late payment. Ganci by now was furious and
tempers were beginning to fray all round. One of the other New
York conspirators, Mazzara, criticized Ganci to his face about
his inability to sort things out. He decided to go to Sicily himself.
This time the mission was more successful. Mazzara managed
to smooth things over with Soresi.

It seems quite extraordinary that there should have been
quibbling over the costs of different suppliers when each transaction would yield hundreds of thousands of dollars. Even more
bizarre was the inefficiency of these 'businessmen'. At times the
story becomes almost farcical. Telephone numbers were lost and
a member of the team had to fly all the way out to Sicily to give
Soresi the number of the payphone outside the Al Dente pizzeria
as he had been given the wrong number. When he finally put a
call through he was unable to get a reply as a member of the
public was using the payphone. The irony is that the elaborate
arrangements for using payphones were useless: they were *all*
being tapped. As soon as they changed from one call box to
another, the FBI would merely apply for another permit for a
wiretap.

Meanwhile, Alfano was still trying to help his uncle talk to his customers direct in New York. Finally Badalamenti called the phone outside the Al Dente pizzeria from Brazil, but neither Ganci nor Mazzurco was there and the phone simply went on ringing. Badalamenti was now exasperated and apprehensive, not least because his friend Tommaso Buscetta had recently been arrested in Brazil, along with his son Leonardo and his nephew Vincenzo Randazzo. Worried that he too was in danger, he went into hiding. When he felt that it was too dangerous for him in Brazil he decided to spend some time in Bolivia.

At the same time the US customs were watching out for Mazzurco's cars. Mike Fahy recalls:

> We're thinking what the hell's going on? They're going to use the cars to import the heroin. It took us about a couple of months to check when the cars were coming over. We had to monitor the wiretaps carefully to get an indication of when those cars were coming in. We went into action again at the customs facilities over in Newark and when the cars came in we stripped them out. We examined them, we tore them apart and put them back together again.

Using fibre-optic cameras, Fahy's team pried into the inner recesses of the automobiles. In twelve hours they stripped four BMWs and three Mercedes down to their component parts and then put them all together again. The cars were completely clean! They sent them on to Lamberti and Mazzurco in showroom condition. As Fahy later commented, 'They had so much cash that they were branching out into legitimate business to hide that cash – and they had a lot of money!'

In the New Year of 1984 a slightly apologetic Alfano telephoned Mazzurco to say that they had lost out on the 'shirts', that is, one potential heroin source, but that his people were exploring two other possibilities. In a spirit of New Year good will, Alfano urged that they should not fight with each other since it was not they but their bosses, Badalamenti and Ganci, who were making the problems. They agreed to try to set up another call with Badalamenti. This time, as Lamberti waited by the newly designated payphone, some uniformed New York City officials came by and scared him off before the call came through. The next day the pizza men heard from Soresi, who told them he was able to provide the 'cheaper paint' immediately but that the 'good stuff' would not be available until March. Lamberti, who took the call, protested that he would not be able to handle the 'big contractor' (their main customer). Soresi told him there was nothing he could do about it.

Faced with the prospect of defaulting on their customer, the pizza men badly needed an alternative source of heroin. Alfano, true to form, was not much help. He told them that he could not contact the 'architect' or the 'engineer', Badalamenti's Italian representatives who liaised with the heroin laboratories. Five days later a call came through from Badalamenti. Lamberti picked up the phone. After exchanging greetings Lamberti explained that they could take care of the 'little jobs', their smaller customers, with Soresi's 'cheaper paint', but that they were in a desperate position with regard to 'more important matters'. Badalamenti must have been pleased to be on top again. He told Lamberti he could provide a stop-gap but that he could not contact his principal supplier at that moment. Lamberti eagerly agreed to take whatever was available on whatever terms they could get.

Although the New York contingent might have been running short of heroin, they still seemed to be able to deal with their smaller customers. During this period Mazzurco turned up at a bar called the Café Italia following a phone call in which he had agreed to bring 'ten shirts'. After he arrived, five other cars pulled up. Each driver took a package out of his car and went inside the café, emerging shortly afterwards with different parcels. A week later the pizza men arranged the delivery of some heroin to a representative of the Gambino family at another café. The drugs were later sold to one of the DEA's team of undercover agents.

The New York group was now becoming increasingly anxious for substantial shipments from Sicily and Brazil. Soresi was in the process of negotiating for a large quantity of high-quality heroin from a secret laboratory in Milan, and Badalamenti was following up the 'stop-gap' supply which would tide them over until the Milan shipment came on-stream. In early February Alfano flew to New York with a small sample of heroin which he gave to Mazzurco. A few days later, on 8 February 1984, a prearranged call from 'Uncle' (Gaetano Badalamenti) in Brazil was received at the Al Dente payphone. Waiting for the call were Salvatore Lamberti and Mazzurco. Mazzurco answered the phone:

> MAZZURCO: Hello . . . hello!
> UNCLE: Hello!
> MAZZURCO: How is it going?
> UNCLE: But we are here. You guys?
> MAZZURCO: Well, thank God.
> UNCLE: Heh, what do you say?
> MAZZURCO: Well, always the same old stories. And you?
> UNCLE: Well, we are here.

This seemingly meaningless banter, a common feature of the thousands of calls made by the Sicilians in pursuit of money and heroin, continued for several minutes. It was almost incomprehensible, but then the conversation became clearer:

> UNCLE: . . . Fort Lauderdale, you know where it is?
> MAZZURCO: Eh, sure I know.
> UNCLE: Eh, from there they will go over there. Will that be fine with you guys?
> MAZZURCO: Well, I think so.
> UNCLE: Eh . . . I think that by the beginning of next week. Or they will come with twenty-two parcels and with eleven parcels, whatever you guys prefer.
> MAZZURCO: Uh, uhm.
> UNCLE: But since with him, it also depends on . . . with the customs there that they have to give him the answer for the thing about the clearance.
> MAZZURCO: Yes.

UNCLE: It's his opinion to come with all twenty-two parcels ... or containers, no?

MAZZURCO: Uh, uhm.

UNCLE: That would be all right for you guys, no?

MAZZURCO: I don't know about the twenty-two.

UNCLE: We have to do it in a way because ... and that's one. In case give me an answer.

MAZZURCO: All right.

UNCLE: Now, there's another thing. I met the guy with the shirts of four years ago.

MAZZURCO: Uhm.

UNCLE: But there's a little problem. But there is another guy here that had, there's 10 per cent acrylic. I understand little about this.

MAZZURCO: But 10 per cent is not bad.

UNCLE: However, I showed it to ... [clears throat] ... to a competent individual, more competent than I ...

MAZZURCO: Yes.

UNCLE: ... and he told me, 'Nothing,' he says, 'it's good ...' he says, 'You have ... it is good cotton ... however,' he says, 'it contains 10 per cent acrylic.'

MAZZURCO: Uh, uhm.

UNCLE: Now ... and that practically ... nothing ... the cost over here is about forty-five cents. And over there it will cost about sixty cents.

MAZZURCO: Uh, uhm.

UNCLE: [clears throat] ... the price is good, and it seems to me ... it seems to me that the things are not ... what price is there right now?

MAZZURCO: [pause] ... Well ... ah ... to really tell you the truth, really ...

UNCLE: It should be good as soon as we talk again, you can tell me, because since now I will continue ... this is one thing. Closed.

Badalamenti went on to talk about the supplier whom they had dealt with four or five years back, mentioning that it would cost 'ninety cents', meaning that the price would be $90,000 a kilo. As New York were selling kilos for about $200,000 dollars this still left a considerable profit. The supplier of the pure heroin would want to keep half of the consignment for himself but he would probably have to operate through the New York group because, according to Badalamenti, 'He does not have an importer's licence.' Badalamenti noted that the '10 per cent acrylic' – cut heroin – would cost the New York buyers $60,000 whereas 'pure cotton' would be an additional $30,000. He reminded Mazzurco, 'You guys already know the trademark because you have sold it over there.'

The conversation ended with typical Sicilian salutations:

MAZZURCO: Many beautiful things.
UNCLE: I embrace you.
MAZZURCO: Bye-bye.
UNCLE: Many things.

In the thousands of pages of transcripts of the Sicilians' coded conversations, this long discussion was the most crucial. It provided an insight into the past deals between Badalamenti and the New York group and it put everyone on full alert for what appeared to be a massive shipment of heroin. The call was also important because it showed that the New York group was now in such a powerful business position that it could trade with both its suppliers at once.

In the next few days there were several more calls relating to the Badalamenti deal in Florida and the problem of taking delivery of the twenty-two containers. Another crucial call was arranged for 14 February. That morning Alfano flew into La Guardia airport, where he was met by Mazzurco. Earlier there had been a summit conference at Catalano's bakery in Queens between Ganci and Giuseppe Lamberti and Mazzurco. It is likely that they were working out how they were going to respond to the Badalamenti proposition and what they would say to Alfano and his uncle when he called. At 3.55 that afternoon the call came through. Alfano answered. Badalamenti gave his nephew a series of instructions about taking delivery of the consignment:

UNCLE: They told you the town over there, no?

ALFANO: No, they still haven't told me.

UNCLE: Aren't they with you?

ALFANO: Yes.

UNCLE: Ask them if they know, or else I will tell you. Listen to me . . .

ALFANO: Tell me.

Badalamenti then gave his nephew the following instructions:

Now before you leave . . . between what there is . . . give a hundred . . . and you bring with you a hundred . . . then I will tell you the name of the hotel. Friday night you will go to sleep over there. Saturday morning they will call you. They will look for Mr Rossi.

Badalamenti, sceptical about the competence of his nephew, repeated several instructions two or three times, asking Alfano if he understood clearly. Alfano promised he did. As usual, he deferred to his uncle, calling him 'sir'. Neither Badalamenti nor the New York operators held the hapless Alfano in great esteem. Badalamenti seems to have preferred to deal with Lamberti and Mazzurco, in the knowledge that they were closer to the men who made the decisions. Later in the same call he revealed to Mazzurco that he had difficulty getting through to the top men:

BADALAMENTI: But why doesn't the boss ever want to come? What is it? What? What does he have? Does he always have things to do?

MAZZURCO: But what do you mean 'things to do'? Eh, he has a tail going after him.

BADALAMENTI: Hah! Anyway . . . you know the town, right?

MAZZURCO: Uh, uhm.

BADALAMENTI: Tell it to my nephew.

The deal seemed to be nearing completion – according to Badalamenti – it was 'on the road'. There was talk of the price being rather high due to a 15 per cent transportation cost, but Badalamenti explained that this money was payment for the man in Florida bringing the shipment over. This is how the conversation ended:

> UNCLE: We will hear each other, okay?
>
> MAZZURCO: So then you will call your nephew?
>
> UNCLE: Give him some money, to my nephew, now, because he has to leave it over there. Because I don't have any more; therefore or else . . .
>
> MAZZURCO: Hah, he has to give it to them. Eh . . . those, those samples that, that he brought to me . . . I gave them to an individual. And day by day I am waiting for them to give me . . . the result.
>
> UNCLE: Listen, he has to leave it there. Therefore, there is nothing to be done. And I don't even have any to be able to send from here. But from here what can I send?
>
> MAZZURCO: I tell you . . . at this exact moment, today . . . it's the same as if, if . . . as . . . squeezing a rock.
>
> UNCLE: You guys have to prepare it. Many regards.
>
> MAZZURCO: Thank you.
>
> UNCLE: Good things.
>
> MAZZURCO: Bye-bye. Bye.
>
> UNCLE: Goodbye.

Badalamenti was instructing the New York buyers to come up with $100,000 for the Florida shipment – money in advance which they were to give to Alfano, who in turn would hand it over to the delivery man in Florida. The demand for this advance payment and the arguments it created would soon lead to the downfall of the multi-million-dollar network that had worked so efficiently for so long. To these drug barons it was a tiny sum of money. Nevertheless it was not forthcoming. A few days later an exasperated Badalamenti said to Alfano on the phone, 'What am I going to do with you?' Alfano then made a series of calls trying to get the $100,000. He failed. Badalamenti insisted on another phone call being arranged with New York. They were reluctant to speak to him, but eventually agreed. Badalamenti got through to Salvatore Lamberti and told him to give his nephew 'eighty' for 'samples'. Lamberti replied that it was very difficult to do as he asked. Badalamenti, in a typically Sicilian understatement, replied that he would be 'embarrassed' if the money was not handed over to his nephew. He also pointed out, 'That guy is on the road. He has not learned that payment was not made . . . that guy is on the street with twenty-two.'

The arguments continued, and relations between New York and their supplier further deteriorated when one of their financial backers pulled out. Acting on instructions from Badalamenti, Mazzurco attempted to transfer some money direct to Brazil through Manfra, Trodella and Brooks, a foreign exchange broker at the World Trade Center, and later on through a Fifth Avenue law firm which Badalamenti had contacted. Both attempts failed. There was another argument about who was going to pick up the heroin in Florida and bring it to New York. Mazzurco claimed that it was Alfano's responsibility, while Badalamenti insisted that Mazzurco should take delivery in Florida. After another high-level meeting in which Ganci took part, the pizza men seem to have made a serious attempt to raise more money. They put 'pressure' on the backer who had pulled out. Ganci remarked coldly that if he said 'No' he would 'put him out of business and, come Monday, we'll have a war'.

The row over who would pick up the heroin was exacerbated by the fact that the New York group was becoming increasingly neurotic about being watched. Alfano discussed the problem with his uncle. Badalamenti ordered him not to deliver the drugs to New York. 'Those are not your affairs, it's their affair,' he instructed him. 'You don't take the walk, they have to.' Although Alfano was willing to make the run, a friend warned him, 'You're not going any place if he [Badalamenti] doesn't tell you first. They'll get used to it if you start carrying for them. You have to stand your ground.'

Essentially there were two problems: the first was that Catalano's men in New York were having difficulty in raising the money for Badalamenti, a difficulty compounded by the fact that they were probably holding money in reserve for their other supplier, Soresi; the second was that they were becoming increasingly cautious. They had recently discovered that Soresi was also having surveillance problems in Italy. He reported to New York that the 'weather was still bad' – Mafia code for police activity. He added that they could have his entire supply as soon as 'the weather' improved.

Perhaps one of the most astonishing aspects of the way the Pizza Connection team planned their huge shipments of heroin was their attitude to police surveillance. They seemed to regard it as an occupational hazard, like the weather itself; it might delay things for a while, but it was never a reason for cancelling anything. Despite their coded conversations and evasive manœuvres in their cars, it never seems to have occurred to them that the surveillance could have been good enough to discover the payphones they used to make their secret calls, nor that the police were sophisticated enough to track their movements. It was a serious miscalculation.

The agents from the different federal departments looked on with some delight as the pizza men began to fall out with each other. Even 'honour among thieves', it seemed, was now unfashionable. The New York conspirators became increasingly frantic to get heroin for their 'big contractor', while Badalamenti in Brazil was increasingly desperate for cash. In the end he became so frustrated that he summoned the hapless Alfano to Madrid. It was the break the investigators were waiting for.

Alfano boarded a flight from Chicago to Madrid. Among his fellow passengers were a team of FBI and DEA agents. Back in New York the FBI were confronted with a dilemma. If they acted now they had a chance of moving in on Badalamenti, but they also had the imminent prospect of two major heroin shipments, one from Sicily and the other from Badalamenti, possibly coming into Miami from South America. There was the tantalizing possibility of confiscating hundreds of kilos of heroin. Weighed against that proposition was the chance that the heroin might never arrive or that it would arrive and they might miss it. At the end of the day, Mike Fahy recalls, there was no argument:

Assistant US Attorney Louis Freeh asked me numerous times, 'Do we want the heroin or do we want Badalamenti?' I said, 'Louis, anybody can get heroin. Get a shot at Badalamenti.'

They took Fahy's advice. Fahy knew now that he would finally meet the rightful owner of the Ford Galaxy that had come in on the *Raffaello* fourteen years earlier. This is how he remembers the last days of the world's longest-running heroin investigation:

> We just keyed in on Alfano's phone. The Bureau out in Illinois keyed in on his phones when we knew that he was leaving. When Alfano left, we knew exactly where he was going. He was going from Chicago to another foreign country and then to Madrid. So we figured that Badalamenti was in Madrid and we had the DEA set it up with the Spanish cops and they followed him.

Back in New York the investigation was reaching a climax. Timing would be of the essence. Once Badalamenti was arrested they would have to move quickly against the other members of the Pizza Connection. But first they had to wait for confirmation from Spain that the operation there had been successful. Everyone was in a state of tension. Fahy recalls the atmosphere:

> That weekend was probably one of the longest I've ever spent on this case. There were some arguments back and forth when this thing was going to be taken down . . . As far as we were concerned, we said we're not taking this thing down until we have Badalamenti.

On Sunday, 8 April 1984, the prosecuting agencies held a meeting to coordinate the arrests and searches that would finally break the Pizza Connection. As they were meeting, a telephone call came through from Madrid. Badalamenti had been arrested.

At 6.00 a.m. the next day the police, customs and FBI teams moved in on the pizza men. It was a carefully planned operation. Mike Fahy explains:

> I used every dog team that we had, twenty-two dog

teams running around to different locations. As soon as we locked everybody up here the Italians just moved in and locked everybody up in Italy. Everybody that we were looking for was locked up in a couple of days. There were thirty-two people between Switzerland, Italy, Spain and the United States.

It was like a well-organized pincer movement the way everything was coordinated. It was good. And then they were all arraigned. We had everybody locked up by 4.00 a.m. and then we had a couple of drinks.

16

The Commission

The LCN [La Cosa Nostra] in New York is much
more powerful than we ever imagined. They have
influence over every major union and industry in
New York City. We've learned that, we've clarified
that, we've documented it. We've also learned that
they control other families in the United States,
something we suspected but weren't able to establish. We are able to do that today.

> Frank Storey, assistant special agent,
> Organized Crime Section, FBI, October 1985

Government can and should be able to promise the
people a solution to the problem of organized
groups that get together, as Robert Kennedy said
in the fifties, as 'an enemy within'. As a government,
we should be able to crush organizations like that.
The people have a right to expect that of government.

> Rudolph Giuliani, US attorney,
> Southern District of Manhattan

When Tommaso Buscetta began to name names to his American
interrogators in 1985 he gave them plenty – the family trees, the
structure of operation of the Commissions in both Palermo and
New York, the murderers in the Mafia wars, the killers of the
'illustrious corpses' – but his decision to talk did more than that:
it undermined the crucial secrecy on which the Mafia depends.
What the US Attorney General called the Mafia's 'myth of

invincibility' was torpedoed in the aftermath of Buscetta's 'honourable treachery'.

On 26 February 1985 the entire New York Commission was arrested. It was, as Rudy Giuliani remarked, 'a great day for law enforcement, but a bad day, probably the worst, for the Mafia. This case charges more Mafia bosses in one indictment than ever before.'

Although the existence of the Commission had been known of for half a century, the authorities had never really been able to penetrate it or come up with convincing evidence of its day-to-day operations. Despite all the books and movies, the Cosa Nostra was still a secret organization and no group was more insulated from the public gaze or the scrutiny of investigators and journalists. When the elderly and 'respectable' Italian–American businessmen were arrested, the reaction was stunned disbelief. As one elderly *capo* was about to be arrested in his elegant suburban home, a Mafia soldier was so surprised that he shouted out a warning to the police, 'Hey, *you* can't go in there!'

For years the leadership of the American Mafia had had an easy sense of security, taking the occasional court appearance in their stride, accompanied by the best lawyers that money could buy. They could usually rely on an acquittal on a technicality or at worst a minor sentence for crimes which bore little relation to the scale of their criminal enterprise.

The average age of the bosses who were arrested in February 1985 was seventy. It was testimony both to their talent for survival and to the failure of the American authorities to uncover their activities. The Commission members arrested were Anthony 'Fat Tony' Salerno, head of the Genovese family; Paul 'Big Paulie' Castellano, head of the Gambino family; Tony 'Tony Ducks' Corallo, head of the Lucchese family; Gennaro 'Gerry Lang' Langella, acting head of the Colombo family; and Phil 'Rusty' Rastelli, head of the Bonanno family (who had in fact been barred from the Commission).

The elderly *capi* were visibly shaken, but their sense of shock soon turned to defiance. Rudy Giuliani, the man who finally brought them to justice, told how they responded to being arrested: 'They were not frightened,' he said, 'they were infuriated.' One small anecdote serves to show the contempt these men exhibited for their fellow Americans.

'Fat Tony' Salerno is indeed fat, well over twenty stone. He emerged from the courthouse in downtown Manhattan after his arrest wearing an expensive coat over his well-upholstered shoulders and a fedora cocked over his head. In his mouth an expensive cigar jutted out like a permanent feature of his facial sculpture. As he descended the courthouse steps network correspondents clamoured for an interview. Salerno brushed past the assembled media and delivered himself of the inelegant but unequivocal response, 'Go fuck yourself.' It was typical of the way the 'Godfathers' reacted to the indignity of arrest.

Bail was set at suitably large amounts. 'Fat Tony's' bail was $2 million. It is a registered fact that Salerno has not worked for forty-five years. For most of us this might present a cash-flow problem. Not for Salerno. He deposited the $2 million in just thirty minutes.

'Big Paulie' Castellano was similarly required to find $2 million bail which he too raised in just thirty minutes. The following day his bail was increased to $4 million. He raised the extra $2 million as well in record time.

The indictment against the Commission was brought under the RICO (Racketeering, Influence and Corrupt Organization) law, which enabled prosecutors to charge an 'enterprise' and those associated with it on the grounds of its being a criminal organization whose purpose is to extort, murder, steal and conspire in all manner of activities. The same statute was being used in the Pizza Connection case.

As Rudy Giuliani readily admits, the case rested on a comprehensive selection of court-approved secret tape-recordings of the heads of the Mafia families 'talking about it, describing what the Commission is, how it operates and what it does'. The tapes confirmed that the Commission was the supreme council – the board of directors – supervising the criminal affairs of the Cosa Nostra. The bosses were also charged with operating a conspiracy within their own Mafia families. Each of them, it was alleged, had an 'underboss', a *consigliere*' and a team of 'soldiers'. Together they 'supervised, promoted and protected the criminal activities of the capos, soldiers and associates of the family. The bosses in return received a part of the illegal earnings of those capos, soldiers and associates.'

It was known that the New York Commission had been quite successful in arbitrating disputes and keeping the peace, since this alternative police force of gangsters and bosses had inevitably drawn attention to itself over the years by its activities. The authorities already knew, for instance, about the way the Commission had dealt with the Bonanno family.

In the mid 1960s Joe Bonanno had become increasingly eccentric. He was antagonizing other families as he tried to expand his territorial interests beyond New York to the West Coast and he was suspected of plotting against fellow members of the Commission. But, as ever, in the status-conscious hierarchy of the Mafia it was family 'business' which caused trouble.

In 1964 Bonanno made his son, Bill, *consigliere* of the family. This blurring of the division between the family of his own blood and the Mafia family which bore his name was received as a slight to Mafia 'ethics'. Nor was his son held in high regard by many of his own soldiers and *capidecini*. One of them remarked, 'You can't take a kid out of a cradle and put him in a tuxedo and let him boss people in the gutter if he can't talk their language.' The Commission sympathized with Gaspar de Gregorio, a long-time member of the Bonanno family who felt personally slighted by Bill Bonanno's promotion at the expense of his own. Rebel members of the Bonanno family rallied to his cause. The Commission was even more annoyed by Bonanno's attempts to expand his influence on the West Coast, and by the suspicion that in 1963 he had instigated a plot to murder two fellow Commission members.

In 1963 the FBI began to bug the office of Samuel Rizzo de Cavalcante, the head of a relatively obscure Mafia family in New Jersey. What interested the authorities was that de Cavalcante was being used by the Commission to act as intermediary between the two factions of the Bonanno family, perhaps in order to drive a wedge between them. Shortly before noon on 31 August 1964, de Cavalcante met one of his captains, Jo Sferra, who was also the business agent for the Hod Carriers' Union in Elizabeth, New Jersey. De Cavalcante referred to 'a little trouble' in New York. 'It's about Joe Bonanno's *borgata* [family],' he told Sferra. 'The Commission don't like the way he's comporting himself.'

'The way he's conducting himself, you mean?' asked Sferra.

'Well, he made his son *consigliere* – and it's been reported, the son, that he don't show up. They [the Commission] sent for him and he didn't show up. And they want to throw [Joe Bonanno] out of the Commission.'

In a later conversation de Cavalcante told Sferra, 'The Commission doesn't recognize Joe Bonanno as the boss any more.'

It was not just Bill Bonanno who refused to appear before the Commission. In a fit of stubborn pride, his father was also refusing. His attitude showed a lack of respect for its authority or, as de Cavalcante put it, 'When Joe defies the Commission he's defying the whole world!'

With a civil war in his own family and a hostile Commission ranged against him, it is hard to understand why Bonanno was not murdered. That he survived was a tribute to his Sicilian cunning and the moderating influence of the Commission. On 21 October 1964 he disappeared, kidnapped by armed men as he was walking through Manhattan with his lawyer. It is thought that the Commission arranged the kidnap in order to settle matters with him, and that he escaped being killed by agreeing to retire gracefully, or at least appearing to do so. Nearly two years later he reappeared looking fit and suntanned. On 17 May 1966 he surrendered himself to a surprised judge at the courthouse in Manhattan's Foley Square. Refusing to say where he had been and faced with the relatively minor charge of obstruction of justice, he 'retired' to his luxurious bungalow in Tucson, Arizona, from where there were reports of frequent visits to call boxes and rumours of his continuing involvement in the Mafia. Whether or not this was true, he had obviously ceased to be a potential threat to the Commission.

But the resentment that Bonanno had stirred among his fellow bosses carried on long after his retirement. In 1983, he agreed to a CBS *Sixty Minutes* interview with Mike Wallace. Shortly after the broadcast, on 28 March 1983, hidden microphones picked up the response of two members of the Lucchese family, the underboss Salvatore Santoro and Salvatore Avellino:

AVELLINO: I was shocked. What is he trying to prove, that he's a Man of Honour? But he's admitting — he, he actually admitted that he had a fam, that he was a Boss of a Family.

SANTORO: Right.

AVELLINO: Even though he says, 'This was my Family, I was like the father.'

SANTORA: He's trying to get away from the image of a gangster.

AVELLINO: Yeah.

SANTORO: He's trying to go back to ahhh, like in Italy. See, when he says, 'My father taught me.'

AVELLINO: Yeah.

SANTORO: His father was a friend of ours in Italy. See, 'cause the town he came from when he came here. He's full of shit, 'cause I know he was a phony, you know he was . . . Like, he says he ain't never been in narcotics, he's full of shit. His own fucking rules he was making piles of money ahh, what's his name was in the junk business. They were in the junk business and they were partners like with him.

AVELLINO: Right.

The *mafiosi* go on to talk about the book that Bonanno had just written.

SANTORO: This cocksucker, you know what he's gonna make, this cocksucker? You know how much money he's gonna make now, his book?

AVELLINO: Is it out already? I knew that they were writing it.

SANTORO: Yeah it's coming out, it's coming out. Because he's quoting from the book . . .

AVELLINO: About what he's . . . about killing people.

SANTORO: Right, right. Now right, now what's gonna happen, Hollywood is gonna come along . . .

AVELLINO: And make a movie.

SANTORO: Make a movie and this guy's gonna be like the technical director. Forget about it, this cocksucker will make a fortune.

AVELLINO: This will be like, the ahh, now they'll say, 'We have the original Godfather.'

The Mafia weren't the only ones to be shocked by the disclosures of Joe Bonanno. Rudy Giuliani bought himself a copy of the book and went through it meticulously, underlining key sections. When one of the assistant attorneys working in his office, Ken Caruso, asked if he could borrow it and noticed the marked sections he asked what he was doing. Giuliani replied, 'If he can write about it, we can prosecute him for it.' Which is precisely what he did.

After his retirement to Arizona, Bonanno had left his family to a troubled succession of leaders – not least of whom was his former *consigliere*, Carmine Galante. Galante was small, about five foot three, bald headed, fat and immensely tough. His constant cigar smoking had earned him his nickname, 'Lillo' – 'Little Cigar'. He had accompanied Joe Bonanno to Palermo in 1957 for the important Sicilian–American Mafia summit attended by Lucky Luciano and a whole host of leading *mafiosi*, including the young Tommaso Buscetta. Galante had then consolidated his interests in Canada, where he had formed a close alliance with the Cotroni family smuggling heroin.

Galante had always been an ambitious and determined gangster. Even during his years inside Lewisburg Federal Penitentiary in Pennsylvania he amassed considerable power. He was feared by prisoners and warders alike. He also served time in the maximum-security G Block which housed the most notorious Mafia prisoners and where Galante was known as 'the *capo di tutti capi* of Mafia row'. One fellow inmate was Vincent Teresa, a high-ranking *mafioso* from New England who left prison to become a highly protected witness. In his view:

> [Galante's] a stone killer. I think he took care of at least eighty hits himself . . . In or out of prison, Lillo is Mr Big and anyone who thinks differently doesn't know what makes the mob tick. He ought to be out of jail soon, and if he is, the New York mobs are in for real trouble. He hated Vito Genovese while he was alive. To him, Genovese was a pimp, two-faced, a man you could never trust. 'When I get out,' he used to say bitterly, 'I'll make Carlo Gambino shit in the middle of Times Square.'

Galante was spared the necessity of carrying out his unseemly threat when he was paroled in 1978 after serving twenty years of his sentence. Carlo Gambino had died a natural death in 1976, at which point the leadership of the Gambino family was taken over by his brother-in-law, Paul Castellano. The leadership of the Bonanno family had passed in 1973 to Phil Rastelli, who was serving a short prison sentence at the time of Galante's release. To Galante it looked like the perfect opportunity to reassert his authority – and not just over the Bonanno family. He wanted more. Teresa had had plenty of time to hear about Lillo's plans:

> There was no doubt in my mind that Lillo planned to take over the New York mobs when he got out. He's got the enforcers, an army of them, to make it stick. He's been off the street for years, but he's still got tremendous influence and respect.

Teresa believed that Galante planned his takeover bid from inside:

> Lillo's brought in an army of men because he wants guys he can depend on when he makes his move. Those aliens are 'made' guys from Sicily, real old country *mafiosi*, mostly young. They've got papers of recognition so they get the same respect in this country that an American

'made' guy has, but they aren't members of the mob in this country. They're well trained, well disciplined. Lillo and [others] are bringing them in across the Mexican and Canadian borders. The old Moustache Petes [traditional rural *mafiosi*] and a few of the smart bosses are recruiting them for just one thing – to bring back respect and honour in the Honoured Society.

These Sicilian *mafiosi* will run into a wall, put their head in a bucket of acid for you if they're told to, not because they're hungry but because they're disciplined. They've been brought up from birth over there to show respect and honour, and that's what these punks over here don't have. Once they're told to get someone, that person hasn't a chance. They'll get him if they have to bust into his house in the middle of the night, shoot him, bite him, eat him, suck the blood out of his throat. They'll get him because they were told to do it.

Once out of prison, Galante surrounded himself with a small Sicilian army – Salvatore Catalano, Cesare 'Tall Guy' Bonventre and Baldassare Amato. Galante wanted wealth and power, so he quickly grabbed control of the heroin trade, which had greatly increased in volume and profit during his enforced absence. He had envied the influence of Carlo Gambino, which had been partially inherited by Paul Castellano, and he was determined to redress the balance by assuming that power himself. It was an ambition that was not shared by the other families nor by the Commission, who saw Galante turning himself into a 'business problem'. Catalano would help solve it.

Phil Rastelli had already been elected as head of the Bonanno family but he stepped down when Galante was paroled in 1978. It looked like an act of deference but in fact Rastelli was just biding his time. The Mafia did not take kindly to someone as brash as Galante. In accordance with another 'honourable' tradition of the Cosa Nostra, the conspiracy to murder him would be constructed by the members of his own family.

Galante's ambition threatened the other families in more ways than one. Since the leadership problems of the Bonanno family, particularly the civil war in the mid sixties, its operations, personnel and business interests had inevitably fallen under the sway of the other families. It was not exactly a takeover, but at times it had come close. In particular, the Gambino family under Paul Castellano had begun to take a benevolent interest in Bonanno family operations. There were many shared areas of expertise in loan-sharking, labour unions, extortion, pizzerias, restaurants, narcotics and hijacking. When Galante threatened the arrangement, the Commission moved. They settled the leadership dispute within the family by simple violence. They authorized the murder of Carmine Galante. The contract fell to Catalano, whose trusted associates, Cesare Bonventre and Baldassare Amato, were Galante's bodyguards.

On 12 July 1979 Carmine Galante was enjoying his customary post-prandial cigar on the patio of Joe and Mary's Italian restaurant in Knickerbocker Avenue, Brooklyn. His bodyguards were with him as always, but that day he was also accompanied by two friends, Leonardo Coppola and Giuseppe Turano.

Three gunmen wearing ski-masks walked in through the back entrance of the restaurant and onto the patio. The first carried a double-barrelled shotgun. He emptied both barrels into Galante. The second killer fired simultaneously with a pump-action shotgun. With the economy of a professional killer, he fired two bullets into Galante and the rest into his guests. His bodyguards drew their guns, but not to defend Galante – Bonventre himself delivered the *coup de grâce* to one of Galante's hapless guests. Amato and Bonventre then got up and walked out of the restaurant with the assassins, their job done.

Amato and Bonventre were close associates also of Giuseppe Ganci. Later they would all be indicted for Galante's murder, together with Phil Rastelli. In a separate indictment the entire Commission of the Cosa Nostra, including Paul Castellano, were charged with ordering the contract. Catalano's immediate reward was the 'licence' to import heroin into New York. In one sense, the beginning of the Pizza Connection was that ruthless killing in Joe and Mary's restaurant. Galante may have stepped out of line, but the trade he worked so hard to build up could not be allowed to die with him. Galante had broken the 'rules' of the Mafia to make obscene profits from drugs. The Mafia killed him. But its rules did not prevent it from continuing to reap those profits.

There had been rumours of a mob contract on Galante for two years, which was hardly surprising as he had made no secret of his vaulting ambition, nor his dislike of the Gambino family. When asked about the risks he might be running he boasted, 'No one will ever kill me, they wouldn't dare.' But he was wrong. The very instrument of his ambition, the Sicilian crew which he had fostered within the Bonanno family, became the means for his destruction. It never seemed to occur to him that the best bodyguards might also make the best killers.

On the day of Galante's murder, Bonanno family captains visited Rastelli in prison to work out the details. Some of the top members of the family gathered at the private social club they often used in Mulberry Street. There were also meetings with Aniello Dellacroce – 'Neil The Lamb' – the underboss of the Gambino family. The murder had been technically approved by Castellano as head of the Commission but other members – Corallo and Salerno – felt that they had not been sufficiently consulted. This typified Castellano's way of operating which over the years earned him increasing hostility from the others.

With Galante out of the running, the way was now clear for Rastelli to take over. Catalano and Ganci took over the management of the Bonanno family trade. As an underboss in the Bonanno family, Catalano reported to Rastelli, who of course would receive some of the profits from the trade. Rastelli, in turn, reported to the Commission, although they were becoming increasingly uneasy about the 'junk business'.

The murder of Galante was a classic gangland slaying. It was part of the ritual – and a tribute to the importance of food in Italian culture – that a man marked for death should be allowed to eat and drink well before being called to account. Many of America's leading *mafiosi* had been murdered after a good meal at one of New York's best Italian restaurants. It was as important a part of the tradition as the ostentatious funeral and the obligatory attendance of the victim's enemies. Lesser minions of the Mafia tended to be chopped up into little pieces or dissolved in acid and thus denied the dignity of a decent Catholic burial. The Mafia is a very class-conscious employer.

But Galante's ghost would return to haunt the Commission. Although murders such as his tend to go unsolved, in this case the investigators were able to pinpoint both his executioners and the men who gave the orders. Using information discovered in the Pizza Connection investigation and gleaned from the testimony of Tommaso Buscetta, the prosecutors brought charges against Catalano and the other Mafia leaders.

As in the Pizza Connection case, much of the additional evidence used to indict the leadership of the Mafia came from surveillance and hidden microphones which recorded their conversations.

The most successful piece of electronic eavesdropping took place in Tony Corallo's car. Although *mafiosi* in the past had tended to favour Lincoln Continentals, Cadillacs and Mercedes, more recently the British Jaguar car had become a prestige vehicle among the rich and famous of Manhattan. Tony 'Ducks' Corallo, so called because of his ability to duck out from a succession of court subpoenas, felt that it was the right car for him: he bought a black model for himself and a white one for his wife. Agents from the Organized Crime Task Force of New York State noted the acquisition with interest. They intended to bug it. As they were unfamiliar with the model, they hired a replica car and practised removing sections of the dashboard in order to place the miniaturized bug out of sight. The only tell-tale sign was a small wire connected to the power supply, but it was unlikely that anyone would notice it. Intensive practice reduced the time for the operation to thirty minutes.

When it was discovered that Corallo was due to attend a grand reception at a restaurant in Huntingdon, Long Island, the task force went into action. Joe Coffey, one of the agents involved in the planning of the operation, recalls the scene:

Finally, D-day came; he went to the affair. We knew he was going to be there a couple of hours. We went and took the dashboard off, installed the bug, put the dashboard back. And – Jesus – they almost got caught a couple of times, you know, because the private security patrol on the parking lot would be riding around and every time they came out, they'd look under the car.

It was raining, so as the agents eased open the Jaguar door they held up a plastic sheet to prevent any drops of water spilling on the expensive upholstery and warning Corallo that someone might have tampered with his car. There were also other surveillance vehicles in the area, some of which did not know what was going on, but fortunately they kept their cover. The bug operated on what they call a repeater system. The device would transmit the conversation to another car equipped with a receiving device which in turn would transmit the signal to the main surveillance van which was equipped with sophisticated digitally locked radio equipment. This meant that they could follow the car from several blocks away without being observed, and still hear the occupant's conversations. The tapes yielded a wealth of material – Coffey explained the kind of information the bug behind the fascia was providing:

Everything – Commission conversations, like who was who, who's what, who was 'made', who was not, who got the money for what operation, labour racketeering and gambling and shylocking. Once they're in the car and Corallo's reading a newspaper, the *New York Times*, and it had just been announced that the US attorney in the Southern District [Giuliani] had appointed six assistants. Corallo says, 'See this, US attorney appointed six new assistants. They're going to need them, because we just "made" six guys.'

Other bugs were planted in Castellano's mansion at 177 Benedict Road, Staten Island, and Salerno's social club, the Palma Boy at 415 East 116th Street, but the Jaguar tapes provided the most vital evidence. As well as giving an insight into the Mafia's affairs, the tapes exposed the way the Commission controlled some of New York's main industries. Just as the authorities had finally brought Al Capone to book on tax evasion charges, so now they were hoping to indict the leadership of the New York Mafia for what might appear to be a mundane crime – corrupt control of the building industry. In fact this was one of the Mafia's most lucrative operations. It shows how easily they can infiltrate and control legitimate business. They had done the same thing on the docks, in New York's fish and meat markets, in restaurants and nightclubs, in gambling, in money-lending and in the labour unions. As the FBI were beginning to realize, there was scarcely a commodity or service from which the Mafia did not get a cut. The overhead would be passed on to the consumer, whether he was the man in the street buying a takeaway pizza for which the mozzarella might be supplied by one of Joe Bonanno's companies, or the entrepreneur who wanted to build a new skyscraper in New York City, for which the concrete and mixing would be controlled by the mob.

The Mafia's move into the construction business was both lucrative and logical. Control of building sites opened up all sorts of possibilities, from putting soldiers on the payroll as non-existent labourers, to holding the investors to ransom by delaying building work through control of the workforce. As with other rip-offs of apparently legitimate businesses, such as the casino and hotel business in Las Vegas, the key to Mafia domination was their control of the labour unions.

The influence of organized crime in the Teamsters' Union has been well documented. At one point it was so extensive that being a senior Teamster official was virtually synonymous with membership of the Mafia. The situation was similar in other unions. Ralph Scopo, president and business manager of the Concrete Workers' District Council, was a soldier in the Colombo family and a key figure in the Commission's control of the construction industry. As president of the union he received an annual salary of $104,000, and $201,000 in 'other disbursements', according to union records. His method in the field of labour relations was revealed by Anthony Rivara, a subcontractor who was working on the Delta Airlines terminal building at La Guardia airport in 1981. He testified that he had had to pay 2 per cent of his multi-million-dollar contract to Scopo or lose the deal. Rivara said that at first he refused to have anything to do with paying anyone off but that he had then been approached by Victor Wortmann, the general contractor for the project. Wortmann was the man who had given part of the contract to Rivara. One day he turned up at the building site and told Rivara to call Ralph Scopo:

> [Wortmann] walked up to me in the mud . . . wearing a three-piece suit. [He said,] 'Go deal with Ralph Scopo.' I called Ralph Scopo right away. I didn't have a signed contract with Wortmann. I wasn't losing this job.

Rivara agreed to give Scopo a down-payment of $15,000, but when he handed Scopo the first instalment, which was only $5000, Scopo started to become suspicious:

> He told me this story about another guy who beat him, who had to go down to a restaurant in Little Italy to meet with [Scopo's] partners and friends. I didn't want to have to go down and sit with three or four guys with big necks.

Scopo was the link between the mob and the construction business. A series of revealing tapes from eavesdropping devices gave a unique insight into the way the system operated. In this conversation, on 19 March 1984, a concrete contractor called Sal d'Ambrosi is asking Scopo if he can get the contract on a $200 million project.

> D'AMBROSI: Everything is upstairs, everything is above, all glass, mirrors, chromes . . .
> SCOPO: But if the job's two hundred million . . .
> D'AMBROSI: Yeah.
> SCOPO: The concrete's gotta be twelve million?
> D'AMBROSI: Yeah. Why can't I do the concrete?
> SCOPO: You can't do it. Over two million you can't do it.

It's under two million, hey, me, I tell you go ahead and do it.

D'AMBROSI: Who do I gotta see? Tell me who I gotta go see?

SCOPO: You gotta see every Family. And they're gonna tell you no. So don't even bother.

D'AMBROSI: If Tommy goes and talks to them?

SCOPO: They'll tell you no. No matter who talks. I know they'll tell you no, I went through this not once, a hundred times. I can't get it for myself. How could I get it for somebody else?

D'AMBROSI: What'd happen if they give me a million at a time?

SCOPO: How can they give you a million at a time?

Scopo then explains the rules for another contract.

SCOPO: First of all the job costs you two points.

D'AMBROSI: Why two points?

SCOPO: That's what they pay. Anything over two million. All the guys in the club, got so much out, pay two points.

The 'club' not only controlled the Cement and Concrete Workers' District Council of the Labourers' International Union, they also had control over Teamsters' Local 282, the union that represented the drivers and workers in the concrete and cement industry. That union was the key to the Mafia's monopoly. It has 4000 members whose jobs consist of driving on and off the construction sites with supplies of sand, cement and anything else needed for the building. If they withdraw their labour everything comes to a halt. Control of that union meant control of the employers and hence the entire industry. It gave the Mafia the leverage to persuade New York's leading cement contractors to form a 'club' which would be run by the Commission. They would decide which company would receive a particular contract and then force rival companies to put in high offers to ensure that they would lose while the chosen company would win.

The Commission operated the scheme on every building site contract in New York which was valued at more than $2 million.

If any of the concrete operators did not like the arrangement or wanted to get out, the Commission would make life so unpleasant for them – they would suffer from inexplicable 'labour problems' and find that their supplies of cement would mysteriously disappear – that they would beg to come back. Ralph Scopo, as president of the union, would assist in any way he could. It was worth his while. In just over one year he and his friends Salerno, Castellano and Corallo extorted the following amounts:

> XLO Concrete Corporation, May 1983: $326,000
> Northberry Concrete Corporation, October 1983: $72,000
> Century Maxim Construction, March 1984: $177,800
> XLO Concrete Corporation, April 1984: $157,000
> S & A Concrete Company Inc., May 1984: $67,000
> S & A Concrete Company Inc., May 1984: $95,000
> S & A Concrete Company Inc., August 1984: $84,000

Altogether just under $1 million – not a bad profit for a minimal investment. It was a perfect business venture. As a direct result of their rackets the Commission made New York City the most expensive place in America to buy concrete. It has been estimated that as much as 25 per cent of the cost of construction contracts in the city goes directly to the Mafia.

With the thousands of other crimes that are committed daily by or in association with the Mafia, unimaginable sums of money are being made. It is almost impossible to estimate how much, but the total amount in 1986, according to the President's Commission on Organized Crime, was $65.7 billion. Other estimates put it much higher. According to the report organized crime reduces the gross national product by $18.2 billion, increases unemployment by 414,000, raises consumer prices by 0.3 per cent and lowers per capita annual income by $77.22. Organized crime is the second largest business enterprise in America – oil being the first – and the most profitable, due to the total non-payment of taxes.

The American Mafia has come a long way from the ill-dressed, impoverished 'Men of Honour' who founded the organization after emigrating from Sicily and southern Italy at the turn of the century. Yet those men, with their rural tradition and sense of family community, were the forefathers of today's *mafiosi*.

Between 1820 and 1930, 4,700,000 Italians emigrated to America, nearly half of them between 1900 and 1910. Eighty per cent were from the south, mainly Sicily. In America they formed street gangs bound together by the fierce loyalty of the family and their common places of origin in Sicily. The major New York families evolved from five different parts of Sicily: the Bonanno family came from Castellamare del Golfo; the Genovese family came from Napolitana; the Lucchese family came from Siciliani; the Colombo family came from Villabate; and the Gambino family came from Palermitana.

With the advent of Prohibition, the opportunity arose for the Italians to move into the supply and distribution of a commodity for which, thanks to the government, there was a limitless demand. With the profits and the experience they gained in the bootlegging business, they formed themselves into better organized and more tightly knit groups than their Irish and Jewish counterparts with whom they originally worked. They became the dominant group in organized crime. With the organizational talent of Lucky Luciano, the foundations were laid for the power and profit enjoyed by today's Mafia.

Since then the 'Honoured Society', in assimilating the values and culture of the land they have plundered, has created a violent distortion of the American dream. Anyone can murder their way to the top and become a millionaire. That they have not, unlike their Sicilian cousins, declared all-out war on the forces of law and order is merely because they reason that the murder of policemen, FBI agents and lawyers would be unproductive. The policy is pragmatic. The families like to be left alone, so they hate publicity, police surveillance and court appearances. They calculate that killing their lawful persecutors would result in more attention and lose them public sympathy and the political influence that they have gained over the years. Although political corruption is not as endemic as in Italy, where, despite recent arrests, the 'Third Level' still manages to survive, there have been instances of corrupt senators, congressmen, policemen, judges and lawyers.

Traditionally, the leaders of the American Mafia families have cultivated the image of leading citizens within their communities. It has given them power among fellow Italians and with politicians who depend on their votes. In addition, businessmen with access to a wealth of funds are frequently welcomed with open arms by American politicians, whose success often depends more on the quantity of the contributions than the quality of the politics. The White House itself has not been untouched by the machinations of the Mafia, resulting in a series of scandals, from the affair of President Reagan's former Labour Secretary, Raymond Donovan, who had become enmeshed with the Mafia through his involvement in the New York construction company Schiavone, to the chairman of Reagan's 1984 election campaign, Senator Paul Laxalt, who was alleged to have accepted personal campaign contributions from Las Vegas mob associates. It is not that the White House is full of *mafiosi*, but that organized crime is now so deeply rooted within the fabric of American society that even those who operate at the highest levels cannot avoid contact.

Through a combination of Hollywood myth, fictional romance and actual fact the Mafia gangster has won himself a permanent place in American consciousness. The modern *mafioso* is one of its heroes along with pioneers, cowboys, movie stars and astronauts. The image is viewed with a mixture of fascination, awe and admiration tinged with a sense of disapproval rather than outright hostility.

The most pervasive corruption of the American dream has been Mafia penetration of the labour unions. The Mafia-infiltrated Teamsters' Union, whose $2 billion pension fund has been used by the Mafia as an unofficial bank, was the only major union to throw its support behind President Reagan. If any further proof were required of the union's Mafia connections it emerged in November 1985 from the evidence of Roy Williams, former president of the Teamsters and a pension fund trustee, in a federal courtroom in Kansas City. Williams admitted that the Teamsters' Central States Pension Fund had long been plundered by the Mafia for large loans to finance both crooked and legitimate businesses. The seventy-year-old Williams, suffering from chronic emphysema and clutching an oxygen bottle, was testifying in the trial of nine alleged Mafia leaders from Chicago, Cleveland, Milwaukee and Kansas City. They were charged with a conspiracy to skim $2 million in profits from the Stardust and Fremont casinos in Las Vegas. The prosecutors alleged that they used a $62.5 million loan from the Teamsters' fund in 1974 to buy the casinos and operate them under the name of the Argent Corporation. Williams admitted arranging the casino loan for the late Nick Civella, boss of the Kansas City Mafia for thirty years. In return, Civella paid him $1500 a month until Williams was elected president in 1981. Williams claimed that he did favours for Civella at the bidding of his superiors, Jimmy Hoffa and Frank Fitzsimmons. Under cross-examination, Williams was forced to confess that in 1979 he had tried to bribe the former Senator for Nevada, Howard Cannon, to block deregulation of the trucking industry. Williams was convicted of bribery in 1982. He admitted that he was testifying in the hope of getting his sentence reduced.

These are among the few public glimpses available of political links with organized crime.

The image of the churchgoing, community-minded citizen so assiduously cultivated by the heads of some of the Mafia families often makes it difficult to believe the darker reality it disguises. When Paul Castellano was making his daily appearances in the federal courthouse in Manhattan's Foley Square in the autumn of 1985, he looked every inch the respectable businessman that he pretended to be. Well over six feet tall, seventy years old, he had a sharp, beak-like nose and quick darting eyes behind wire-rimmed glasses. His hair, thinning on top, was carefully groomed with oil. He seemed fit and alert. He greeted friends with a smile and a handshake and was especially polite to the wives of his co-defendants. He did not look very different from the teams of expensive lawyers who surrounded him. In the evenings he would be driven home in his limousine to his mansion on Staten Island, described as a miniature White House.

Castellano had two attorneys, one of whom was James la Rossa, reputed to be one of the best defence lawyers in the city. He had defended many alleged Mafia bosses and had once declared, 'From all of my experience, both as a former Justice Department employee and as a defence attorney, I've never seen evidence that there is a Mafia or any real connection with Italy in any fashion.'

La Rossa's 'non-Mafia' client with 'non-Italian' connections had an interesting pedigree. He was a cold-blooded killer, though of such exalted power that he would never have had to carry out the executions himself. Others would do that for him. He could order a contract with less anxiety than most people order a meal in a restaurant. Castellano did not hesitate to kill to advance his business interests, to settle an inter-family dispute as in the case of Galante, or to avenge his so-called personal 'honour'.

When 'Big Paulie' found out that his daughter's husband was playing around with another woman he was furious. His daughter was pregnant and became so agitated by her husband's infidelity that she eventually had a miscarriage. Castellano intervened. He ordered his son-in-law's execution. The man was invited for an evening out at the club used by the Gambino family in Brooklyn. Afterwards he was invited to a nearby apartment. Unsuspecting – after all he was married to the boss's daughter – he walked through the front door. Seconds later an assassin pushed a knife expertly through the centre of his heart. The murder was carried out with surgical precision in order to minimize the flow of blood. They did not want any unseemly evidence on the floor of the apartment. The killers then dragged the body to a shower room and dumped it on the floor. They switched on the shower to wash away the blood, and then started to cut up the body. The boss, Roy di Meo, a captain in the Gambino family who was in charge of the contract, got angry because his men were taking so long to chop up the corpse: 'Listen,' he said impatiently, 'I'll cut – you wrap.'

The police learnt the entire grisly story from one of the men who carried out the contract. The pieces of body were placed in a garbage bag and disposed of later. It was a routine operation. More than twenty other murders were arranged at the same location using the same method. To most people the story is horrific, but to the men carrying it out it was a night's work. To the hawk-nosed man with his well-cut suits, sitting in his mock White House mansion on Staten Island, it was a matter of honour. His daughter may have been deprived of her husband, but family honour had been restored.

In the autumn of 1985 Castellano was in serious trouble. Although he headed the biggest Mafia family in New York, the Gambino family, with an estimated strength of 250 members, he was facing a series of trials which threatened to be so time-consuming that they would prevent him from carrying out his job as chief executive of the family enterprises. According to Joe Coffey, who has specialized in the investigation of organized crime, a day in the life of a Mafia family boss takes in more meetings than the chairman of a major corporation:

> His day is taken up with meetings, almost every day, and every meeting has a purpose, a purpose which is the dollar sign: how much money you might get, all day long. In some cases all night long. That's all it is; it totally revolves around the dollar. And they all have girlfriends. They'll do their business, then they'll go to their girlfriends. In fact, if we can get to put bugs and wiretaps in their girlfriends' apartments, that's where we go because we know that's where they talk.

The importance of these meetings came to light in one of the thousands of wiretaps recorded by the authorities. The police learned how viciously the bosses reacted when a humble soldier failed to make a meeting. This is a *capo* in the Gambino family, John Gotti, berating a soldier for missing an appointment:

> GOTTI [screaming]: Why am I burning my fucking balls? I waited three days for you.

SOLDIER: My wife just called me . . .

GOTTI: Your wife just called you, ha! I'm missing you for three days. She tells me she told you yesterday.

SOLDIER: She hasn't told me yesterday.

GOTTI: She just told Willie she told you yesterday. You telling me your wife's a fucking liar?

SOLDIER: Well, then, she lied then. She didn't tell me.

GOTTI: Well, let me tell you something. I need an example. Don't you be that fucking example! You understand me?

SOLDIER: Listen, John . . .

GOTTI: Listen, I call your fucking house five times yesterday! Now, if your wife thinks you're a fucking dusky, or she's a fucking dusky, and if you're gonna disregard my mother-fucking phone calls I'll blow you and that fucking house up.

SOLDIER: I never disregarded anything you say . . .

GOTTI: This is not a fucking game. I'm not gonna miss meets for three days and nights, yeah? My fucking time is valuable!

SOLDIER: I know that . . .

GOTTI: Now you get your fucking ass down here and see me tomorrow.

SOLDIER: I'm gonna be there all day tomorrow.

GOTTI: Well, never mind 'you be there all day tomorrow'. And *never* make me have to do this again, 'cause if I hear anybody else 'calling' you within five days I'll fucking kill you. Now you make sure you get your ass out here tomorrow! Maybe you're all fucking liars. [Slams the phone down]

The *capo* was hardly exaggerating.

With the constant round of court appearances that Castellano now faced, he would not have much time for meetings or for girlfriends. In the first of the trials he was accused of operating a car-theft ring. This may seem a rather modest field of criminal endeavour for a man who was worth millions until it is remembered that the head of a Mafia family takes a cut on every major crime committed by his soldiers. Failure to pay the 'tax' or feudal dues to the boss can result in premature and permanent retirement. The car-theft operation was a multi-million-dollar enterprise. It was supervised by Roy di Meo. He recruited professional car thieves to steal selected cars to order, often a specified model, colour and size of engine. They dealt only in high-quality automobiles like Mercedes and BMWs. The thieves would be paid a few hundred dollars for a night's work. Alternatively, because many were junkies, they would be paid in drugs. Di Meo would then sell the car for $20,000 or more. They selected areas of New York where there would be a high concentration of quality cars, like Howard Beach in Queens – a residential area full of luxury cars but relatively free of police patrols.

One of the men whom di Meo recruited was a short fat ugly man with glasses and a thick New York accent called Vito Arena. He was a skilled mechanic and he knew how to steal virtually any car you wanted. He could also 'chop it out' – change the engine ID so that all trace of the car's origin would disappear. Sleazy garages in Brooklyn known as 'chop shops' would be used to cut out the identifying marks on the car. Mechanics like Arena would be paid considerably more than the street thieves.

When the car had been given a new identity and the sale made, usually to clients in the Middle East, di Meo would be chauffeured up to Castellano's mansion, where he would hand over thousands of dollars in cash. It was a trip he would make practically every night of the week. Although he apparently never saw Castellano, he had no doubt about whom he was ultimately working for.

Early in 1983 an off-duty New York City detective was having dinner with his wife in a restaurant in Suffolk County. There was a short fat bespectacled man seated at a nearby table who looked remarkably familiar. Suddenly the detective realized who he was. He left his table and made a discreet call from the restaurant payphone to the Suffolk County police. Within minutes they arrived and arrested him. He was Vito Arena.

Arena had become a confidant of the Gambino family, and federal and state authorities had been investigating the Gambino family car-theft operation for some time. The investigation had become even more important when a series of murders associated with the operation confirmed links with organized crime. Joe Coffey, formerly in charge of the Organized Crime Homicide Squad, had been drafted in to the US Attorney's office in the Southern District to look into the murders. When Arena was arrested he was immediately brought to the Foley Square office building where Coffey was working. Joe Coffey has been out on the streets with Mafia hoods for most of his police career. He describes them all as 'low-life swine'.

One Sunday afternoon in the presence of police chiefs, attorneys involved in the car-theft case and Joe Coffey, Vito Arena began to talk. His first words were: 'I want to talk about a homicide I did.'

He went on to describe one murder, then another, then another. A litany of killing poured out of his fat lips. The details are unpleasant, but they reveal more than most 'shock horror' press reports or Hollywood films about the reality of the Mafia.

The first murder he described was the killing of Joseph Scorney. Scorney had been one of Arena's partners in the car-theft ring. The murder had been the idea of a mutual friend, Richard di Nome, who convinced Arena that Scorney wanted to squeeze him out of the profits. 'Scorney and I and Richard di Nome were walking into the auto chop-shop in Brooklyn,' Arena told the police. 'As we were walking in I shot him in the back. He turned round and fell to his knees and he said, "Vito, what are you doing?" 'I'm killing you, you motherfucker,' Arena replied, putting the gun into Scorney's mouth and pulling the trigger. Scorney was still not dead, so di Nome picked up a five-pound sledgehammer and bludgeoned his head. They then loaded the body into a fifty-five-gallon oil drum and poured in eight bags of cement. The head was still sticking out of the drum so di Nome took a shovel and chopped it off. He then pushed it into the concrete so it was level. The two men took the barrel away in the back of their car and drove it to the south shore of

Long Island, where they dumped it in the water. They then headed for Chinatown and sat down to dinner.

When Arena had finished talking, Coffey asked him if he could take them to the place where the drum was dumped. Arena said he could. They drove out to Long Island. He showed them where it had sunk into the water. Arena was proving to be a valuable informant with a photographic memory. Coffey recalls:

> Two days later we went there with a scuba team and we found the barrel with the body in it, exactly the way he described it. He described the clothing he [Scorney] had on, three and a half years on, and he also told us that in his left breast pocket we'd find his wallet, which we did. Not only did we find his wallet with his ID in it, but we found his dentist's name in it which helped in the positive ID.
>
> Why did Arena turn around and why did he become an informant? He was a homosexual – he was captured with his lover who was also wanted and all he wanted was to be incarcerated with his lover. That was the whole deal.

Even for Coffey and his colleagues, who were virtually unshockable, Arena's statements were a sickening glimpse of the awful kingdom controlled by well-dressed men like Paul Castellano. When Arena later repeated his litany of horror for the benefit of the court, in the presence of both Castellano and the jury, two of the women jurors put their heads in their hands, horrified by the acts he described. It was a natural reaction. Castellano as usual sat impassively. He might as well have been listening to the weather forecast. His whole demeanour was that of a bored businessman, even though he was facing the probability of a severe prison sentence and at least twelve months of daily court appearances where he would be forced to listen to the scum he had once employed.

When Arena was cross-examined by la Rossa the proceedings descended into black comedy. Arena had apparently become convinced that he was going to be a 'star', and wanted to discuss his publicity potential for books and films with a literary agent. Arena had seriously suggested to his literary agent that his part in the movie could be played by Tom Selleck. He openly admitted that he was cooperating with the authorities to get leniency for his lover, and his testimony became positively surreal when he admitted that, in addition to demanding Bruce Springsteen records, bigger steak portions and plastic surgery for his homo-sexual partner, he had also asked for an operation to have fat sucked out of his cheeks, chin and neck. La Rossa then asked Arena, 'Did you say you needed a nice profile because you look like a Cyclops?'

With a straight face Arena responded, 'I felt that my appear-ance was awful.'

'Is that the word you used?' asked la Rossa.

'Yes,' he replied.

'Did you say that?' repeated la Rossa, for the benefit of an incredulous jury.

'I thought it would help my appearance,' answered Arena.

'Did you further tell Mr Mack [the federal prosecutor], "La Rossa is going to dress up all the defendants, and I am going to look like a bad guy." Did you say that?'

'If you look at the baby faces on them and you look at me . . .'

If you came across Vito Arena in a novel about the American underworld, the character would be ridiculous. In the sober surroundings of Courtroom 306, with the head of the American Mafia on one side of the table and the pudgy hit man a few feet away in the witness-box, it was reality at its most unreal.

Besides his two lawyers, Castellano was constantly attended in court by his faithful bodyguard and driver. Tommy Bilotti was an overweight gangster who took considerable care in the selection of the clothes for his wide and heavy frame. The mere weight of his presence was enough to intimidate, and he also had a reputation as a skilled handler of a baseball bat in its application to the human body. With his bright blue suits, thin lips, dark curly hair and duck-like gait, Bilotti was an essential prop to the 'B'-movie quality of 'Big Paulie's' world. During breaks in the court proceedings and the lunchtime recess, Bilotti would be seen shepherding the elderly 'godfather' through the streets of Manhattan, talking softly and occasionally putting a protective arm around him. Bilotti was Castellano's link with the outside world, relaying decisions and messages essential to the continued business success of the Gambino family. Although he had no formal title within the family, Bilotti's proximity to Castellano gave him power and authority.

John Gotti, a Howard Beach *mafioso*, felt that his chances of promotion within the Gambino family were frustrated by the favouritism Castellano was showing Bilotti. Gotti was a forty-five-year-old hood with a reputation for physical violence. He was also impatient and ambitious. Castellano had prevented Gotti expanding his business interests from hijacking trucks and selling stolen goods into the more lucrative rackets which he himself controlled. Gotti's jealousy of Bilotti and dislike for his boss were shared by other members of the Commission. They had never forgiven Castellano for assuming the leadership of the Gambino family just because his sister had married Carlo Gambino. Their resentment had festered for a long time. Secret FBI tapes now reveal how the other top *mafiosi* reacted to Castellano. The following conversation was recorded in Casa Storta, a restaurant in Brooklyn. The guests were Gennaro 'Gerry Lang' Langella, acting boss of the Colombo family, one of his captains, Dominic 'Donny Shacks' Montemarano, and Angelo Ruggiero, nephew of the Gambino underboss, Aniello Dellacroce. Langella kicks off by grousing that Castellano owes the Colombo family $50,000 as part of a union racket that they had been running together. He says that Castellano is now lying about his debt:

LANGELLA: [It's an] out and out lie.
RUGGIERO: Paul [Castellano] told me that.
LANGELLA: It's a lie.
RUGGIERO: Paul told Neil [Dellacroce]. Paul told me.
LANGELLA: This is not the truth. Is he insinuating something?
RUGGIERO: Well. That's Paul.

They move on to discuss the problems within the Gambino family and the tension between the different factions.

LANGELLA: What did I say, Donny, after the holidays, what would happen?

MONTEMARANO: Neil and Johnny [Gotti] will die.

LANGELLA: That's it. I made a prediction, and you know why.

MONTEMARANO: Just what you see is going on.

RUGGIERO: It's getting worse and worse . . . he [Castellano] don't want nobody around him carrying pistols to meets . . . I never go on a meet with a pistol. It's a shame.

LANGELLA: That man [Castellano], most of his guys got guns, and you know he ain't going easy [i.e. it will be difficult to kill him].

RUGGIERO: No, I know and Neil knows it and Johnny knows it. If anything happens to Johnny and Neil, I'll come and see you, 'cause I don't trust those . . .

LANGELLA: I don't blame you, it's not a nice way to live today.

RUGGIERO: To me, he badmouths everybody. He badmouths his own family.

Castellano's problems reached a climax with the Commission indictment. Other FBI tapes recorded Tony Salerno and Tony Corallo constantly insulting him. At one point the driver of Corallo's bugged Jaguar, Salvatore Avellino, complained about having to deliver large envelopes of cash to Castellano at different restaurants around New York City: 'Forget "Thank you" – "Thank you" I don't expect,' complained Avellino. 'Twenty thousand, thirty thousand, fifty thousand . . . I can't even fucking carry them.'

Another complaint that was voiced on the tapes was that Castellano could not control Teamsters' Local 813, even though he had collected a $50,000 pay-off to guarantee labour peace from an employers' association. But he did not know how soon his problems were going to come to an end. His court commitments weakened his power. Family business was neglected and delegated and, worse, his fellow Commission members now had even more reason to gang up against him. The fact that the security of his own house had been violated by an FBI bug, which had somehow been placed in his living room and dining room, meant that his authority as head of the Commission was seriously undermined. When the other members of the Commission found out what he had been saying about them when their lawyers gained access to some of the tapes, they were furious. Among other things, he was heard discussing what should have been confidential Commission business with Tommy Bilotti, whom they considered to be merely a driver. Castellano had broken the rules.

When the Gambino family underboss, Aniello Dellacroce, died on 2 December 1985 aged seventy-one, the family lost the one man able to keep the peace between Castellano's supporters and the rest. Dellacroce, also known as 'Neil the Lamb', was in charge of street bosses like John Gotti who so bitterly resented Castellano's leadership. On the day Dellacroce died Castellano made it known that he wanted his confidant, Bilotti, to take over as underboss. It was a decision that would remove Castellano forever from the courtroom. He would never have to worry again about the confessions of Tommaso Buscetta.

Just six weeks after Buscetta first appeared to testify in that Manhattan courthouse, Castellano went out to dinner at Spark's restaurant. Third Avenue and Forty-sixth Street were full of warm American Christmas cheer. A jolly Santa Claus clanged a bell and wished the world a merry Christmas.

Bilotti eased the black Lincoln to the kerb. The two men got out of the car, the old man tall and forbidding, the young one short, built like a bouncer. Bilotti as usual put a protective arm around his 'godfather'. It was a gesture almost of intimacy. That Christmas night it provided no protection. Three men in fedora hats and trench coats appeared out of the crowd, drew handguns from their coats and put six bullets into Castellano, six more into Bilotti. As the crowd panicked and backed away one of the killers walked coolly up to the bodies, inspected them and then shot Castellano once more in the head. The three men then ran off, as one eye-witness said later, 'like businessmen jogging for a cab'.

It was New York City's most sensational gangland slaying since the murder of Carmine Galante in July 1979, which had ironically been approved by the man who lay dying outside Sparks restaurant. The only break with tradition was that Castellano had not been allowed to die on a full stomach.

Organized crime investigators immediately suspected the hand of John Gotti, whose career prospects had been thwarted by both Castellano and Bilotti. It later emerged that Gotti had been spotted making the rounds of several important mob social clubs before the hit. He would undoubtedly have needed the approval of the Commission for a murder as significant as the killing of 'Big Paul' Castellano.

Although murders of men of his standing are increasingly rare in an organization which has striven to appear legitimate, they are a clear indication of the blunt violence which characterizes the Mafia.

The head of the Gambino family and the boss of the New York Commission was dead. So was his probable successor, Bilotti. The ageing 'board of directors' was losing its grip, facing life sentences in the courts of America and Italy. Now the new generation had to salvage what it could from the wreckage wrought by Giovanne Falcone, Rudolph Giuliani and the greatest traitor in the history of the Mafia, Tommaso Buscetta.

17

The Mafia on Trial

SAL AVELLINO: We're gonna knock everybody out, absorb everybody, eat them up . . . whoever stays in there is only who we're allowing to stay in there.
FAZZINI: You got big plans.
AVELLINO: Well isn't that the truth?

Organized Crime Task Force bugged conversation between Salvatore Avellino, Thomas Ronga and Emedio Fazzini in a Jaguar automobile NY Reg. No 7099 AMT, on 28 June 1983

On 8 September 1986 the ruling Commission of the American Mafia went on trial. Sitting in courtroom 306, two floors beneath the Pizza trial at the federal courthouse, were the elderly men who had reigned over the New York families. A woman watching the proceedings from the public benches exclaimed: 'They don't look like Godfathers, they look like grandfathers.' She was right, but then appearances can be deceptive. Their presence had been made possible by the rigorous application of the RICO (Racketeering, Influence and Corrupt Organization) statute, the federal law which enabled the prosecutors to indict entire Mafia families on the grounds that they were 'continuing criminal enterprises'.

To everyone's surprise the defence admitted in their opening statements that the Mafia existed. The admission was qualified by the suggestion that membership of the organization did not mean you were a criminal. It was the myth of the 'Men of Honour'. The success of the defence would rely on the readiness of the jury to believe that the Mafia could be synonymous with peaceful activity. That such a proposition could even be entertained in 1986 was in itself something of an admission.

One of the defendants, Carmine Persico, decided to conduct his own defence. Persico, the head of the Colombo family, was also known as 'the Snake' – although apparently his girlfriend 'Tootsia' was the only person foolish enough ever to call him that to his face. 'The Snake' had spent so much time in court-rooms that he felt his understanding of the legal process was as good as anyone else's. He was probably right. With a large bulbous nose, the expression of a bloodhound and a face that had been compared to a tombstone, Persico endeared himself to the court and the press with his 'Godfather-like' speeches and mannerisms.

According to the government, Carmine Persico

> ... killed his first human being in 1951, before his eighteenth birthday. His mother ordered older brother Allie Boy, who was in the car with Carmine at the time of the murder and was arrested with him, to 'take the rap', so Allie Boy pleaded guilty to the murder and went to jail for the killing. Charges against Carmine Persico were dismissed and he became the scourge of his neigh-bourhood, developing the reputation that he could not beat you with his hands, but that he was deadly with a gun or a pipe. His violent crimes earned the respect of older Mafiosi, and he became a 'made' man when others his age were getting their first jobs. He boasted to Fred DeChristopher [his cousin] of being one of the trigger-men chosen by the Commission to gun down boss Albert Anastasia in a Manhattan barbershop in the mid-1950s.

The prosecution revealed a succession of wiretaps, videotapes, witnesses and meetings which provided a fascinating glimpse into the inner world of the most powerful men of the American Mafia. Highlights included 'Fat Tony' Salerno boasting that 'If it wasn't for me, there wouldn't be no mob left. I made all the guys. And everybody's a good guy.' The conversation was secretly recorded at the Palma Boy Social Club, Fat Tony's seedy Harlem headquarters at 416 East 115 Street. In the same conversation, Salerno grouses with Tony Corallo, head of the Lucchese family, about his inability to control an underling:

> SALERNO: I can't talk to no one. I used to do anything I wanted with the guy. All of a sudden. Since this fuckin' shit with this kid there, when this kid did that fucking job there, see.
> [Background laughter.]
> CORALLO: Tony, he's, he's, he's –. One thing, get rid of them, shoot them, kill them, but then, you know, you can't go on. It's disgusting. Well, here's to your health and fuck everything!

In a conversation taped inside the bugged black Jaguar, Corallo seethes with rage about the soldiers in different families who are dealing in narcotics. Corallo begins by complaining to his driver Sal Avellino about an article in the *New York Times* about the different Mafia families of New York City:

> AVELLINO: Had a write-up about our family?
> CORALLO: Yeah.
> AVELLINO: About you?
> CORALLO: Castellano, the junk business, that we in this junk business and all that shit. Like, ah, Tom, Tom was the, the, the Underboss, the Consigliere is the other guy, and all that shit. I hope we didn't make a fuck-up. I hope there's nobody that we took in the last shot ... Now I couldn't be any fuckin' plainer than I was with some of these guys ... Anybody fuckin' with junk, they gotta be killed. That's all. Fuck this shit. They look forwards over here to us. What do they think they do. Christ sakes.
> AVELLINO: Sure, this is the whole fuckin' problem. Is the junk. They don't care about the gambling and all that other bullshit. They never did. It's the money ...
> CORALLO: It's just the fucking junk ...
> AVELLINO: That's where all the appropriation of the money is, though.

CORALLO: We're not involved.

AVELLINO: I know, but the only way they could get money and keep their jobs going is they need the appropriations from the government and the only way they can get the appropriation is on junk. They can't get appropriations on gambling and every, all this other shit. Big money is what I'm talking about, millions and billions. You heard D'Amato the other day, 'We gotta put more of this on,' you know. Only, he didn't say, 'To eliminate organized crime.' He says, 'To eliminate organized crime in the *narcotics* business, in the *heroin* business.' He didn't say nothin' about in gambling, and unions. He just says, 'Narcotics.' That's where they appropriate all of these millions.

CORALLO: You think they know we're not in it?

AVELLINO: Right.

CORALLO: They know who's in it.

AVELLINO: They know.

CORALLO: Now, of course, you cannot be in the narcotics business and put it on your fucking stomach . . . You gotta be exposed to it. You gotta go out on the street, you got to *sell* it. You can't be in the junk business without goin' in the fuckin' streets and selling this cocksucking shit. We should kill them. We should have some examples. Alright? Alright. We should make some examples . . . Say, we'll kill the first cocksucker. You know, we'll *kill em* . . . anybody with us, anybody near, comes near us, you know, we'll kill em. Don't worry, that gets to their fucking ears. See.

Even as they were talking, the foul-mouthed Tony 'Ducks' Corallo was the target of a major investigation initiated by New York State Organized Crime Task Force. Ironically, it had little to do with narcotics but a lot to do with his control of unions, the garbage disposal industry and construction. Corallo's dislike for drug dealers was shared by other members of the Commission. Because of the drug activities of the Bonanno family, they decided to exclude Phil 'Rusty' Rastelli, from the Commission, despite the fact that he was the head of that family.

Corallo and Salerno had known for years that the Sicilians were bringing massive quantities of heroin into their city. There was little they could do about it now – except curse and swear. Referring to the Bonanno family, Salerno's voice was full of contempt: 'They're all junk men,' the ageing mobster snarled. Such contempt, coming from two powerful members of the Commission, created major problems for Rastelli, but did nothing to interrupt the heroin trade. In a conversation in the Palma Boy Social Club at 10.00 a.m. on 31 January 1984, listening FBI agents were astonished to hear the inside power machinations of America's most powerful criminal institution:

> SALERNO: Now, I told him up there, eighty times. I must have said it eighty times. I says, 'But he *cannot* sit on the Commission.' So he come back about four weeks ago and he said, uh, 'You know, uh, Rusty likes to meet us. Let's meet him,' he says, 'and we'll straighten it out.' Well, there's nothin' to straighten out, I told the kid. 'He wanted to be the Boss, make him the fuckin' Boss,' I said. I said, 'As far as the Commission, they don't want him. That's all.' Now, if we meet, we see what goes on. Whether they come to the meet, who the fuck knows.

In the talks between Fat Tony, Salvatore Santoro ('Tom Mix'), the underboss of the Lucchese family, and Christie 'Tick' Furnari, his *consigliere*, there was some confusion over what Paul Castellano had said. Some thought he had okayed 'Rusty' to be on the Commission, while others thought he had merely okayed his accession as head of the family. The problem was still unresolved exactly a month later. Catalano's heroin deals were giving the Bonanno family a bad name. But Rastelli was still keen to become accepted by the Commission. He was like a very rich businessman desperate to become a member of the most exclusive club in town, only to find that the membership committee were excluding him on the grounds that they didn't like the business he was in. When Rastelli complained to Tony

'Ducks' Corallo, the fat grey-haired *mafioso* gave him some advice. 'Take care of your family first,' counselled Corallo. 'Straighten out your family and when you straighten them out, then we talk about the Commission.' Rastelli never did straighten out his family, nor did he ever join the Commission. Although not part of the Commission trial, Rastelli was arrested, tried and convicted under a separate racketeering indictment. He is currently serving a twelve-year jail sentence.

One member of his family who did have the honour of being indicted alongside the Commission was Anthony 'Bruno' Indelicato, a tall, good-looking man with a sallow complexion, dark Italian features, gold wire rimmed glasses and a taste for lightweight fawn-coloured suits. In his early forties, Indelicato was something of an oddity, surrounded as he was by the geriatric grandees of the American Mafia. He was a contract killer with a $3000-a-day cocaine habit and an arsenal of heavy-calibre handguns and semi-automatic rifles. He lovingly tended his armoury and on one occasion drove along in a car while dipping the bullets from a handgun into a vial of cyanide before replacing them in the chamber of the gun. Indelicato had himself narrowly escaped death in one of the Bonanno family's ceaseless feuds. His continuing survival was due not least to the high regard in which he had been held by the Commission. Indelicato had been one of the gunmen who had driven up to Jo and Mary's restaurant in the summer of 1979 to shoot Carmine Galante after his lunch. The Commission had ordered the contract.

On 13 January 1987, Richard Owen sat down behind his desk. He was a distinguished-looking man in his sixties, wearing glasses that perched halfway down his nose. He perused the familiar documents and photographs that lay in front of him, then he peered over the top of his spectacles at the elderly men seated around him. Judge Richard Owen sentenced each member of the Commission to 100 years in prison.

The only one to receive a lighter sentence was Indelicato. He received forty years for the murder of Galante. Judge Owen read out his sentence to each defendant in turn, starting with Fat Tony Salerno, who betrayed not the slightest reaction to the Judge's accusation: 'You have essentially spent a lifetime terrorizing this community to your financial advantage.' The 75-year-old head of the Genovese family shuffled out of the courtroom with the aid of his walking stick. He would die in prison. The only man to lose his grip was 72-year-old Salvatore Santoro, the underboss of the Lucchese family and a frequent companion to Corallo inside the black Jaguar. Sitting beside his boss, the elderly 'Tom Mix' started to rant at the judge: 'You're in the driver's seat, your honour,' he said with a heavy note of sarcasm, 'and you're doing a good job.' When the judge agreed with him, Santoro exclaimed, 'Why don't you give me a hundred years too?' The judge complied, but not before Santoro had to be restrained from walking out of the courtroom.

Ralph Scopo, the heavyweight Colombo family soldier, who throughout the trial had tried to convey the image of a working man from a union by wearing loud check shirts worn with the collar outside the jacket, also gave vent to his injured sense of justice. As Owen waved surveillance pictures of Scopo attending a Commission meeting on Staten Island, Scopo stood up and protested that he had merely been walking down the street at the time. Owen smiled. There was nothing any of them could say when faced with the hundreds of photographs and the hours of tapes. The Commission of the American Mafia had convicted itself.

18

Man of Honour

Nothing brings a man greater honour than the new laws and new institutions he establishes. When these are soundly based and bear the mark of greatness they make him revered and admired. Now, in Italy the opportunities are not wanting for thorough reorganization. Here he would find great prowess among those who follow, were it not *lacking among* the leaders.

MACHIAVELLI,
The Prince: Exhortation to liberate Italy.

It was bitterly cold. The wind-chill factor had brought the temperature down to a bone-freezing level. The DEA agent who had been responsible for his protection waved to us in the street.

He too was feeling the biting wind. He recognized us. He was going to escort us to meet Tommaso Buscetta. Nobody would know the exact location, until moments before seeing him. Buscetta would be brought to neutral ground, ensuring that no one would have any indication of where he had come from, where he was living or where he would return after our meeting. Once with him, all personal communication with the outside world would be cut off. No incoming or outgoing telephone calls, no going out and coming back. The security would be absolute.

With dark curly hair, an expensively knitted Italian silk jersey, a gold chain on his wrist and a fashionable black-faced gold watch, the 59-year-old Sicilian looked fit and well, and younger than his age. He looked less careworn than a man whose family has been destroyed. He looked like a successful and casually dressed Italian businessman. It had taken two years of painstaking negotiations to finally meet 'The Godfather of Two Worlds'. Tommaso Buscetta had agreed to give an exclusive television interview for a BBC Television documentary. It would be the first time that a former member of the Sicilian Mafia had ever spoken on television. Over the next two days Tommaso Buscetta talked on- and off-camera. He confirmed everything he had stated in his confessions. He spoke warmly of Christina his wife. In particular he was proud of her intelligence and her ability to speak so many languages. He was full of warmth and affection for his surviving family. He spoke of the tragedy of losing his children and of the hatred felt for him by the Corleonesi, in whose opinion he was one of the lowest forms of life, 'a worm'. He described his loathing for Pino 'Scarpazzedda' Greco, the man responsible for murdering his relatives.

In the spring of 1987, Buscetta's most hated enemy, Pino Greco, was still on the run. Four hundred and seventy-four *mafiosi*, including leading members of the Corleonesi, were still on trial in the specially-built maximum security bunker in Palermo, Sicily. Adjoining the Ucciardone prison, to which it was connected by an underground tunnel, this bunker had cost the Italian government the equivalent of £18 million to construct. The trial had opened on 10 February, 1986. The *sentenza* (indictment) ran to forty volumes and 8007 pages. It charted the Mafia's control of the heroin trade and the vicious killings of the Corleonesi. It was a tremendous achievement, yet the cost had been heavy. On 28 July 1983, Judge Rocco Chinnici, the man who had initiated the judicial proceedings against Michele Greco and the Corleonesi, had been blown up by a massive fifty-pound car bomb detonated outside his Palermo apartment. Giovanni Falcone, Paolo Borsellino, Leonardo Guarnotta and Giuseppe di Lello have continued his work, and acknowledge their debt to him in the judicial papers: 'It should be a matter of record, that this investigation was begun three years earlier by Examining Judge Rocco Chinnici who paid for his dedication with his life.'

Tragically, the arrests following Buscetta's confessions have not prevented further killings. On 23 February 1985, industrialist Robert Parisi and his driver were shot by a Mafia commando team of eight men. President of the local football team and vice-president of the Palermo Business Association, Parisi was murdered over a dispute concerning a pay-off to the Mafia from the street lighting contract managed by one of his companies. Five days later another businessman was killed: Pietro Patti had refused to pay L500,000 protection money. His young daughter, nine-year-old Gaia, was critically wounded. Both attacks were seen as indications that the Mafia had been seriously damaged by the confessions of Tommaso Buscetta and the subsequent judicial onslaught. Its success had caused something of a cash flow problem for the Sicilian Mafia: deprived of much of the income from heroin, disrupted by arrests in many of the families and the fact that several bosses were on the run, the smooth running of the multi-billion-dollar business gave way to desperate moves to rebuild illicit profits.

The setback was mitigated one month later by the arrest of Pippo Calò in Rome. Head of the Porta Nuova family and Buscetta's boss, Calò is one of the most powerful and important Mafia leaders ever to have been caught. His base in Rome had put him in touch with leading Italian financiers and politicians of the 'Third Level'. He had acted as the Mafia's treasurer and their ambassador in Rome. Known as 'Mario', he had eleven apartments in the city and three villas in Sardinia. On arresting him, the police seized eleven kilos of pure heroin. More disturbing was the discovery of T4 plastic explosive and detonators concealed in a wall behind a cellar. Investigators now have evidence that Calò, and the Mafia, participated in the terrorist bomb attack on the Naples–Milan express on 23 December 1984. The bomb was planted on the 904 train at Florence, and exploded as the train was going through the tunnel. Fifteen people died and 150 were injured in the carnage. Thirteen kilos of explosive had been put inside a suitcase on a luggage rack in the corridor of a second-class compartment. It was one of Italy's worst terrorist attacks. Investigators believe it was planned by the Mafia, a neo-fascist group and members of the Camorra, the secret Naples crime organization with whom Calò had forged an alliance. The motive may have been no more than the desire to divert the attention of the Italian state away from the Mafia's activities, and onto an upsurge in terrorism. If so, it was a brutal calculation.

On 2 April 1985, fifty kilos of the same type of plastic explosive was used in an attempt to assassinate Carlo Palermo, a Sicilian magistrate from Trapani who was investigating arms and heroin smuggling. Miraculously, the magistrate escaped, but a woman and her children in a passing car were blown to pieces by the explosion.

On 28 July 1985, Palermo police chief Giuseppe Montana was shot and killed by the Mafia. He had been in charge of a squad briefed with hunting down fugitive *mafiosi*. Nine days later his close friend, Antonio Cassara, the highly respected deputy head of the Palermo Flying Squad, was cut down by a hail of two hundred bullets from several Kalashnikovs. After his murder, more than half of the agents in his squad asked to be transferred out of Sicily. Their requests were granted. The apparent ease with which Cassara and Montana were murdered dealt a devastating blow to morale, particularly that of the magistrates who were working on the final stages of the indictment for the maxi-trial. Giovanni Falcone, in particular, was bitter. The men who had been killed had been instrumental in preparing the investigations and charges and in debriefing the *pentiti* (witnesses) who had decided to follow in the footsteps of Tommaso Buscetta. For example, Cassara had persuaded Ignazio Lo Presti (before he disappeared) to give him the names and business connections of leading Palermo *mafiosi*. He had also cultivated one of the highest ranking *pentiti* codenamed 'First Light': none other than Salvatore Contorno. Another was 'White Flower', whose identity remains a secret.

Whereas in the past the Mafia could take arrest and trial in their stride, the new Mafia realized that the determination of men like Cassara and Montana, supported by a strong judiciary, was all too likely to lead to convictions rather than acquittal. In the aftermath of their murders, in a series of rare interviews with Italian newspapers, including *Panorama* magazine, *La Repubblica* and *Corriere della Sera*, Falcone made some astonishing statements:

> For months and months we have asked for men and the means to support our investigations ... but little has been done. There is something that is even worse. By now the Mafia understands very well that if they kill Ninni Cassara or Giovanni Falcone, the state reacts weakly. Certainly, there are the solemn funerals; solemn declarations. But then, nothing happens. And in the meantime, they have taken from us an essential part of the struggle against the Mafia.

With a hard realism, Falcone admits that because of the arrests that followed the confessions of Tommaso Buscetta, the Mafia has been working hard to recuperate, by renewing their 'prestige' and infrastructure. The assassinations showed that their military power remained intact.

Falcone, while disillusioned by the murder of his colleagues, remains loyal to the belief that the Mafia can still be destroyed: 'The recent Mafia war has selected the best, most ferocious, the real killers. For this reason, the Mafia immediately attacks anyone who tries to settle into their territory. When Commissioner Montana discovered the secret hideout of wanted *mafiosi*, he had to be stopped at any cost. The same thing happened to Cassara.' Falcone is now under even greater security. His own recent wedding was attended by a procession of armoured alfettas and an escort of heavily armed bodyguards. When asked if he is ever afraid, the beleaguered magistrate replies: 'We all have fear. The problem is to overcome it. I often reflect on a saying that strikes me: "The courageous only die once; the scared die a thousand times a day."' Finally, when asked what he thinks the *mafiosi* think of him, he replies: 'This

I cannot know. I do know what a leader like Buscetta thinks because he told me personally: "I asked to talk to you because among us it's said that you have no other *padrone* but your conscience. Therefore, you're a man I can trust".'

Already Falcone is experiencing a backlash against the success represented by the mere holding of the maxi-trial. People murmur that it was much better when the magistrates were not so determined, that they are making things worse for the ordinary people. At a higher level, there is still a suspicious amount of obstruction, which leaves the magistrates in no doubt as to the hidden power of the organization with which they are dealing. Even among his neighbours Falcone finds little support: 'The tenants of my building applauded when I moved. A lady in Palermo society told me the other day, "But what makes you do it? Why don't you leave things alone and enjoy life?" I told her, "Signora, if I did not know you, I would take your words for a warning from the Mafia".'

The investigations into the murders of Cassara and Montana were posthumously rewarded. On 20 February 1986, in a dawn raid on a remote farmhouse twenty-four miles east of Palermo, the *carabinieri* arrested 'the Pope': Michele Greco. It was hailed as the most important Mafia arrest in the post-war period. The news was immediately transmitted to Bettino Craxi, the Italian Prime Minister, then on a state visit to Bonn. Michele Greco had been a fugitive for years. He was found with false identity papers and had grown a moustache to disguise himself. It was a welcome boost in morale to police and magistrates, especially as the trial, in which Michele Greco was one of the leading defendants and was being tried *in absentia*, had recently opened. Now he could attend in person.

Eight weeks later, Tommaso Buscetta and Salvatore Contorno were flown over from America to Sicily, surrounded by impenetrable security. Their testimony made headlines in Italy. Yet it was as much their mere presence as the weight of their words which would dismay and convict their fellow *mafiosi*.

Buscetta took a seat directly facing the judge and the members of the jury and removed a pair of tinted glasses. The Mafia defendants were in cages at the back of the courtroom. Their most hated enemy was now surrounded by a human screen of armed *carabinieri*. It was later decided that even this physical shield of protection was insufficient. The next day, a bullet-proof glass booth was erected. Although RAI, Italian State Television, were recording the whole trial, they were forbidden to take any pictures revealing Buscetta's face. The most dramatic moment came when Pippo Calò, the head of Buscetta's Porta Nuova family, was allowed to come down to the front of the court and sit down just a few feet away from Buscetta. There followed an extraordinary interchange.

Calò accused Buscetta of merely repeating things he had learnt from the film of *The Godfather*! 'How does he know I am a *capo*?', queried Calo with an affected air of mocking good humour. 'How do I know?', replied Buscetta. 'Because I was part of your family . . .' Each man was struggling to control the intense hatred he felt for the other, Calò with an air of irony and detachment, Buscetta with rigid self-control, but this finally broke down. Calò began to mock and taunt Buscetta by claiming that he had been a great friend of his brother, Vincenzo, who had been disapproving of the way Tommaso conducted his family life; also that Buscetta had abandoned his son, Antonio, when he was imprisoned. Calò was onto a raw nerve and he knew it. Buscetta began to become enraged: '. . . in four hundred pages of interrogation, I have never touched on the personal family life of anyone . . . yes, you were a friend of my brother, and at the same time, together with the whole Commission, you were planning the murder of my brother and my nephew!' Calò did not let up. He continued to goad Buscetta, accusing him of abandoning his wife, Melchiorra, and their children; of being a man who went from woman to woman with no thought of his family. Buscetta exploded: 'The brother of my wife, and my sons, my son-in-law, and cousins, you have killed all my family, but you have not been able to kill me'.

Calò smiled: 'Don't you worry . . .' In the Sicilian code, Calò was saying 'We'll find a way.' Buscetta, barely controlling his rage, asked permission of the President of the court to make a new statement. 'Of course,' said the President. 'What's this?' taunted Calò, 'the latest thing . . . ?'

'Yes,' replied Buscetta, with icy calm, 'the latest thing . . . When I was in prison, I opened the newspaper and I read that a person had disappeared. This person, that I read about in the newspaper, was a member of *your* family, of the family of *Calò* . . . When I came out of prison, at the first meeting with Calò, I asked him, "Giannuzzu, why has be disappeared?" And Calò answered me, "Eh, the Commission have done it . . ." And I said to him: "But you could have said to the Commission that this is a brave young man, that he is a worthwhile person, that he was in prison, convicted for Mafia association, for six years and that he had suffered enough?" I carried on but Pippo Calò finished by saying: "Yes, yes, but I could not have done anything less", and he stopped the argument. Then I went to the Fondo Favarella and confronted Michele Greco. I said to him: "Why was it decided to strangle and drown Giannuzzu?" Michele Greco said to me: "Eh, he was too close to Gaetano Badalamenti!" And I replied, "Solely for that reason?" He said to me: "That alone . . ." I said to him: "Michele, could it not have been avoided?" "No, it was inevitable . . ." This man who was murdered, Giannuzzu, was called Giovanni Lallicata, and he was from the family of Porta Nuova, the family of Signor Calò, and Signor Calò presents himself here with a face of an innocent man!"'

Buscetta had got his own back but the taunts continued. Calò accused Buscetta of being a liar and causing great suffering. 'You think only of your own suffering,' replied Buscetta, 'never of the suffering of others. I have ruined no one . . .'.

'No one?' responded Calò with a note of heavy sarcasm. 'And what about all these people facing you? Turn around and look, we are five hundred in the cages, and how many families have you ruined? Three thousand people. Turn around, Buscetta!'

In one of the cages at the back of the courtroom lounged a portly and elegantly dressed man, smoking an enormous cigar. He had a cell all to himself. It was Luciano Liggio, the boss from Corleone, the man whom Buscetta believed had begun the degeneration and decline of the traditional Mafia when he had murdered the head of his family, Michele Navarra from Corleone, thus establishing the cycle of intrigue, murder and betrayal which would become the hallmark of the 'Honoured Society'. Liggio's several years in prison had not prevented him from issuing commands and death warrants through his loyal lieutenants Bernardo Provenzano and Salvatore Riina. When he had been visited by the magistrates in prison the previous summer, Liggio had pretended not to know who they were. He greeted them with the mocking words: 'You are the men sent by Tommaso Buscetta!' Apart from that, Liggio told the magistrates nothing.

There remains the chilling probability that Liggio and Michele Greco will continue to run the Mafia from prison, overseeing its regeneration. History has shown how the Mafia can renew itself, as it did after the Second World War, and again, following the first Mafia wars. Ironically, there is to be yet another massive public works project for Sicily: a nine-year development programme has been recently approved by the Italian government. The funds may be just what the Mafia needs to help it back on its feet and to recruit a new generation. There are even signs that a new war may be in progress. On Sunday 21 September 1986, seven armed men burst into a small bar in Porto Empedocle and fired into a crowd of people. They killed four members of a local Mafia family including Giuseppe Grassonelli and his son Luigi. Two innocent bystanders were also mown down in the hail of bullets. The Grassonellis were said to be involved in a bitter feud with another Mafia family over control of drug trafficking. Although it was reported that at least a hundred people had witnessed the attack, while taking the traditional Sunday evening stroll through the town, no one came forward. It was the all too familiar cycle of violence, death and silence.

Whether the successful bringing to trial of the Pizza Connection and the Commission, along with the maxi-trial in Sicily, are enough to destroy the Mafia as an organization is doubtful.

Certainly they have inflicted unprecedented damage on both sides of the Atlantic. Yet it is probable that the Mafia can never be totally annihilated by outside forces. What the example of Buscetta and the pressure of the last few years may have achieved is an acceleration of the process of self-destruction. As the Mafia wars have demonstrated, those most successful at destroying the 'Honoured Society' have been its own members; first through the shoot-outs of the 1960s, and later through the vicious tactics of the Corleonesi. In challenging the Italian state by murdering its representatives, they forced the government to retaliate; in attacking their enemies with relentless terror, they generated a powerful resentment which would find its apotheosis in the declarations of Tommaso Buscetta.

In both Italy and America there has been a remarkable increase in the number of people willing to betray the Mafia, either through self-interest or motivated by the prospect of immunity. Most recently, during the trial of John Gotti, the new head of the Gambino family, it was revealed that the New York State Organized Crime Task Force had 'turned' Dominick Lofaro. Lofaro had been arrested on a heroin charge, and agreed to go back on the streets 'wired'. At considerable risk, he secretly taped meetings with Gotti and others. It is the first time that an active member of a Mafia family has been working with the authorities. Law enforcement is succeeding in turning the organization against itself.

In Italy, the 'Men of Honour' have been transformed by their wholesale involvement in the heroin trade, the revenue for which would come from their counterparts in America. Narcotics became the source of both power and money, but provoked an increased determination by law enforcement agencies to destroy the organization responsible for so much misery and death. Ironically Paul Castellano, the elderly head of the New York Gambino family, had issued an edict that no one in his family should deal in heroin. In the early 1980s, at the height of the Sicilian Connection, Castellano ruled that any family members dealing in narcotics would be executed. He also forbade anybody arrested on a narcotics charge since 1962 from ever becoming a member of his family. The edict created great tension within the Gambino family. Investigators now have evidence that rival Gambino Captain John Gotti and his crew were worried that they would be 'whacked out' on Castellano's instructions. Some members of the Gambino family realized that their involvement with narcotics had brought a lot of heat on the Gambino family and ultimately on Big Paul himself. Thus, when their protector Aniello Dellacroce, the Gambino underboss, died of cancer on 2 December 1985, they moved first. Fourteen days later Castellano and Bilotti were shot dead in the centre of Manhattan. As with the last major Mafia execution, the murder of Carmine Galante, the motive was power-play directly related to the trade in narcotics. Castellano had been right: the concrete and poultry business was a lot safer.

There is no doubt that the narcotics trade has altered the Sicilian and American Mafia. Although it became the Mafia's most lucrative enterprise, it has also generated more murder, violence and betrayal than any other criminal activity. As the profits spiralled, so did the need to protect them, hence the assassination of the 'Illustrious Corpses''. In Sicily, 'honour' became purely a matter of power, derived from the destruction of one's enemy and the elimination of competition. The Corleonesi became the dominant power but in the process made so many enemies that not even they could kill them all.

Their victory would return to haunt them when Tommaso Buscetta decided to talk.

With a new identity, Tommaso Buscetta is living quietly in the United States. He enjoys American television, Charles Bronson movies and the occasional game of football. He knows that the Mafia still want to destroy him and he has accepted the idea of dying. He is not afraid for himself, only for his family. Yet Tommaso Buscetta remains confident that the Mafia can be destroyed. In Sicily, he believes that the new generation will no longer have need of the Mafia. In America, he is convinced that the organization is virtually finished. He appears genuinely to cling to the belief that the Mafia he knew as a young man was worthy of respect. Men like Michele Greco changed the rules. Although there is more than a grain of truth in Buscetta's analysis, there is also an element of delusion. The vision of the Mafia as an organization dedicated to truth and justice does not correspond with reality. Whether it is an outright lie, a genuine conviction or chronic self-deception is something only Tommaso Buscetta himself knows. Buscetta undoubtedly has a lot more to say, not least about the 'Third Level'. He continues to deny that he was ever involved in the narcotics trade – to admit to such ignominy would destroy the image.

In the eyes of the world, Tommaso Buscetta would like to be seen as the last 'Man of Honour'.

On 11 February 1987, the nephew of Gaetano Badalamenti, Pietro Alfano, was shot by two gunmen in the middle of Manhattan. He was hit in the back by three bullets, one of which lodged in his spine. He is now partially paralysed. Within forty-eight hours the FBI had tracked down his assailants. They were Frank Bavosa, Giuseppe Amico and Philip Ragosta.

Six days later, on 17 February 1987, Pasquale Conte, a 61-year-old businessman, was arrested. Conte was accused of organizing the $40,000 contract on Alfano. He was also charged with receiving $5000 payment on every kilo of heroin imported from Sicily and running a $10 million heroin conspiracy.

It was the first time that he had been arrested. When his house was searched, guns were found in every room. Conte had been running a chain of supermarkets with a $53 million turnover. He was also a captain in the Gambino crime family and an associate of Salvatore Catalano.

On Friday 13 March 1987, John Gotti, head of the Gambino family, and six of his associates were acquitted of armed hijacking, loan-sharking, illegal gambling and murder.

Bibliography

Printed sources:
Bonanno, Joseph, *A Man of Honour*, London, Andre Deutsch, 1983
Calvi, Fabrizio, *De La Mafia de 1950 à Nos Jours*, Paris, Hachette, 1986
Clark, Evert and Horrock, Nicholas, *Contrabandista*, New York, Praeger, 1973
Cornwell, Rupert, *God's Banker: The Life and Death of Roberto Calvi*, London, Allen and Unwin, 1984
Dalla Chiesa, Nando, *Delitto Imperfetto: Il Generale, La Mafia, La Societa Italiana*, Italy, Arnoldo Mondadori Editore, 1984
Demaris, Ovid, *Captive City: Chicago in Chains*, New York, Lyle Stuart, 1969
Demaris, Ovid, *The Last Mafioso*, New York, Bantam Books, 1981
Fava, Giuseppe, *Mafia da Giuliano a Dalla Chiesa*, Italy, Editore Riuniti, 1984.
Galante, Pierre and Sapin, Louis, *The Marseilles Mafia*, London, W. H. Allen, 1979
Galluzzo, Lucio, *Tommaso Buscetta: L'Uomo che Tradi'se Stesso*, Italy, Musumeci Editore, 1984
Galluzzo, Lucio and La Licata, Francesco, *Rapporto Sulla Mafia Degli Anni 80; Gli Atti del Ufficio Instuzione del Tribunale di Palermo*, Italy, Saverio Lodato, 1986
Jannuzi, Lino, *Cosi Parlo Buscetta*, Italy, Sugarco Edizione, 1986
Kruger, Henrik, *The Great Heroin Coup: Drugs, Intelligence and International Fascism*, Boston, South End Press, 1980.
Lamour, Catherine and Lamberti, Michael R., *The International Connection: Opium from Growers to Pushers* (trs. Peter and Mary Rose, New York Pantheon Books, 1974.
Lernoux, Penny, *In Banks We Trust*, New York, Anchor Doubleday, 1984
Lewis, Norman, *The Honoured Society*, London, Collins, 1964
Maas, Peter, *The Valachi Papers*, London, Panther Books, 1970

McCoy, Alfred, *The Politics of Heroin in Southeast Asia*, New York, Harper and Row, 1972

Moldea, Dan, *Dark Victory*, New York, Viking Penguin, 1986

Newsday, Staff and Editors, *The Heroin Trail*, London, Souvenir Press, 1975

Orecchia, Giulio, *Mafia, Camorra Ndrangheta*, Gianpaolo Rosetti, Tullio Pironti Editore, 1982.

Pantaleone, Michele, *Mafia e Droga*, Italy, Rinaudi, 1966

Reid, Edward (ed.), *The Grim Reapers*, Chicago, Henry Regnery Co., 1969

Servadio, Gaia, *Angelo La Barbera: The Profile of a Mafia Boss*, London, Quartet Books, 1974

Servadio, Gaia, *Mafioso*, London, Secker and Warburg, 1976

Short, Martin, *Crime Inc.*, London, Thames Methuen, 1984

Stajano, Corrado, *Mafia: L'Atto d'Accusa dei Giudici di Palermo*, Editori Riuniti, 1986

Talese, Gay, *Honor Thy Father*, New York, World Publishing, 1971

Teresa, Vincent with Renner, Thomas C., *My Life in the Mafia*, London, Hart-Davis MacGibbon, 1973

Yallop, David, *In God's Name*, London, Corgi, 1985

Documented sources:

Gli Atti d'accusa dei Giudici di Milano, *Sindona*, Italy, Editori Riuniti, 1986.

Tribunale di Palermo Ufficio Instruzione dei Processi Penale. Mandato di Cattura contro Giovanni Abbate + 365, 12 November 1984

USA v. Anthony Salerno, Paul Castellano, Aniello Dellacroce, Gennaro Langella, Anthony Corallo, Salvatore Santoro, Christopher Funari, Philip Rastelli, Ralph Scopo. US District Court, Southern District of New York.

USA v. Paul Castellano et al. US District Court, Southern District of New York.

USA v. Jorge Asaf y Balla, Tommaso Buscetta, Carlo Zippo, Giuseppe Catania et al., US District Court, Eastern District of New York.

Affidavit in the matter of the Extradition of Tommaso Buscetta.

Parliamentary Commission of Inquiry into the Mafia in Sicily, 1976

'The Sicilian Connection: south-west Asian heroin en route to the United States', Report by Senator Joseph R. Biden to the Committee on Foreign Relations and Committee on the Judiciary, US Senate, September 1980.

Twelve Cases of Individual Mafiosi, ed. Girolamo di Causi, The Anti-Mafia Commission, Rome, 1971.

BIBLIOGRAPHY

Interview with Tommaso Buscetta, *Il Mattino*, 20 November 1973

Interview with Giovanni Falcone, *Panorama* Magazine, 10 August 1985.

'Alleged Assassination plots involving Foreign Leaders', An Interim Report of the Select Committee to Study Governmental Operations with respect to Intelligence Activities, United States Senate, 20 November 1975.

'A Decade of Organized Crime', Pennsylvania Crime Commission Report, 1980.

'Procedimento Penale Contro Michele Greco ed Altri', Procura della Repubblica di Palermo.

'Organized Crime and Illicit Traffic in Narcotics', US Senate Permanent Sub-Committee on Investigations, 1964.

Schweizer Illustrierte, 15 July 1985, 2 September 1985, 30 September 1985.

'Containing the Mafia', Richard A. Finney, *Chief Executive*, 23, Spring 1983, pp 34–37.

'The Mafia in Canada', *McLean's* Magazine, 7 March 1964.

New York Times series on Narcotic Trafficking, Nicholas Gage, 24 April 1975.

'Organized Crime and the World of Business', Quebec Police Commission. Report of the Commission of Inquiry on Organized Crime and Recommendations.

'The Fight against Organized Crime in Quebec', Quebec Police Commission. *Ibid*.

'The Cash Connection: Organized Crime, Financial Institutions and Money Laundering', President's Commission on Organized Crime: Interim Report to the President and the Attorney General, October 1984.

Annual Report, 1984, of the Select Committee on Narcotics Abuse and Control, House of Representatives, 3 January 1985.

Memorandum of Law: LJF: mer9–1184A/1B. [Indictment of Gaetano Badalamenti et al.].

Declaration of Paul Waridel to Magistrate Paolo Bernasconi, 30 April 1985, Lugano.

Report on Organized Crime to the United States Senate Committee on the Judiciary, July 1983

Interview with Giovanni Falcone, *La Repubblica*, 13 April 1985.

De-briefing of Benedetto Buscetta, January 1973, New York

De-briefing of Tommaso Buscetta, July 1985: DEA

De-briefing of Giuseppe Catania, September 1973, New York

De-briefing of Michel Nicoli, January 1973, New York
De-briefing of Claude Pastou, April 1973, New York

Interviews:
Tommaso Buscetta, Drug Enforcement Administration, New York
Salvatore Contorno, Drug Enforcement Administration, New York

Tom Angioletti, Drug Enforcement Administration, Rome.
Paolo Borsallino, Investigating Magistrate, Palermo
Joe Coffey, New York State Organized Crime Task Force.
Michael Fahy, Special Agent, US Customs, New York.
Giovanni Falcone, Investigating Magistrate, Palermo.
Kevin Gallagher, Drug Enforcement Administration, New York.
Rudolph Giuliani, US Attorney, Southern District, New York.
Richard Martin, Assistant US Attorney, Southern District, New York.
Charles Rose, Assistant US Attorney, Eastern District, New York.
Frank Storey, FBI, Organized Crime Section, Washington.
Tom Tripodi, Drug Enforcement Administration, Washington.

Additional interviews were conducted in Italy, Brazil, Switzerland and the USA with various law enforcement agencies who wish to remain anonymous.

Index

INDEX

Operation
  Caesar 119–20
  Springboard 105
Ormente, 'Big John' 75
Orsini, Guido 84–5
Owen, Judge Richard 295–6

Palermo 26, 44–5, 47
Palma Boy Club 271, 291, 294
Paraguay 99
Parisi, Robert 299
Pastou, Claude 81–2, 96–7, 105–6
Pelletier, Customs Officer Lynn 97–8
Persico, Carmine 291
Piancone, Louis and Michael 216
Pimtacuda, Father, SJ 161
Pisciotta, Giulio 60–61
Pizza Connection 17, 26, 215–218
Porta Nuova family 40–41, 69, 130, 134
Pozza, Michel 201, 224
Prestifilippo, Mario 165
Provenzano, Bernardo 165

Rastelli, Phil 266, 267, 269, 294–5
refining heroin 47
Rendo, Mario 158, 163
Riccobono, Rosario 165
RICO law 261, 290
Ricord, Auguste 19–82, 90, 99–100
Riina, Salvatore 86, 113, 115, 126, 128, 136–7, 165
Rizzo, Joseph 93
Rognoni, Virgilio 155
Romano, Giuseppe 85, 169, 170
Rose, Charles, Assistant US Attorney 16, 27, 28–30, 109, 185, 190
Rossini, Enrico 237–8
Rotolo, Antonio ('Carlo') 132–3
Ruggiero, Angelo 286–7
Russo, Colonel Giuseppe 116

Salamone, Antonio 78, 139, 140, 143, 146, 148, 223, 237
Salerno, Anthony (Fat Tony) 260–261, 275, 287, 292–4, 296
Salvo
  Ignazio 138, 157, 158, 205–6, 209, 212

Nino 138, 157, 158, 206–9, 211, 212
Sansone, Fabrizio 171, 173, 178, 189
Santapaola, Benedetto (Nitto) 150, 159, 163, 164, 165
Santoro, Salvatore 264–6, 296
São Paulo 99
Sarti, Lucien 81, 95, 104–5
Scaglione, Pietro, Procuratore Generale 114–115
Scarnatto, Raffaello 172–3
Schiaparelli pharmaceuticals 46
Scopo, Ralph 272–5, 296
Scorney, Joseph 283
Settimo, Antonio (Tony) 91, 93
Sicilian separatism 40
Sindona, Michele 26, 118, 135
Sirchia, Giuseppe (Pippo) 68–9
Sollena, Salvatore 117
Soresi, Giuseppe (Peppino) 223, 244–5, 247, 256
Spadolini, Prime Minister 152–3
Spatola, Rosario 77–8, 126
Staccioli, Paolo 171, 173, 177–8, 189
Steiner, Sylvia, prosecutor 184–5
Storey, Frank 224–5, 246
Strollo, Anthony 74
swearing-in ceremony 34–5
Swiss banks 234–240

Teamsters' Union 273, 278
Teresi, Mimmo 142, 143
Terranova
  Judge Cesare 121–2
  Signora 122, 124–5
Third Level 25, 43, 57, 197, 277, 299
Title Three surveillance 224–5
tobacco smuggling 42
Trafficante, Santo jr 102–3
Tramontana, Giuseppe 83–4, 85, 89, 90, 109–110, 170
Trapani, Giuseppe 42
Tripodi, Tom 49, 118–120
Tuma, Superintendent Romeo 177, 182, 184, 186–7

Ucciardone prison 111, 129, 298

319